Ramón María del Valle–Inclán

# Lights of Bohemia

*Luces de bohemia*

*Drawing by John Lyon of Valle-Inclán*
*after a painting by Ignacio Zuloaga*

ARIS & PHILLIPS HISPANIC CLASSICS

Ramón María del Valle–Inclán

# Lights of Bohemia
## *Luces de bohemia*

*Translated from the 1924* Opera Omnia *edition of the Spanish text with an introduction and commentary by*

John Lyon

Aris & Phillips is an imprint of
Oxbow Books, Oxford, UK

ISBN 9780856685651

First published 1999, reprinted with corrections 2006

Printed and bound by CPI Group (UK) Ltd, Croydon, CR0 4YY

A CIP record for this book is available from the British Library.

# Contents

# Illustrations

To the memory of Toni Turull,
colleague and friend,
who for me will always be
the *Preso catalán*

# Preface

With only two minor adjustments, the Spanish text printed here is taken from A. Zamora Vicente's *Clásicos Castellanos* 1973 edition of the play, which, in turn, is based on the Renacimiento *Opera Omnia* edition of 1924. This latter version was revised by Valle-Inclán himself and is generally accepted as the definitive text. I have not included details of the numerous variants between this edition and the original twelve-scene version which appeared in the review *España* in 1920 (31 July to 23 October), since these are comprehensively listed both in Zamora's *Clásicos Castellanos* edition and his invaluable book, *La realidad esperpéntica: Aproximación a 'Luces de bohemia'* (Madrid: Gredos, 1969).

The Introduction and Commentary were written mainly with the non-specialist in mind, although it is hoped they will also be useful to students of Spanish literature at university level. The notes are on the English text and points of translation are discussed only in exceptional cases. The editor has preferred to omit comments on the structural aspects of the play from the Introduction and incorporate these into the scene-by-scene commentaries at the back of the book.

I would like to acknowledge a particular debt of gratitude to Dru Dougherty's excellent collection of Valle-Inclán's lectures and press interviews, *Un Valle-Inclán olvidado* (Madrid: Fundamentos, 1983), a mine of information which has been constantly on my desk during the preparation of this book. Finally, my thanks are due, as always, to my wife Elizabeth for many helpful suggestions and patient checking of the typescript.

John Lyon, Bristol, 1993.

*Façade of the Banco Español de Crédito seen from the Calle de Alcalá in 1911. Drawing by Dionisio Baixeras Verdaguer.*

# Introduction

## 1. *Lights of Bohemia* in context

**Valle-Inclán's earlier theatre**

Ramón María del Valle-Inclán (1866-1936) was a dramatist, novelist and, to a lesser extent, a poet. His career as a writer follows a somewhat unusual trajectory from an initial traditionalism in his youth to revolutionary iconoclasm in his middle and later years. In his early work he makes no attempt to reflect contemporary society and appears uninterested in the national psychoanalysis and reappraisal which preoccupied many of his literary contemporaries around the turn of the century. At that time creative writers and intellectuals were trying to come to terms with the collapse of the last remnants of empire abroad and chronic political and social crisis at home. Their response to these problems associated with Spain's emergence into the twentieth century was, with few exceptions, a quest for the nation's 'essential identity' in its history, tradition and the character of its people. This search for the national essence, though not unmixed with nostalgia, should not, however, be confused with a merely reactionary kind of traditionalism. For Angel Ganivet, Miguel de Unamuno and Azorín,[1] tradition was not just in the past; it was profoundly embedded in the living present and contained the seeds of the future. Valle's form of traditionalism was less regenerationist in spirit. His portrayal of archaic societies was an indirect response to the society of his own time and an implicit rejection of its values and assumptions. But their appeal for Valle was almost entirely a heroic one. His idealization of the feudal lord, Montenegro, in his *Comedias bárbaras* ('Barbaric Comedies') and his cult of the world of Carlist traditionalism in his trilogy of novels on the Carlist war were a heroic gesture of defiance to an institutionalized bourgeois world that was taking their place.

Apart from its heroic appeal, traditionalism for Valle was tied in with his aesthetic convictions. His basically Symbolist philosophy was that all art aspired to a stasis and its purpose was to detect the archetypal forms and patterns which reveal the essential unity of being beneath the changing surface of the world. José Antonio Maravall has pointed out that tradition in the social order was, for Valle, equated with that unchanging essence so valued by the artist.[2] It was not so much an aesthetic of exploration and analysis as of revelation of hidden norms, harmonies and links. This quest for what T.S. Eliot called the 'still point of the turning world' had, in his view, to be accompanied by an attitude of disinterested contemplation on the part of the artist. Valle-Inclán, like his

---

1    Pseudonym for José Martínez Ruiz.

2    J.A. Maravall, 'La imagen de la sociedad arcaica en Valle-Inclán', *Revista de Occidente*, 44-5 (1966), pp. 225-56. The relevant passage is on p. 253.

Irish contemporaries Yeats, Synge and, later, Joyce, was strongly opposed to the analytical approach or to the imposition of any ideology in art, to anything, in fact, which elevated the intellect or personality of the writer above the collective reality that he was contemplating.

One of the central principles behind Valle-Inclán's early drama was its collective emphasis. His reported pronouncements lay great stress on the collective nature of the theatre, both in the sense that it should grow out of a collective culture and that it should, in turn, reflect that culture in its content. He believed that the essential purpose of the theatre was to reflect, as impassively as possible, broad collective identities.[3] Perhaps the most successful examples of this are the first two plays of his *Comedias bárbaras, Aguila de blasón* ('Heraldic Eagle') in 1907 and *Romance de lobos* ('Ballad of the Wolves') in 1908, which are set in a late nineteenth-century Galicia and portray a decaying feudal order in the form of a conflict between the ageing patriarch Don Juan Manuel de Montenegro and his degenerate sons who try to dispossess him. In these plays the characters are conceived archetypally as products of a natural landscape and a certain cultural tradition. They are given no individual past, no individual problems, no unique inner life which impinges on the action. The forces which determine their behaviour — primary instincts (lust, greed), tradition, heredity, caste — are not seen as the attributes of individuals, but as collective forces which work through characters. The conflicts that exist in these plays are not highlighted as 'problems' or 'issues', but woven into a broad tapestry, and what dominates overall is not conflict but a sense of interdependence and continuity, between characters and landscape, past and present, heroic figures and their choral accompaniment and even between elements which appear incongruous and contradictory, such as lust and death, greed and religious fear.

The collective emphasis continues in works of lesser importance such as *Cuento de abril* ('April Story') in 1909 and *Voces de gesta* ('Epic Voices') in 1911. The first is a medieval verse fantasy which ironically contrasts the ascetic warlike culture of Castile with the delicate lyrical tradition of Provence. The second is a rather more solemn and monolythic celebration of Carlist traditionalism, emphasizing its nature as a living force in the hearts of a people, rather than as a political doctrine. *La marquesa Rosalinda* in 1912 reverts to the more ironic mode with a stylized and balletic presentation of the cultural contradictions in eighteenth-century aristocratic society between the dogmatic moral intransigence of the Castilian tradition and the free-thinking, 'pagan' influences coming from France and Italy. From *La marquesa* onwards, incidentally, Valle discovered the dramatic potential of stimulating a dual response in the audience. *La marquesa* is subtitled 'a grotesque and sentimental farce'. This duality started off as half-lyrical, half-comic and ended up as a blend of the tragic and the grotesque, which is

---

3    "I believe that the supreme aspiration of art, and especially of the theatre, should be to record, reflect, give the impression of the life of a whole people or race." Translated from an interview with José López Nuñez in *Por Esos Mundos*, 1 January 1915 (reprinted in Dru Dougherty, *Un Valle-Inclán olvidado: entrevistas y conferencias*. Madrid: Fundamentos, 1983 pp. 52-64).

what we see in *Divinas palabras* ('Divine Words'), published in 1920. Here Valle presents a tableau of rural Galicia which has none of the heroic nostalgia of the earlier *Comedias bárbaras*. It reflects incongruous and conflicting attitudes coexisting within the culture: inherited moral attitudes, codes, taboos, stemming from its religious tradition, and what could be described as natural, instinctive drives of sensuality, lust and greed. These are depicted not so much in conflict, as entangled in ironic, serio-comic contradiction. Again the nearest equivalents in English are to be found in Irish literature. J.M. Synge's *The Tinker's Wedding* (1908) is based on similar contradictions between pagan and Catholic elements in the itinerant and sedentary components of a community.

The emphasis Valle placed, certainly up to *Divinas palabras*, on the collective nature of his theatre links him to both Synge and Yeats, but, more than either of these writers, his outlook is dominated by a belief in determinism. His vision of life is one in which nature and landscape mould regional and national character, language shapes thought, and collective cultures determine the behaviour of individuals. He wrote in a letter to the theatre director C. Rivas Cherif: "Every day I am more convinced that man is not governed by his ideas or degree of education. I imagine there is a determining influence of environment, heredity, physiological defects, etc. and that the motivation for our behaviour is totally divorced from our conscious thoughts...: It is only man's pride that makes him think he is a thinking animal."[4] He then goes on to add that the *Comedias bárbaras* (particularly *Cara de plata* in 1922) were written with this notion very much in mind. The protagonists of the *Comedias* are completely devoid of any duality between self and society or of any conflict between a private and a public self. The natural background and the cultural tradition in which they live are seen as the determining forces which bind classes and individuals in an interdependent relationship. The primary passions which motivate the characters are rooted in the collective rather than the individual psyche. As the author's work develops from the early *Comedias* to *Divinas palabras* and *Cara de plata* ('Silver Face'), then finally to the late one-act plays included in his *Retablo de la lujuria, la avaricia y la muerte* ('Altar-piece of Lust, Greed and Death') published in 1930, these instinctive passions become increasingly dominant, the characters they possess become increasingly dehumanized and the general tone increasingly grotesque.

Valle-Inclán's deterministic outlook was always a double-edged sword. It could produce a heroic kind of literature, in which the individual was enhanced by the forces of nature and tradition working through him. The early *Comedias* clearly come over as a celebration of the heroic, a hymn to a dying breed of rural patriarch. Montenegro is undoubtedly a larger-than-life figure, heroic even in his sins and remorse. But this same outlook could also produce a literature of automata, manipulated by the forces not of nature, but of society (social myths, stereotypes, the power of rhetoric). Valle-Inclán's

---

4    C. Rivas Cherif, 'La Comedia bárbara de Valle-Inclán', *España*, 409, 16 February 1924 (reprinted in Dougherty, *Un Valle-Inclán olvidado*, p. 147, n. 177).

transition to a more anti-heroic view of life became evident from about the middle of the First World War. Contemporary political and social events made an increasing impact on his writing. He wrote some reports from the war front in 1916 for the Madrid newspaper *El Imparcial*,[5] as a result of which he became aware of the limitations of his heroic preconceptions about warfare. About the same time he also became aware of the enormous gap between myth and reality in Spanish public life. One of the first references to this appears in his book on aesthetics *La lámpara maravillosa* ('The Marvellous Lamp') in 1916. He claims that the attitudes enshrined in the very texture of the Castilian language are based on a view of Spain's place in the world which is three centuries out of date. "We are no longer a race of *conquistadores* and theologians", he writes, "and yet our language continues to sustain that fiction. The route to the Indies is no longer ours, nor are there Spanish Popes in the Vatican, yet the baroque hyperbole, imitated from Latin when it was master of the world, still survives in our language."[6] He compares the myths which sustain Spanish pride to the light from a star which had long ceased to exist. As Valle's awareness of this gap increased, he became less content to contemplate, enhance or mythify reality impassively and turned to a more subversive style. From 1920 onwards, he enters into areas which he had previously considered ephemeral, that is, history, politics and contemporary urban reality. He sets out to undermine the illusions of grandeur, heroic myths and inflated rhetoric which had clung to the Spanish psyche since the days of empire. These included the implicit belief in having a privileged historical destiny or in being the standard-bearer of imperishable values supposedly rooted in the national character and the Catholic tradition. The juxtaposition of this heroic mythology with the unheroic realities of contemporary life is perhaps the most consistent unifying feature of the four plays Valle baptized *esperpentos* or 'grotesques': *Luces de bohemia* ('Lights of Bohemia') in 1920, *Los cuernos de don Friolera* ('The Horns of Don Friolera')[7] in 1921, *Las galas del difunto* ('The Dead Man's Best Suit') in 1924 and *La hija del capitán* ('The Captain's Daughter') in 1927. In one of his descriptions of the new genre, Valle compares this contrast of heroic myth and grotesquely inadequate reality to a mouse running around inside a suit of armour. The warrior had died a long time ago, but the mouse continues the charade.[8]

*Lights of Bohemia*, originally serialized in the review *España* in 1920, later revised and amplified in book form in 1924, represents a turning point in Valle-Inclán's theatre. It was written after a seven-year absence from the life of the capital and the professional stage in his native Galicia, during which the author had had time to reflect on his work and its relevance to the social situation in Spain. In *Lights of Bohemia*, Valle abandons some of the Symbolist principles which had formed the basis of his earlier work, such as

5    These were published the following year in book form under the title *La media noche: visión estelar de un momento de guerra*.

6    Translated from *La lámpara maravillosa* (Buenos Aires: Espasa Calpe, 1948), p. 52.

7    Published in the present series under the title of *Mr Punch the Cuckold*.

8    From a lecture given in the Ateneo in Burgos as reported by *El Castellano* (Burgos), 23 October 1925.

the ahistorical approach and the distant authorial perspective, immersing his reader/spectator in the maelstrom of contemporary Madrid and adopting a more attacking, subversive attitude. The play considers — as subsequent *esperpentos* also do — the relevance of the hero in the modern world. The situation of Max Estrella is that of a former 'heroic' figure — associated with Romantic literary archetypes of syphilitic, garret-dwelling poets heroically undergoing poverty and starvation for the sake of their art — who is left stranded on the beach of a commercialized, materialistic and turbulent society which regards him as an irrelevance. Society has changed, history has moved on, and the 'hero' is left as a quaintly anachronistic survival. Before examining the impact of this change on the central character and his response to it, it is necessary to sketch in the historical and social background of Spain in the second decade of the twentieth century.

**The historical and social background**
For the most part, *Lights of Bohemia* reflects social conditions in Madrid (and, to some extent, Barcelona) between about 1917 and 1920.[9] However, it was not Valle's intention to paint a historically exact or chronologically accurate picture. The play also includes allusions to events outside this time-frame, such as those surrounding the 'Tragic Week' in Barcelona in 1909 and the subsequent polarization of public opinion centred around Antonio Maura or the massacre of the Spanish garrison at Annual in Morocco in 1921. These events, along with others, such as the Bolshevic Revolution, the appointment of García Prieto as prime minister (1917) and the death of Galdós (1920) are all lumped together as topical occurrences in the play. With similar disregard for chronology Valle also extends the life of his former literary colleague and old friend, Rubén Darío, who, in historical fact, died in 1916 before many of these things had happened. Rather than a historically exact snapshot, Valle is presenting a faithful synthesis of the confused events of this period, a kaleidoscopic background for his central characters.

Historically speaking, Spain was undergoing a disintegration of its constitutional monarchy, owing mainly to the inability of the political parties to support it. The fragmentation of both the Liberal and Conservative parties made sustained government impossible and attempts to form alliances or national governments generally foundered on the deep-seated divisions between the different components. Since the debilitated parties could not provide strong government, the king, Alfonso XIII, began to take a more active role in politics, particularly in the appointment of political leaders. As a result of this, he had to rely increasingly on the armed forces to provide order and stability. The army, always poised to intervene and 'save' the nation, eventually took over, with the complicity of the king, in the military coup led by Primo de Rivera in 1923.

---

9    I wish to acknowledge a general debt to Raymond Carr's *Modern Spain: 1875-1980* (Oxford, 1980) and *Spain: 1808-1975* (Oxford, 1982) and Gerald Brenan's *The Spanish Labyrinth* (Cambridge, 1967) in writing this section.

The social unrest which forms the background to *Lights of Bohemia* had been endemic, particularly in Barcelona, since the late nineteenth century, although it was greatly exacerbated by more recent historical factors like the colonial wars in Morocco, the Russian Revolution and the First World War. The events of the *Semana Trágica* ('Tragic Week') in July 1909 were sparked off by the call-up of Catalan reservists to defend Spanish mining interests in Morocco. The workers' protest strike degenerated into a confused and leaderless orgy of anti-clericalism in which over 20 churches and some 40 convents were burnt. The repression that followed was swift and severe, with some 175 workers shot in the street and summary execution of the ringleaders. The political repercussions of this episode were far-reaching, since they eventually brought about the fall of the government, the resignation of the then prime minister, Antonio Maura, and a split in the Conservative party which would later prove to be an important contributory factor in destabilizing parliamentary government in Spain. The Russian Revolution sent shock waves all over Europe and stimulated the rise of the labour movement. For the first time in history the anonymous masses found a voice and a leading collective role on the world's stage. The events leading up to the Revolution and its eventual triumph naturally fuelled the militancy of organized labour and brought to the boil an already dangerous situation between capital and labour which had been simmering since the 1890s.

It was, however, the 1914-18 war which imposed the greatest strain on the Spanish economy and thereby created the greatest tensions between capital and labour. Politically, the war served as a catalyst for polarizing ideological opinion within the country. Support for Germany was associated with support for 'order' and 'authority' as against 'decadence' and was embraced by the Conservatives. While for the Liberals, Socialists and Republicans, support for the Allies was synonymous with support for 'civilization' against 'barbarism'. Raymond Carr suggests that, in part, the industrial unrest of the later and post-war years in Spain was the product of rising expectations.[10] The war undoubtedly created a boom in Spain's manufacturing industries and, to a lesser extent, in its agriculture. Prices rose and factory workers wanted a share of the profits they were creating. Many strikes for higher pay were successful because employers with full order books were loth to jeopardize their profits. Despite the resistance of the employers to wage demands, the general effect of the war was to strengthen the hand of the anarchist-dominated unions. Once the war was over, however, the foreign markets for Asturian coal and Bilbao steel disappeared, the industries closed down and arable land reverted to scrub. Workers were thrown out of work or went on to short time for reduced wages. José Gutiérrez Solana in his book *Madrid callejero* ('The Streets of Madrid') describes the food queues he saw in the summer after the Great War: "... an endless line of hungry people waiting with the utmost patience and resignation from early evening until sunrise, when the market stalls opened, to buy, just a little more cheaply, half a litre of oil, a few handfuls of beans or lentils, while the shopkeepers and

---

10    Carr, *Modern Spain*, p. 82.

speculators laughed and raised their prices".[11] In the post-war slump, the social unrest was the product of unemployment and deprivation. The trade unions continued to organize strikes in support of wage claims but, faced with intransigent employers, with far fewer prospects of success. The strikes became more political and revolutionary in character. Anarcho-syndicalism, which had begun as a philosophy of libertarian anarchism gradually declined into bomb-throwing terrorism.

'Monte benéfico de Satanás' *by Santiago Regidor, showing a food queue in Madrid.*

---

11   J. Gutiérrez Solana, *Madrid callejero* (Madrid: Trieste, 1984), p.193. This book was originally published in 1923.

The social unrest in Madrid as depicted in *Lights of Bohemia* was most probably inspired by the general strikes of August 1917 and March 1919, although the labour war continued unabated right through to Primo de Rivera's military dictatorship in 1923. The socialist-backed general strike of 1917, though important as the first revolutionary strike in Spanish history, was ill prepared and far from universally supported. It was this very lack of solidarity which caused many of the disturbances. Strikers tried to compel shops and bars to close and police went round the city trying to keep them open. Trams were attacked by strikers in an attempt to paralyse the public transport system. Workers of striking factories led attacks on others who had decided to continue working. Unamuno describes how some individuals reported at the *Ministerio de la Gobernación* and volunteered their services as 'honorary policemen'.[12] Díaz-Plaja claims that the continuing influence of the ex-prime minister Maura was still capable of polarizing popular opinion, despite the fact that he held no official position either in government or in his party.[13] The official reaction to this unrest was typically ferocious. Martial Law was proclaimed, the Cavalry and Infantry were divided into small detachments to patrol the city and stone-throwing strikers were dispersed by rifles and machine guns.

The employers, for their part, formed themselves into a Federation to combat labour militancy and the power of the unions. In Barcelona they were in no mood for compromise and used any weapons that came to hand. In addition to lock-outs and the refusal to employ militants and recognize anarchist-dominated unions, they met terrorism with terrorism, hiring gunmen to engage in guerrilla warfare with the militants of the unions (in particular, the C.N.T.) or to assassinate their leaders. According to Brenan, the total number of political assassinations in Catalonia between 1919 and 1923 was over 700[14] and Carr claims that in January 1921 there were twenty-one assassinations in the space of 36 hours.[15] In their struggle against the unions, the employers received enthusiastic assistance from an army by now totally beyond government control. As the political parties became less capable of governing, the army grew more impatient to intervene and right-wing opinion began to see military intervention as the only solution to the nation's problems.

In November 1920, under pressure from the Employers' Federation, the government appointed as Governor-General of Barcelona General Martínez Anido, a hard-liner who did not hesitate to use illegal methods against 'anarchists' and 'revolutionaries'. These included using hired gunmen to shoot certain syndicalist leaders on sight, making arrests and shooting the prisoners on the way to prison for allegedly 'attempting to escape', or releasing prisoners and having gangs of gunmen shoot them down before they could reach the relative safety of their working-class territory. Martínez Anido and the

---

12    For a documentary account of these events see F. Díaz-Plaja, *España, los años decisivos: 1917* (Barcelona: Plaza y Janés, 1970), pp. 71-91 and *El siglo XX: historia de España en sus documentos* (Madrid, 1960), pp. 371-7.

13    *España, los años decisivos: 1917*, p. 81.

14    *The Spanish Labyrinth*, p. 74, n.2.

15    *Modern Spain*, p. 90.

employers were engaged on a policy of creating panic and instability, deliberately provoking acts of violence in order to bring about the total suppression of anarcho-syndicalism by the authority of the state. For this reason, many of their arrests and assassinations were directed at the more moderate anarchist leaders, who were trying to reach a negotiated settlement with the government. The situation was further complicated by the presence of free-lance *agents provocateurs* and mercenary groups who acted either as informers or assassins for one side or the other and who frequently incriminated or killed totally innocent people, particularly when business was slack.

The most dominant figure in Spanish politics during the first two decades of the twentieth century was undoubtedly Antonio Maura, who is referred to several times in *Lights of Bohemia*. A self-made lawyer-politician from Majorca, he succeeded Francisco Silvela as the leader of the Conservative party in 1903 and first became prime minister for a brief period in 1904. Maura was a devout Catholic of austere character and uncompromising convictions. His principal aims were the reform of local government and the electoral laws. He wished to release what he referred to as 'the real Spain of the neutral masses' from the scourge of *caciquismo* or local political bosses and ensure fair and representative government by a programme of reform from above. Maura had the attitudes of a high tory who ruled by divine right. He never wavered from his conviction that the 'neutral masses' he was about to liberate were natural Conservatives and that any dissenting voice was the unrepresentative opinion of rabble-rousing demagogues, who should be suppressed in the name of order. It was his determination to convert his ideological views into law which led to the polarization of Spanish politics. During his ministry from 1907 to 1909, his response to the labour troubles in Barcelona united the forces of the Left against him. The terrorist law of 1908 resulted in a pact between the Liberals and the Republicans to drive him from office. The events of Barcelona's 'Tragic Week' in July 1909 and the ensuing repression and executions of anarchist leaders, particularly that of Francisco Ferrer, who at the time was not even in Barcelona, created a violent rift in Spanish politics, split the Conservative party and brought about Maura's resignation in 1913. Support for Maura continued to exist during his exile from party politics in the form of what Raymond Carr calls 'street Maurism'. That is to say that Maura became the rallying cry for quasi-fascist malcontents and violent youth. This atmosphere of warring factions between his supporters ('Maura sí') and his opponents ('Maura no') and the presence of right-wing vigilante groups such as *Acción Cuidadana* (Citizens' Action) are reflected in the social background of *Lights of Bohemia*.

Maura directed his appeal to a 'true Catholic' or 'essential' Spain, an appeal which supposedly transcended all political partisanship and one which would later be echoed by the dictator Primo de Rivera and the Falange in their efforts to by-pass the democratic process. Maura's supporters saw him as a messianic figure who would one day return from the political wilderness, with the backing of the army, as the saviour of the nation. Possibly to the disappointment of his followers, Maura did not become an extra-parliamentary dictator. Instead he was merely to become prime minister in one of a series of national or coalition governments which assumed power after the general strike of 1917. From the end of the First World War to 1923 Spain had ten changes of government. The Liberals were split between the followers of the Count of Romanones and García Prieto, the Conservatives between Maura and Eduardo Dato, the Republicans were against the principle of the monarchy, and the King was busy playing politics to defend his own position. In the rapidly worsening social situation in Barcelona, the capital and rural Andalusia, where anarchist influence was very strong, the politicians proved incapable of governing and the army, as is so often the case in Spanish history, piously accepted the task of national salvation.

## Bohemian life in Madrid

Historically speaking, literary bohemian life has rarely been a purely aesthetic phenomenon. The Romantic bohemia of the mid-nineteenth century in France (Gautier, Gérard de Nerval, Musset), elegaically evoked in Henri Murger's *Scènes de la Vie de Bohême* (1847), with its quasi-religious cult of Art, was quickly followed by a more revolutionary and socially-conscious bohemianism between about 1855 and 1875, exemplified in the works of Jules Vallès, whose book *Les Réfractaires* (1866) sees the role of Art as the defence of the underprivileged in society. The rampant capitalism of the latter part of the century with its concomitant social injustice created a sense of rootlessness in the artist, always in rebellion against bourgeois institutions, yet torn between dedication to his art and solidarity with the struggles of a rising proletariat. These tensions between artistic and social allegiances can be observed in the *fin de siècle* bohemianism of Montmartre (Paul Verlaine, Catulle Mendès, Tristan Corbière, François Coppée and others, with occasional reinforcements from Spain and Latin America, such as Alejandro Sawa and Rubén Darío). Alongside the devotees of beauty and form were poets like Coppée, who wrote of the lives of the poor and deprived. Art and social concern were constant, though occasionally uneasy, bedfellows in the literary reviews of the period, *La Plume* and the prestigious *Mercure de France*.

The same debate between 'pure art' and social protest or awareness divided opinion in Spain's rising literary generation at the turn of the twentieth century. United in their opposition to the traditionalist values reimplanted by the Restoration of the monarchy in 1874, they were nevertheless divided between the various ideologies on offer: socialism, anarchism, republicanism, symbolism or decadentism, to name but a few. To those unsympathetic with their views, writers of this generation, whether or not they were aesthetes and whatever political and social causes they espoused, became known pejoratively as *modernistas* ('Modernists'). The extent of the social function of the artist was central to most of their polemics. The pages of literary and socio-political magazines such as *Don Quijote* (1892-1903), *Nuestro Tiempo* (1903-26) and *Alma Española* (1903-4) are full of articles on the nature of the artist's responsibility in a society in which a rise in the urban proletariat and a widening gulf between capital and labour, as well as chronic hunger in Andalusia, was producing some of the most profound social unrest in Europe. To what extent was the creed of 'pure art' tenable in a society where hunger and injustice were rife? *Alma Española* reflects all shades of opinion from defenders of aestheticism to champions of outright social commitment.[16] However, the dominant view that emerges from the reviews of the period is in favour of a fusion of art and the social question, a reconciliation of art and utility. Modernism in literature and the intellectual revolution which embraced a wide range of iconoclastic doctrines were frequently associated with the same breaking of traditional moulds as anarchism in politics. In fact the review *La Anarquía literaria* ('Literary Anarchy') was founded on the premise that there is an equivalence between literary/aesthetic and social/political renovation.[17] Many bohemian artists and writers, particularly around the turn of the century, became attracted to the theory of anarchism. They strongly identified with the proletarian's sense of alienation from society, and their feeling of frustration and impotence in a climate of social disintegration led them to embrace a wholesale rejection of the past, existing institutions and the status quo. Ernesto Bark (who is caricatured in *Lights of Bohemia* as Basilio Soulinake) constantly returns in his writings to the theme of the interdependence between art and social revolution and refers to the literary bohemia of his time as the 'intellectual proletariat', a term which, in view of the meagre rewards given to literary creation, translation and journalism, at least had a basis in economics.

This is the view one might derive from the literary magazines of the period. The Madrid bohemian set of the early 1900s, as recalled by contemporaries in their memoirs (Pío and Ricardo Baroja, Alberto Insúa, Eduardo Zamacois and others) comes over as rather less high-minded in their devotion either to art or to social questions. Alberto Insúa, for instance, describes the night life of Madrid just before the time of the 'Tragic Week' in Barcelona:

> *It was a Madrid in which everybody knew one another and it was not difficult to place people with their appropriate names, nicknames and reputations: such and such an aristocrat with a yen for low life; such and such a lady who enjoyed not being one on certain nights of the week; such and such a famous writer or dramatist who never returned home on his own two feet unsupported by his fellow revellers; such and such a celebrated matador who chose the most elegant and expensive cabaret to regale his admirers with real champagne; such and such a brilliant poet who remained faithful to his 'manzanilla' and was a specialist in the art of 'cante jondo'. And many more types of illustrious and talented bohemians, as well as bohemians whose only inspiration was the spirit of raw alcohol.* [18]

---

16  *Alma Española: Nov. 1903 - Abril 1904,* ed. Patricia O'Riordan (Madrid: Ediciones Turner, 1978).

17  The *Propósito* of the first and only issue of this review is reprinted in I. Zavala, 'Fin de siglo: modernismo, '98 y bohemia', *Cuadernos para el diálogo,* Col. los Suplementos, 54, Madrid, 1974.

18  A. Insúa, *Memorias* (Madrid: Editorial Tesoro, 1952), p. 567.

Insúa describes the atmosphere of Madrid at the time as highly politicized, but represents the bohemian elements as keen only in their efforts to avoid contact with politics. According to these sources, few bohemians seemed prepared to starve to safeguard the 'purity' of their art or to carry out the proletarian revolution. Ricardo Baroja concedes that some were genuinely inspired by a passion for their art, but claims that their interest in and knowledge of politics were extremely limited. At most, they felt a romantic sympathy for a mystically-orientated kind of anarchism.[19] His brother Pío took a less charitable view, not only denying their political interest, but claiming that the artistic interest was, in many cases, a pretentious veneer to conceal a tendency to idleness, alcoholism and malicious gossip.[20] Both Pío Baroja and Rubén Darío had had considerable experience of the bohemian life in their youth and later rejected it as a corrosive and pernicious influence. Darío, as we see in *Lights of Bohemia*, rejects the life while still being under its influence.

The poet, novelist and journalist Alejandro Sawa (1862-1909), widely accepted as the model for Max Estrella, was a man who embodied all the contradictions of bohemian life, between his social and aesthetic convictions as well as between his life and his beliefs. He was regarded by many of his contemporaries as the archetypal bohemian, whose talent and intellect were undermined by alcohol, idleness and the irregularity of his lifestyle. His writings — particularly his journalism — reveal a serious concern for the social and political issues of his day. He rebukes his countrymen for their indifference towards the disaster of Cavite in the Phillipines, where the Spanish fleet was blown out of the water by the United States navy.[21] In an article entitled 'The Lies of History' he roundly condemns the inculcation of empty imperialist values in Spanish education and advocates the exercise of will power and political action, conspicuously absent from his personal life.[22] He was well-read in revolutionary literature, formed part of the founding group of the socialist review *Germinal* and wrote with anger and indignation on the plight of the poor, the hungry and the homeless. At the same time, Sawa believed passionately in art and literature as an ideal self-sufficient world. He was a devotee of the French *Symbolistes* and revered the poetry of Verlaine, whose work he did much to disseminate amongst his own contemporaries and the rising *modernista* generation. Yet there is no evidence in his writings of any conflict either between his devotion to aesthetics and his social convictions or between his self-destructive lifestyle and his evident awareness of a need to respond to the tragedy of his social context. These are the latent contradictions which Valle-Inclán was to depict in his portrayal of Max Estrella.

---

19    R. Baroja, *Gente del '98* (Madrid: Cátedra, 1989), pp. 51-2.
20    P. Baroja, 'Nuevo Tablado de Arlequín', *Obras Completas,* vol.V (Madrid: Biblioteca Nueva, 1948), p. 93.
21    *Alma Española,* XV, February 1904.
22    'La historia que miente', *La Anarquía Literaria,* July 1905 (reprinted in Zavala, 'Fin de siglo').

It should not be assumed that Max Estrella was conceived as a literary re-creation of Alejandro Sawa. There are aspects of Sawa's personality which do not appear in Max and dimensions of Max's character which, as far as we know, are at variance with Sawa's. Max Estrella, like most literary characters, is a composite figure, containing elements of different people of Valle's acquaintance, not least of the author himself. However, the parallels both of circumstances and character are sufficiently striking to be worth recording.

Alejandro Sawa was undoubtedly the most dominant personality of an older and more impoverished generation of bohemians who frequented the taverns of Madrid in the early 1900s before the construction of the Gran Vía.[23] Between 1890 and 1896 he had lived in the Latin Quarter of Paris, where he had made the acquaintance of Verlaine and other leading French writers. This period had such a profound influence on his life that his subsequent existence in Madrid, up to his death in 1909, seemed to him like banishment. Like his literary counterpart, he had a French wife and one daughter and lived in an attic flat surrounded by the memorabilia of his Parisian heyday.[24] The parallels with Sawa's sad final years in Madrid are more specific. His suicidal despair after losing his collaboration with the newspaper *El Liberal* is referred to by Valle-Inclán in a letter to Rubén Darío.[25] Like Max, he went blind and had to dictate his literary and journalistic work to his wife. His last years were marked by ill health and encroaching madness. His letters and the testimony of friends speak of his increasing sense of abandonment and oblivion, a feeling of anachronistic irrelevance in an indifferent society, which is central to Valle's portrayal of Max Estrella. A letter to Rubén Darío dated 31 May 1908 reveals a touch of bitterness and self-pity, as well as a degree of prophetic insight:

*How can a man like me die like this, in obscurity, assassinated, as it were, by all those around him, without his death, like his life, having the least significance, other than a purely anecdotic interest as an isolated example of rebellion against the society of his time?* [26]

---

23  Pío Baroja (*Obras Completas*, V, p. 93) draws a distinction between an older and more impoverished generation of bohemians who frequented the taverns and those of his own more dandified generation who preferred the cafés. The speed of social change was possibly accelerated by the creation of the Gran Vía from about 1906. Many of the smaller streets in the centre where the cheap taverns were situated were demolished to make way for more modern buildings. See Gutiérrez Solana, *Madrid callejero*, ch.1.

24  The journalist Nicasio Hernández Luquero, in an article for *El País* (7 March 1909) on the occasion of Sawa's death, confirms at least one detail about his room mentioned by Valle-Inclán in the play. This is the signed and dedicated photographs of well-known French writers (Zola, Hugo, Musset) which adorned his walls. This article is quoted in Allen Phillips's excellent monograph *Alejandro Sawa: mito y realidad* (Madrid: Ediciones Turner, 1977), p. 26.

25  Dictino Alvarez (ed.), *Cartas de Rubén Darío* (Madrid, 1963), p. 70.
26  Dictino Alvarez, pp. 65-6.

Some of the details of Max's death and burial are also mentioned by contemporary commentators in connection with Alejandro Sawa. Eduardo Zamacois remembers the point of a nail sticking through the plain pine boards of Sawa's coffin[27] and Alberto Insúa vividly recalls the coffin lying on the floor and the burial attended by 'four or five friends who, between them, had paid for the funeral'.[28]

Zamacois has given us what is perhaps the most complete portrait we have of Alejandro Sawa.[29] He records the larger-than-life histrionic quality which earned him the nickname of 'Alejandro, the Magnificent'. Like Max, he was a man of the large gesture, the commanding presence and the theatrical pose. "Even when he was asking for something, he appeared to be issuing a command", Zamacois observes. He then relates the anecdote of being invited to a drink by Sawa in a bar. Upon being ordered to serve drinks and, in addition, lend the poet five pesetas, the bar owner nervously remonstrated with him and passed him a piece of paper with a long list of previously contracted debts. Sawa ignored this with olympian disdain and continued talking to his guests, until the bar owner became so embarrassed that he withdrew the list and pushed five pesetas across the counter. Sawa was a man whose life and personality overshadowed and outlasted his work, a man who cultivated his image with the greatest care, yet possessed an inner conviction in the supremacy of his art, which neither poverty nor blindness could dislodge. He wore his tattered clothes — large broad-brimmed hat, large necktie, large walking stick — with the aristocratic pride of one who serves a noble cause and carries the torch of an honoured tradition.

Other contemporary accounts paint a less heroic picture. Pío Baroja portrays him as a vain and envious individual, with little real talent and generous only with other people's money. He recalls an incident which neatly illustrates the central paradox of the sponger and the aristocrat in Sawa's character. Having allowed Baroja to pay for a round of drinks, Sawa asked him for three pesetas. Baroja explained that he did not have the money on him.

*'Do you live far from here?', Alejandro asked me with his arrogant air. 'No, quite near.' 'Good. Go home and fetch the money.' He spoke with such authority that I went home and brought him the money. He came out to the door of the tavern, took the money and said: 'You may go now.'* [30]

Zamora Vicente shrewdly observes that this negative side of Sawa's personality finds its expression, not in Max Estrella, but in his grotesque shadow, Don Latino.[31] This

---

27    E. Zamacois, *Años de miseria y de risa* (Madrid: Renacimiento, 1924), p. 195.
28    *Memorias*, p. 547.
29    *Años de miseria y de risa*, pp. 189-95.
30    *Obras Completas*, VII, (Madrid: Renacimiento, 1949), p.735.
31    A. Zamora Vicente, *La realidad esperpéntica: Aproximación a 'Luces de bohemia'* (Madrid: Gredos, 1969), p. 47.

theory is reinforced by a number of biographical coincidences. Don Latino is given the same birthplace as Sawa: Seville. Valle has Latino go around with a dog, a practice adopted by Sawa in his later years, partly because of his blindness, but also as an extension of his personality. Finally, Latino claims to have done translations for the French publishers Garnier while resident in Paris, which, in Sawa's case, was true. The fact that Valle-Inclán chooses to unload the negative aspects of the original model on to the character of Don Latino reflects, on balance, a sympathetic though not uncritical attitude to Sawa, as well as to Max Estrella. When Sawa died, Valle wrote a short letter to Rubén Darío in which he said that he had wept in front of his coffin "for him, for myself and for all the poor poets".[32] There is an evident sympathy in the tone of this letter which would later be transferred to the portrayal of Max. Moreover, there is evidence of self-identification with Sawa and a feeling of a tragic destiny, borne out by the text of the play, common to all those poets marginalized by society. Although this feeling is tempered in *Lights of Bohemia* with objective criticism (Max does not remain entirely unsullied by the times he lives in, nor does he continue to believe in the supremacy of art in that contemporary context), the letter quoted does express an attitude of nostalgia for all that was dignified and heroic in the bohemian life and of regret at its inevitable passing.

## 2. Analysis of the play

*Lights of Bohemia* is the first play which Valle places in a totally contemporary setting. All the action takes place in the streets, bars, cafés and newspaper offices of Madrid in the immediate aftermath of the First World War and the Russian Revolution. The social and political conditions — strikes and demonstrations, political assassinations, clashes with the police, workers' meetings in the *Casa del pueblo*, the right-wing backlash in the form of vigilante groups like 'Citizens' Action' — are the consequences of these historic events. The turbulent and politicized atmosphere is a palpable presence throughout the play, created by allusions to police patrols, street clashes resulting in the death of innocent people and damage to property, arrests and prisoners shot 'while attempting to escape'.

The play is crammed with topical references to contemporary figures in politics, literature, journalism and bullfighting. Many of the characters are based on real-life contemporary counterparts.[33] In addition to the case of Max Estrella / Alejandro Sawa, already referred to, other characters have been reliably paired with their historical equivalents: Zarathustra with the bookseller Gregorio Pueyo, Don Peregrino Gay with Ciro Bayo, the well-known traveller and eccentric, Basilio Soulinake with the bohemian anarchist and writer, Ernesto Bark, the Minister of the Interior with ex-man of letters and ex-bohemian, Julio Burell. Dorio de Gadex (pseudonym of an obscure contemporary

---

32  Dictino Alvarez, p. 70.
33  For further information see the appropriate notes in the Commentary.

journalist and poet) and, of course, Rubén Darío, appear as themselves. The current literary and intellectual fashions are reflected in the dialogue of the bohemian 'Modernists': the adoration of Verlaine and the deprecation of Galdós, the disdainful attacks on the political establishment and the Spanish Academy, the vogue of theosophy and Madame Blavatsky. Popular feeling in the streets and bars is manifested in the vilification of Maura and Romanones, in gossip about the drunkenness of the journalist Mariano de Cavia, and the legendary rivalry between the bullfighters Joselito and Belmonte.

There is something deliberate and almost aggressive about the topicality of *Lights of Bohemia*, to the extent that the contemporary allusions run the risk of obscuring the more durable aspects of the play. Indeed, for Valle-Inclán, whose art had always been associated with the quest for stasis and the maintenance of artistic distance, contemporary reality had always represented flux, transience and confusion. His decision to immerse himself in the ephemera of contemporary history naturally owes a great deal to the circumstances, but it also comes over as a challenge which he issues to himself, that is, a challenge to confront the heroic world of his imagination with the real society he lived in.

As has already been pointed out, Valle-Inclán's cult of the heroic past had always implied an attitude towards his own time. Consequently, given the right circumstances, a more direct expression of this antipathy to his historical present was a more logical development than might at first appear. If we examine Valle's attitude to this contemporary world in *Lights of Bohemia*, we can see that his main attack is not against cruelty or injustice as such but against institutionalization, commercialization and the progressive 'bourgeoisification' of life and society, not so much against policies and political leaders as against public attitudes. Lizard-Slicer and Zarathustra are the representatives of these commercial ethics. They embody a conservative commercial class for whom social order is a higher priority than social justice. The Press has become the docile mouthpiece of Authority. The police have become the mindless tool of state bureaucracy and the forces of order kill innocent children in the defence of private property and 'honest commerce'. Art has become, in the Minister's words, 'a marketable commodity'. Max claims that even the religious sensibility of the Spaniards has been institutionalized, that Heaven has become 'a Church fête with no hanky-panky which the Children of Mary may attend with the permission of the parish priest' and that the great enigmas of life and death have been transformed into 'the tittle-tattle of old crones doting over a stuffed cat'. The harshest criticism is reserved for the unheroic, life-reducing aspects of modern existence which trivialize even what is noble and generous.

The scenes interpolated in the 1924 version of the play (2, 6 and 11) seem to convey a more explicitly political viewpoint. There is a clear identification on Valle's part with the Catalan prisoner. What in earlier work had been sympathy with a traditionalist rural *pueblo* now transfers itself to a revolutionary urban working class. Referring to the current strife in Barcelona, Valle overtly condemns, through this character, the capitalist organization of society, the commercial exploitation of workers and the forces of order who defend it, and advocates the abolition of inherited wealth and the revolution of the proletariat. These radical attitudes, however, perhaps owe more to Valle's long-held anti-bourgeois views and instinct for heroic extremes than to a reasoned political position. José Antonio Maravall argues convincingly that, for the later Valle-Inclán, the real appeal of revolutionary anarchism was the epic-heroic nature of its mystical vision.[34]

It would be a distortion of Valle's intentions to see the play exclusively as an indictment of contemporary values or of the capitalist system. This new social and political awareness must be set against the attitudes of the blind poet through whom we perceive this society. The focus of this first *esperpento* is the relationship between modern society and the artist, and, more specifically, the metamorphosis of the artist's 'heroic' image by an unheroic context.

The vision of man and society formulated in Scene 12 of *Lights of Bohemia* is a complete reversal of the heroic view, since it implies that collective social pressures have become the controlling agents over the life of the individual. Valle's earlier creations such as Bradomín and Montenegro, though formed by their setting and tradition, are nevertheless conceived on a plane above the trivialities of organized society and historical developments. Valle-Inclán himself had always asserted the artist's duty of remaining independent of his historical situation by the exercise of will. In *La lámpara maravillosa*, he establishes this as the first norm of his aesthetic discipline: "Be like the nightingale which looks not at the ground from the green bough on which it sings".[35] Max Estrella is one nightingale who is unable to maintain this sublime aloofness from his historical situation. The social and political unrest of his country, his own precarious circumstances and the changing values around him inevitably leave their mark and change his views.

In both *Lights of Bohemia* and his second *esperpento*, *Los cuernos de don Friolera* ('The Horns of Don Friolera'), Valle creates protagonists who in a former age might have been considered tragic and heroic figures. The literary archetype he had in mind for Don Friolera is clear enough: the hero of an honour drama, a contemporary Othello. Max Estrella's literary antecedents are more confused. They are partly classical, since his blindness is related in the text to that of Homer, Hermes and Belisarius. But the archetype which emerges most strongly from the character's behaviour and circumstances is a Romantic one, the bohemian artist of 'uncompromising integrity', blind, penniless and syphilitic, who lives in a garret and dies in the street. In both plays it is the surrounding contemporary context which renders the heroic archetype absurd; life makes a mockery of literature.

Valle-Inclán's *esperpentos* were part of a general shift in European sensibility after the First World War which questioned the mythology surrounding the hero. This was not so much the burlesque of a literary institution which had fallen into disrepute as a feeling that the very nature of twentieth-century life militated against the heroic. The vision of

---

34    *Revista de Occidente*, 44-5 (1966), p. 253.
35    *La lámpara*, p. 18.

James Joyce was to treat the present as a travesty of the past, while trying to synthesize the heroic archetypes with the unheroic present. Later Bertold Brecht set about dismantling the hero (and indeed the whole apparatus of heroic tragedy) in plays like *The Life of Galileo*. Valle-Inclán's Max Estrella is a bohemian poet in the heroic mould marginalized in a prosaic society. The social context is shown as a concave mirror which distorts Max's image into that of a clown. The attitudes of the various characters with whom he comes into contact serve to underline his anachronistic irrelevance. They either exploit him, deceive him, despise him or pay hypocritical lip-service to his 'genius'. His values are systematically degraded, as he is robbed by Latino, ignored by his so-called colleagues, frustrated in his attempt to relate to the proletariat and compelled by necessity to accept money from a government slush fund. Valle-Inclán emphasises the hero's decline into terminal irrelevance by killing him off three scenes before the end of the play, after which we see how society's mirror distorts his death, his burial and finally his memory.

The importance of *Lights of Bohemia* lies in Valle's perception of the alienating effects of history, in the realization that our view of the hero depends on and is changed by the historical context and that the hero's values cannot survive in isolation. Those values have to be corroborated and endorsed by a collective context — a consensus — and where that corroboration is lacking they become irrelevant and absurd. Scene 12, in which Max Estrella in effect retrospectively assesses his situation, alludes metaphorically to this metamorphosis of the 'hero'. The image of the distorting mirror evidently refers to the changed social context. ("All our cherished heroes have wandered into a hall of distorting mirrors." "Reflected in a concave mirror, even the most beautiful images become absurd.") In other words, the greater or lesser value we attribute to any person, quality or action is ultimately determined by the prevailing moral climate. The figure of Don Latino is consistent with this emphasis on the metamorphosis of values, since he is not only a degraded foil to Max, but also takes his place in the eyes of society when he cashes in on Max's lottery ticket and his literary works, and receives the Drunk's accolade of 'privileged mind' at the end.

The main dramatic interest of the play lies in the ambivalent nature of Max Estrella's response to a situation in which he has become an irrelevance. How far does he remain a helpless victim of his situation and how far is he able to overcome it? *Lights of Bohemia* is unique in Valle's work in that it shows a central character who is fully aware of the social forces acting upon him. It is this awareness, which prevents him from being a totally conditioned individual and gives the play its extra dimension. There is a conscious element of self-doubt and self-accusation in Max, revealed in part by his association with Don Latino. Latino is like a grotesque shadow of the protagonist, a sychophantic imitator and a constant reminder to Max of his own absurdity and potential — perhaps real — inauthenticity. Latino is, above all, a fake, a pseudo- intellectual and a false friend. He cheats Max out of money (Scene 2), refuses to lend him his overcoat and take him home (Scene 4), protests love and admiration for Max, yet is too cowardly to defend him (Scene 5), is pretentious in his intellectual aspirations while being profoundly ignorant (Scene 9), sees only play-acting in authentic human grief (Scene 11), steals the dying Max's wallet (Scene 12) and neglects to assist Max's family when he wins the lottery prize (Scene 15). Yet, with all his depravity, Latino's function is not simply to enhance the nobility of Max's character. On the contrary, Max's association with Latino clearly argues a degree of self-identification and dependence. He sees the debasement of values so evident in Latino as a distorted reflection of himself. He despises Latino, just as he despises himself a little, particularly after accepting money from the Minister. His attacks on Latino are, in part, attacks on himself. Is he really any better than 'a pedlar of lousy literature by instalments'? He associates with Latino to remind himself that, besides being an anachronism, he could also lose his authenticity as an artist and as a man.

The only thing that prevents Max from becoming a Don Latino is the honest acceptance of his own degraded image. Max salvages some authenticity from his situation by the only means available to him, by means of artistic distance, by standing outside himself and observing himself dispassionately. In the early scenes of the play Max strikes many of the tragic, rhetorical or self-pitying attitudes that he will later reject as inappropriate to the circumstances. Scene 6 with the Catalan prisoner and Scene 8 with the Minister of the Interior lead him to a more objective view of himself. Scene 8, in particular, is the turning point, when Max goes to demand satisfaction for his honour and ends by accepting a cash payment on a regular basis. After this scene Max realizes that he is tainted by the society he lives in and directs his sardonic humour against himself. A new spirit of self-deprecation and clowning runs through the later scenes. Max even makes his own death into an elaborate charade in which he lays himself out in preparation, orders the funeral dirge to be sung and utters the calculatedly untragic last words of "Good night!" This is his clownish response to a world which has denied him a tragic exit.

Max's antics stem partly from a feeling of guilt and self-disgust, but they are also a bid for authenticity and freedom in a fight against historical inevitability. Friedrich Dürrenmatt's Alfred Ill *(The Visit)* and Romulus *(Romulus the Great)* are both anti-heroes who turn defeat into victory by accepting the version of history that is imposed on them, whilst managing to retain a hold on human values in a dehumanized and dehumanizing world. Max Estrella, created some thirty years earlier, is a 'hero' in this mould. The world is making him into a clown and he knows it. Like Dürrenmatt's Romulus who, confronted with the imminent collapse of the Roman Empire, decides to breed chickens, Max consciously accepts the role of clown and plays it to the end in order to make a fool of historical necessity. His self-destructive humour is the expression of a marginal kind of freedom. Alone of all Valle-Inclán's protagonists, he is permitted this modest triumph over determinism.[36]

---

36   F. Dürrenmatt in his now classic essay 'Problems of the Theatre' sees parody as a way of regaining artistic freedom: "In laughter man's freedom becomes manifest, in crying his necessity" *(Theatre in the Twentieth Century,* ed. R.W. Corrigan, New York: Grove Press, 1963, p. 73). Alan E. Smith *('Luces de bohemia* y la figura de Cristo', *Hispanic Review,* 57

It is perhaps the ambivalence of Max's response — poised between self-accusation and liberating humour, impotence and heroic resistance — and the consequent ambivalence of Valle's treatment — critical and ironic yet nostalgically affectionate — that constitutes his richness as a dramatic character. Another aspect of this ambivalence is his attitude towards art and the demands of social justice. Max Estrella, like his historical counterpart Alejandro Sawa, is typical of many *déclassé* writers and artists at the turn of the century who were drawn to the proletarian cause chiefly because they identified with their sense of marginalization by middle-class society.[37] Max, however, unlike Sawa, is made to realize that this desire for association inevitably comes up against an unbridgeable gulf. The scene with the Catalan prisoner reveals the similarity of the plight of the artist-intellectual to that of the worker (the Prisoner's description of himself as a 'pariah' would undoubtedly have struck a chord in Max), but underlines the mutual irrelevance of their separate worlds. They speak different languages. Max's bohemian hyperbole never quite harmonizes with the Prisoner's ideological solemnity. This and other scenes interpolated in the final version give the lie to Max's claim in Scene 4 that he is a 'man of the people'. Scene 11 not only emphasizes the artist's irrelevance to the people's cause by portraying him as a helpless onlooker to the tragic killing of a babe-in-arms, but also suggests a moral incompatibility between devotion to art and the pursuit of social justice. In such circumstances, Max feels a sense of guilt and shame at his poet's calling and bohemian way of life: "Barbarian rabble! All of them! All of us! The poets ... we're the greatest rabble of the lot!" As with the other paradoxes in his ambiguous hero, the author leaves this tension between his bohemian artistic lifestyle and the clamouring of his conscience for social justice as an unresolved contradiction.

Max Estrella's assertion that our lives are not a tragedy but a travesty might lead us to conclude that Valle was negating the whole idea of tragedy. If, however, we take Scene 12 of *Lights of Bohemia* in conjunction with other reported comments on the *esperpento*, it becomes clear that this is not the case. Valle repeatedly made the point in his later theoretical pronouncements that the *esperpento* consisted in the inadequacy of contemporary 'heroes' to measure up to the reality of tragic situations:

> *Spain is a vast stage set for a tragedy, a tragedy beyond the capacity of the actors to perform. They are like cardboard men without passions or ideals, who appear ludicrous decked out in their heroic trappings.*[38]

> *The facts of life — its sadnesses, its loves — are always and inevitably the same. What changes is the cast, the protagonists of that life. Formerly, the main parts*

---

(1989), pp. 57-71) approaches the same paradoxes of triumph through defeat, life in death and freedom in the acceptance of inevitability via an interesting exploration of the parallels between Max Estrella's final binge and the Passion of Christ.

37    See Clara E. Lida, 'Literatura anarquista y anarquismo literario', *Nueva Revista de Filología Hispánica*, XIX, 2 (1970), pp. 360-81.

38    Francisco Madrid, *La vida altiva de Valle-Inclán* (Buenos Aires: Poseidón, 1943), p. 345.

*were played by gods and heroes. Today, well, what can I say? Formerly, destiny weighed upon the shoulders of Oedipus or Medea and the suffering was borne with pride and dignity. Today that destiny is the same, with the same fatality, the same grandeur, the same suffering ... but the men who sustain it have changed. The actions, the anguish, the responsibilities are the same as those of yesterday. The men are different, too diminutive to support their burden. Hence the contrast, the sense of the incongruous and ridiculous.*[39]

Clearly what is being denied is the existence or the possibility of the tragic hero (at least in the classical mould), not the spirit of tragedy itself. Valle-Inclán believes in the essentially tragic destiny of of his protagonists, while seeing them as comically unequal to that destiny. But this raises a further question. Does he think of this tragedy as a traditional abstract standard, unattainable by those gesticulating contemporary clowns who aspire to it, or does the *esperpento* begin to take comedy into the area, described by Dürrenmatt and practised by much of the Theatre of the Absurd, in which it becomes the only way of expressing a fragmented, paradoxical, incomprehensible and essentially *tragic* world?

There is at least one statement which unambiguously affirms Valle's intention to express the tragic through the medium of the comic or grotesque:

*You all know that in ancient tragedy, the characters progressed towards their tragic destiny with all the appropriate tragic attitudes and gestures. In my new genre I too lead my characters towards a tragic destiny, but use instead ludicrous attitudes and gestures. In real life there are many human beings who carry their tragedy within them, yet are incapable of an elevated attitude and whose actions are consequently merely grotesque.*[40]

*Lights of Bohemia* seems to be an attempt to seek a new sense of the tragic by delving into the comic paradoxes of contemporary society. Max Estrella's claim that the tragic sense of Spanish life can *only* be conveyed by an aesthetic criterion of systematic distortion suggests that the distortion is there not to deny tragedy but as an alternative route to it. In the play Valle achieves a dynamic tension between tragic and grotesque elements. The posturing of the bohemian poets clashes with the reality of death on the streets, the hollow sentiments of Don Latino with the real despair of the protagonist. Valle consciously avoids making Max's death into the tragic culmination of the action, to stress the point that, in the eyes of society, his death is as irrelevant as his life. And it is this irrelevance to the society around him which consistently turns Max's tragedy into farce. The last three scenes are thus a conscious and *dramatic* use of anti-climax in

---

39   Dougherty, *Un Valle-Inclán olvidado*, p. 192 (from an interview with José Montero Alonso, prologue to Valle-Inclán's 'Vísperas de la Gloriosa', *La Novela de Hoy* (Madrid), 418, 16 May 1930).

40   Dougherty, *Un Valle-Inclán olvidado*, pp. 107-8 (from an interview in *Diario de la Marina* (Habana), 12 September 1921).

which circumstances undermine the tragic dignity of his wake, burial and memory. Perhaps 'try to undermine' would be more exact, since, despite the accumulation of anti-tragic details, the tragedy obstinately refuses to die. The humour is anti-tragic in that it does everything to reduce the conventionally tragic or heroic stature of the protagonist, yet, in doing so, heightens and reinforces his authenticity and hence the tragedy of his situation.

The humour of the play is partly in this juxtaposition of attitudes and circumstances, but it is also, as we have seen, a conscious response on the part of the central character. It is the degree of empathy that Valle allows his audience with Max Estrella which accounts for the play's distinctive tone of ironic pathos, not unlike Sean O'Casey's *Juno and the Paycock* (1924) or *The Plough and the Stars* (1926). O'Casey was exploring the territory of hybrid emotions in drama about the same time as Valle was working on his *esperpentos*. The ironic, anti-heroic treatment of the Irish Troubles, the amalgam of grotesquerie, tall talk, hunger and death in O'Casey's Dublin strongly remind us of the 'grotesque farce, sparkling wits and empty stomachs' of Valle-Inclán's riot-torn Madrid. But whereas the comedy in O'Casey is usually associated with self-regarding escapism or false heroics, whose impact turns intentionally sour as the social tragedy intensifies, the comedy of Valle's play is partly a function of the protagonist's self-knowledge. It is humour as an antidote to despair, humour as catharsis. Once we have glimpsed the despair beneath, the self-destructive humour acquires a liberating force and a sense of humanity regained against all the odds, an almost heroic quality, quite different from the escapist ramblings of Boyle and Joxer in *Juno and the Paycock*. Although the humour in *Lights of Bohemia* is a response to a historical rather than a metaphysical situation, it shares with the Theatre of the Absurd this anti-deterministic quality of creating an opposition to the controlling mechanisms of life. Like Ionesco's Béranger (*Rhinoceros* and *The Killer*), Dürrenmatt's Alfred Ill (*The Visit*) or Romulus (*Romulus the Great*) and even Hamm in Beckett's *Endgame*, Max represents Valle's bid to re-invent the heroic and redefine the tragic in a non-tragic world.

## 3. *Lights of Bohemia* and Valle-Inclán's idea of the theatre

So far we have considered the *esperpento* as a devaluation of certain heroic qualities and attitudes by the social and historical context and the protagonist's human response to this state of affairs. However, as Max makes clear in Scene 12, the sense also extends to the artistic response (see Commentary). The only coherent response to a grotesque reality, he claims, is for art itself to become grotesque: "We must distort our expression of reality in the same mirrors that distort our reflections and the whole miserable charade of Spanish life." The classical norms of beauty, harmony and proportion no longer apply in a context which has rendered them meaningless. The urgent need is now to reflect a reality which is a travesty of these norms, while retaining some sort of artistic objectivity and discipline. This is what Max is referring to when he speaks of a 'systematic distortion' which operates with the mathematical impartiality of a concave mirror. The purpose of 'systematic distortion' is more explicitly brought out in the Prologue to *Los cuernos de don Friolera*. The artist should regard his characters as the puppeteer regards his puppets. Identification with individual characters leads to a loss of total perspective, just as feeling sorry for the horse in a bullfight precludes one from experiencing the total aesthetic emotion of the spectacle. The artist's viewpoint should be above laughter and tears. He should view his creatures with the same uninvolved amusement as if he were watching the comedy of the living from the viewpoint of the dead. The theory is more rigorously applied in *Don Friolera*, in which the puppet convention is consistent throughout — in characterization, gesture, movement, décor and language. Perhaps here it could be said that Valle had come close to the mathematically consistent distortion which, in Max's words, "is no longer distortion", presumably because it has become the norm. In *Lights of Bohemia*, however, it is debatable whether Valle does in fact apply the systematic distortion referred to by Max Estrella. Although certain characters (Zarathustra, Minister of the Interior, Basilio Soulinake) and evocations of atmosphere (e.g. the café in Scene 9) reveal strong elements of caricature or literary stylization, others are portrayed 'straight' or with evident sympathy on the author's part. Certainly Max's wife and daughter, the Catalan prisoner, the Mother of the dead child and, most of all, Max himself could not be described as 'distorted' or in any way dehumanized. It is always dangerous to confuse precept with practice in a writer's work and *Lights of Bohemia* is a good illustration of this point. It is more a play about a man who comes to see life as an *esperpento* than an example of the literary theory propounded by its protagonist.

There are other aspects of *Lights of Bohemia*, which, despite its status as the first *esperpento*, reveal it as a work of transition between Valle's former heroic image of the world and his later anti-heroic view. The physical descriptions of Max Estrella highlight the statuesque, heroic qualities which had previously been associated with Montenegro and the *Comedias bárbaras*. Like Montenegro, Max's movements and body language evoke heroic antecedents and confer on the character an archetypal status. The 'tousled head and sightless eyes' give him 'a classical-archaic air reminiscent of the busts of

Hermes'. The hieratic gesture of raising one arm in salutation has an air of imperial grandeur, despite the hint of bombast. His motionless form, after the dialogue with the Catalan prisoner, is a tragic expression of unspoken grief. In fact the quality of stillness in word and gesture is perhaps what most distinguishes Max from his surroundings.[41] The visual images which depict those surroundings are more in line with the abrupt angularity of the puppet theatre, animated cartoon or silent-screen comedy which typified the later *esperpentos*. Whereas Max is generally seen in repose, those around him are frequently caught in the middle of grotesque action. Don Latino, for instance, intervenes in the discussion 'like a cowardly dog snapping from between his master's legs' (Scene 2). Dorio's arms raised aloft in what appears to be a parody of Max's gesture succeed only in resembling the plucked wings of a chicken (Scene 4). The embrace between Max and the Minister of the Interior in Scene 8 is a clear example of a deliberate contrast between authentic tragedy and contemporary sham: Max "with arms flung wide, his head high, his dead eyes tragic in their stillness", while the Minister "pot-bellied and larded with greasepaint, responds with the effusive alacrity of a ham actor in a French melodrama". As elsewhere in his work, Valle draws on debased literature and bad acting to exemplify what he saw as the inauthenticity of his age.

The transitional nature of *Lights of Bohemia* is also revealed in Valle's handling of the dramatic rhythm. Many of the later plays (not only *esperpentos*) are structured on the basis of a sustained, frenzied action, with an accelerating rhythm, crammed into a limited time-frame, rather like a machine spinning out of control: the mounting frenzy of passions and movement in *Cara de plata*, for example, or the crazy escalation of cause and effect in *La hija del capitán*, in which a murder based on mistaken identity is turned to advantage by different groups or individuals and finally results in the downfall of a government. This type of dramatic structure was to a large extent the result of Valle's reassertion of his deterministic philosophy, to show human beings dancing to the tunes of social imperatives or blindly driven on by passions of pride, lust and greed. The ultimate purpose of this was to give theatrical expression to Valle's new feeling of tragic emptiness and inauthenticity in human affairs. To dramatize a world indulging in empty histrionic activity, Valle consciously uses the well-worn clichés of popular melodrama and the breathless dynamic action associated with certain products of the silent cinema. *Lights of Bohemia* has a restricted time-frame (evening twilight through to dawn on one day and dusk to nightfall on another), but none of the frenetic movement that characterizes some of the later plays. The rhythmic progression of its scenes is created by variation of mood and tempo rather than the driving force of the central action. This in turn is determined by its different thematic emphasis, not the agitation of creatures

---

41  In his reply to a survey on the artistic importance of the cinema (*ABC*, 19 December 1928), Valle-Inclán censures the actors of the silent screen for debasing the art of cinema by the abuse of melodramatic gesture and grotesque facial movement, claiming that economy of movement had always been the hallmark of great acting, whether comic or tragic. He refers to Grecian statues as a 'school for tragedians'.

programmed by instinct or manipulated by forces beyond their control, but the implicit struggle of a conscious awareness to resist the dehumanizing pressures upon it.

The visual quality of *Lights of Bohemia* — and indeed of almost all Valle's theatre — has been commented on by many critics. Valle had a life-long interest in painting and the plastic arts and a life-long fascination with the power of the visual image. He claimed that, as a race, Spaniards were stirred more deeply by what he called a 'plastic' representation than by a conceptual explanation. To support his case he cites various forms of popular ritual, such as the bullfight, Holy Week processions and the Mass, all of which communicate via visual ceremony.[42] The theatre, which lives by its capacity to communicate collectively, should, he believed, follow the same path. He evidently had his own ideal of the theatre in mind when, in 1923, he said: "Nowadays I always write with a possible performance in mind, in which the emotion is conveyed by the plastic vision."[43] His interest in visual communication was given a significant boost after about 1920, when he became aware of the silent cinema. Valle's fascination with a dynamic artistic medium which heightened visual awareness by totally obliterating the sense of hearing is reflected in certain incidents from his later plays.[44]

"Before starting to write", Valle said in an interview with José Montero Alonso, "I need to see the characters physically and in detail. I need to see their face, their shape, the way they dress, the way they walk."[45] He also needed to visualize the settings his characters inhabited and through which they moved, not just to 'create atmosphere', but as a prerequisite to creating the situation and writing the dialogue for a scene. In another interview he maintained that it was a common misconception "to believe that the situation creates the scenery ... because, on the contrary, the scenery creates the situation".[46] In other words, the physical settings in a play should not be merely places where it is dramatically convenient for the action to unfold, but a presence which contributes towards moulding the dramatic situation. He illustrates this principle of how a scene derives its vitality from the immediate physical surroundings by quoting the examples of the graveyard scene in *Hamlet* and, elsewhere, the sofa scene in Zorrilla's *Don Juan Tenorio*.[47] Action and dialogue generally draw their life and stem directly from the physical properties of a scene. The tension rarely derives from the manipulation

---

42   See Luis Emilio Soto, 'Valle-Inclán y el teatro nuevo', *La Nación* (Buenos Aires), 3 March 1929 (reprinted in Dougherty, *Un Valle-Inclán olvidado*, pp. 180-88).

43   From an interview with C. Rivas Cherif, *La Pluma*, January 1923.

44   The most notable example is the stage direction describing the death of Sócrates Galindo in *Las galas del difunto*: "The awkwardness of the movement and the grimace which distorts his face give the impression of life reflected in a convex mirror. The words can be divined from the facial expression and the sound of falling feet from the angle of the legs. It is an instant in which everything is pregnant with silence and the meaning is amply conveyed by a distressingly self-evident visual image."

45   Dougherty, *Un Valle-Inclán olvidado*, p. 191.

46   *Ibid.*, p. 263 (from an interviw in *Luz* (Madrid), 23 November 1933).

47   Interview in *El Imparcial*, 8 December 1929 (reprinted in Dru Dougherty, 'Valle-Inclán ante el teatro clásico español: una entrevista olvidada', *Insula*, 476-477, July-August 1986, p.18).

of or dramatic irony created by a plot. The action generates its own energy and gathers its own momentum from within. Everything is presented as happening in the present. Time itself in the later plays is presented, not in terms of hours, days, weeks or years, but visually through the passage from light to dark and dark to light, in a succession of 'present' images which rarely solicit our memory of the past or interest in the future.

*Lights of Bohemia* gives the impression of having been conceived along these lines, as a series of physical locations rather than a developing plot or theme. The scenes are structured in a semi-independent form, to the extent that it was possible for Valle to interpolate three new scenes in the final version with only minimal adjustments to the original twelve. The storyline in itself reveals very little. It tells us that Max Estrella needs money, that he is cheated by Latino and the bookseller, that he has to return his lottery ticket and later recovers it after pawning his cape, that he gets drunk, is arrested and then released, that he is given money by the Minister, has a farewell supper, meets a prostitute, witnesses a cross-section of the public reacting to an act of police brutality and finally dies of exposure outside his own tenement building. Three more scenes show reactions to his death, burial and the debts he left behind him. Valle-Inclán does not develop his themes through a closely-knit plot or by intensive concentration on a situation. Instead, he proceeds by constructing scenes which radiate from a central dramatic axis (the artist and his historical context) and illuminate that axis from different angles.[48] Valle seems to apply to dramatic construction the same criteria as he applies to the syntactical structure of a paragraph, that is, the suppression of logical links and the reliance on juxtaposition and sensation. He said in a lecture given in Buenos Aires in 1910: "Anyone can relate two ideas with a 'however', a 'nevertheless', an 'in spite of', a 'like' or a 'but'. It is very difficult to relate them through a slow gradation of thought and feeling. There is nothing like feeling for deciding what should come first and what should follow in a sequence of clauses. They should be connected not by any grammatical conjunction or logical relationship, but by sensation alone."[49] There are certain logical links in the thematic and character development of *Lights of Bohemia* which are left to emerge from the context rather than pointed in the dialogue. This is particularly true of Max's psychological development in the play, where Valle allows simple juxtaposition of attitudes to suffice. The self-doubt arising from Max's encounter with the Catalan prisoner and the self-disgust at accepting money from the Minister are never rationalized in explanatory dialogue. Yet the nihilistic and abrasive humour with Rubén Darío, the self-deprecation with the prostitute Lunares, the feelings of guilt in Scene 11 and the increased concern with his approaching death are all seen to have a causal relationship with those earlier scenes 6 and 8. This relationship is signalled only by a change of register in Max without further signposting to forge the link in the reader's or spectator's mind.

48 See Francisco Nieva, 'La visualización del tema en Valle-Inclán', in *Busca y rebusca de Valle-Inclán* (Simposio internacional sobre Valle-Inclán 1986), ed. J.A.Hormigón (Madrid: Ministerio de Cultura, 1989), vol. 1, pp. 387-90.
49 F. Madrid, p. 187.

The silent cinema may not have been the original inspiration for Valle's technique of presenting direct action in multiple self-contained scenes, but it certainly served to confirm and clarify many of his aesthetic convictions. From references in interviews, letters and other written comments on the cinema, there can be no doubt that he took it seriously and recognized its potential as an artistic medium. He was clearly fascinated by the cinema's revolutionary treatment of time and space, the immediacy of its visual impact and its ability to create dynamism and tension via montage. The cinematic technique of montage, implied statements through the juxtaposition of images, reinforced one of Valle's most enduring aesthetic principles: the need for impassivity in art. It also presented an alternative to the exclusive reliance on plot or narrative as a method of continuity. The principles behind montage were, in Valle's view, by no means the exclusive prerogative of the cinema. He adapted these principles in all his later novels and advocated that the theatre should also follow this example: "We must create a theatre of direct action, without narrative or explanatory dialogue or single sets; a theatre which follows the example of the contemporary cinema which, without the spoken word or vocal registers, simply by using a dynamic flow and variety of images and locations, has been successful all over the world."[50] Some clues as to how Valle envisaged this adaptation of cinematic montage to the theatre may be gleaned from his most detailed comments on cinema made in 1921.[51] After deploring the inanity of trying to adapt complex theatrical plots to the silent screen (a film of Benavente's *Los intereses creados* was made in 1918),[52] Valle sketches out his idea for a scenario of a Holy Week procession in Seville, in which the element of plot or narrative would be negligible and meaning would be communicated exclusively through the visual sense. The juxtaposed images pick out all the tensions and contrasts of the scene, the inherent drama of religious fanaticism and pagan sensuality: the religious procession with its images of candles, mitres and cowls surrounded by a variagated public with dark faces and flashing eyes, the pallor of the suffering Christ and the warm sensuality of the night, the dancer Pastora Imperio ('barefoot, penitent and provocative') singing a religious *saeta* and the strains of a lover's mandolin serenading at a window. It is precisely this quest for inherent tensions which characterizes so much of Valle-Inclán's drama (e.g. *Divinas palabras*), a dramatic tension which lies not so much in the linear structure as in the total situation, from the counterpoint of scenes and incidents to the very texture of the language. In *Lights of Bohemia* there is, as we have seen, an all-pervasive inherent contradiction between the essentially tragic nature of Max Estrella's destiny and the social context which renders it and him absurd. There are also the contradictions within Max's shifting and ambivalent responses. As the scenes progressively illuminate this

50    Dougherty, *Un Valle-Inclán olvidado*, p. 264.
51    According to Dougherty, these comments were originally made 'towards the end of 1921' in *Cine mundial* (New York), although they were later reprinted in *El Cine* (Madrid), 512, 4 February 1922 and *El Bufón* (Barcelona), 15 February 1924. See *Un Valle-Inclán olvidado*, p. 264, n. 303.
52    *La Ilustración Española y Americana*, 30 October 1918.

central dramatic axis, we are stimulated by the presence of an unresolved contradiction which deepens and widens in our minds in the course of the action. If we think of the play in terms of plot and character with the perspective of conventional drama, the final scenes inevitably appear anti-climactic and irrelevant. If we focus our attention on the fundamental tensions at the heart of the play, they acquire relevance and poignancy. Following what he sees as the cinema's example, Valle consciously devalues the importance of the narrative line from its central position as metaphor for the theme to that of a functional framework around which he elaborates the harmonies and counterpoint of his composition.

Valle-Inclán saw the cinema as a commercial threat to the theatre, but also as a possible source of artistic salvation. He considered the Spanish theatre to be in a state of decline as a result of French neoclassical influence infiltrating into the country during the second half of the eighteenth century. This influence, which he claimed was alien to the national tradition, had led to the visual impoverishment and emotional constriction of Spanish drama. The trend had degenerated during the course of the nineteenth century into the formula of the 'well-made play' popularized by Scribe and Sardou and the bourgeois comedy as practised by Bretón de los Herreros. Valle was thus reacting against a theatre which had become, in his view, emotionally trivial, limited in conception and mechanical in execution. He wanted above all to get the theatre out of the drawing room, to liberate it from middle-class domestic situations and the mechanistic neoclassical concept of unity. The great lessons to be learned from the cinema were its qualities of visuality and dynamism. In a letter to C. Rivas Cherif written in December 1922, he explains his dramatic purpose as "fusing the three neoclassical unities (of action, time and place) into a dynamic process". He refers to the process of compressing and filling time by a dynamic succession of scenes from which would emerge a broader sense of socio-cultural unity.[53] In addition to Valle's well-known emphasis on the life of the collectivity, we also have here a rejection of an externally-imposed, mechanically-conceived type of unity (cause-and-effect linkage of a plot building to a single climax, twenty-four hour maximum duration and single set) in favour of a more organic — and more cinematic — concept of rhythm and continuity.

*Lights of Bohemia* is the first play Valle wrote which reveals specific cinematic influences. These include examples of metaphorical montage, often involving animals: the trick of light which makes Zarathustra's nose appear to be bent back on his ear juxtaposed with an image of the parrot with its beak tucked under its wing or Max Estrella slumped in a doorway juxtaposed with a dog urinating in the street, its rheumy eye "like a poet's, raised towards the last star before dawn". There are unmistakeable examples of close-ups. The camera lens zooms into the number of a lottery ticket on the table, a tear in the Minister's eye, a bullet-hole in the child's temple, a nail sticking

---

53    See J. Caamaño Bournacell, 'Valle-Inclán y el concepto del teatro' in *Mélanges à la mémoire d'A. Joncha-Ruau* (Provence University Press, 1978), pp. 501-15 (reprinted in Lyon, *The Theatre of Valle-Inclán*, p. 206).

through the pine boards of a coffin. A succession of close-ups records the different expressions of a common emotion when the Pot Boy returns to the bar in Scene 3. Clearly these would be impossible to reproduce on a theatre stage and it was not part of Valle's intention that theatre should vie with the cinema's mobility and control of viewpoint. These effects have no theatrical function and fulfil a descriptive role in the printed text. They are however an indication that the general inspiration of the cinema was very much in the author's mind in his attempt to work towards a theatre which would unite the visual excitement of forms, movement and light with the power of the word, traditionally associated with the theatre.[54]

In *Lights of Bohemia* we can perhaps see an embryonic form of this fusion. The 'stage directions' are not descriptions of theatrical sets but visualized atmospheres. They are designed to create not so much a background for the action as an emotional response and visual excitement in the audience. They are essentially locations defined by light and shadow — twilight, candlelight, acetylene lamp, gaslight, oil lamp, electric light, arc light, moonlight, dawn — rather than detailed reproductions of reality. The directors of the two major Spanish productions of the play to date, José Tamayo and Lluis Pascual,[55] both discarded total naturalism, not simply because it would have been impractical, but, more importantly, because it would have been artistically wrong. They also discarded, for similar reasons, an intellectually conceived style of schematic expressionism. Both directors opted for a broadly impressionistic design with dramatic chiaroscuro in the manner of the later paintings of Goya. Valle imagined his scenes, much as Goya painted his canvasses, with a dramatically selective eye for light and shade, grouping and gesture. The general social climate is conveyed, visually and aurally, in a predominantly cinematic way, that is, by direct impact on the senses. Wider social events, either complementing or contrasting with the foreground action, are suggested by the movement of figures or shadows in the background, possibly projected on to a screen,[56] and a continuous soundtrack of riot noises, clattering of horses' hooves, running feet and sporadic gunfire successfully blends scenes of varying mood and tempo into a uniform climate of popular unrest.

The power of the spoken word had always meant more for Valle-Inclán than the capacity to express ideas or convince by means of argument. The total significance of words was not restricted to their conceptual meaning. "The supreme beauty of words" he writes in *La lámpara maravillosa*, "is revealed only when ... their musical essence is

---

54    Valle explicitly states the desirability of this union in an interview with Federico Navas, *Las esfinges de Talía o encuesta sobre la crisis del teatro*, Imprenta del Real Monasterio de El Escorial, 1928 (reprinted in Dougherty, *Un Valle-Inclán olvidado*, pp. 166-70).

55    In 1971 and 1984 respectively.

56    Rafael Osuna points out that in the 1920s there were one or two examples of mixing filmed sequences and live performance on the Madrid stage. See 'El cine en el teatro último de Valle-Inclán', *Cuadernos Americanos*, 222 (1979), pp. 177-84 and 'Un guión cinematográfico de Valle-Inclán: *Luces de bohemia*', *Bulletin of Hispanic Studies*, 59 (1982), pp. 120-28.

savoured, when the human voice, by virtue of tone and register, imbues them with their full range of meaning"(p. 60). Valle himself stressed the importance of tone and register in *Divinas palabras*. In an interview several months before its first performance in November 1933, he described it as a work of "infinite nuances" and "varied rhythms within an indestructible melodic unity". He continues, "The voices are extraordinarily important. That's why it will have to be rehearsed as if one were rehearsing an orchestra."[57] The principal requirement for good dramatic writing was thus a sensitivity to tone and register, which was what ultimately determined the emotional response of an audience.[58] In *Lights of Bohemia*, Valle tries to encapsulate the essential flavour of a heterogeneous yet compact society, Madrid of the 1920s, in its language. The social layers and their corresponding idioms are intermixed in a heady linguistic cocktail. The literary bohemian element has an eclectic language all its own, at once esoteric and plebeian, in which gypsified argot and street slang is laced with rhetorical flourishes, classical allusions and literary quotations. Popular speech shows itself in its purest form in characters like the Gravediggers or the Concierge, but reveals the imprint of constant exposure to cultured influences in the Pot Boy and, occasionally, Henrietta, or veers towards the idiom of the underworld and criminal fringe in the King of Portugal and Fantail the Pimp. In Lizard-Slicer popular speech is contaminated with social pretensions to commercial respectability and in the Asturian nightwatchman with the jargon of municipal authority. Conversely the agents of law and order (Pitito) are not above expressing their highly official sentiments in the unofficial language of the streets. Nor are the essential voices of reaction, such as Don Filiberto and the Minister, totally devoid of literary aspirations or bohemian nostalgia.

It was perhaps these linguistic paradoxes that attracted Valle to the subject matter. There is little doubt that he uses the different registers to underscore certain dramatic changes or confrontations. We have already seen how Max's change of attitude towards himself and others is left implicit in the different tones he adopts after the climactic Scenes 6 and 8 which significantly lower his self-esteem. It is the contrast of linguistic registers that creates the humour of Max's confrontation with officialdom (Scenes 4 and 5) and gives a philosophical point to the parallel dialogues between Rubén Darío and Bradomín and the two Gravediggers in Scene 14 (see Commentary). In the case of the Catalan prisoner it serves a more subtle purpose. Although the content of the dialogue may suggest what some critics have seen as a meeting of minds, Valle insists on maintaining a tonal distinction between the two characters which continues to indicate

---

57　From *El Sol*, 25 March 1933 (reprinted in Dougherty, *Un Valle-Inclán olvidado*, p. 250, n. 293).

58　"Thesis drama was a confidence trick devised by a handful of pseudo-writers without imagination. The thesis was almost invariably misguided. And even if they had a magnificent doctrine to impart, they couldn't have done it in the theatre by means of rational argument. The general public can only be moved or entertained and what moves us in the theatre is the tone, not reason or argument" (translated from Dougherty, *Un Valle-Inclán olvidado*, p. 262).

an unbridgeable gap between the artist-intellectual and the working man. In Scene 11 Valle exploits the stark contrast between the Mother's passionate anger and grief and the chilling abstractions of those commenting on the situation around her.

*Lights of Bohemia* is not particularly helpful in clarifying what Valle-Inclán meant by the *esperpento*. The text, as we have seen, does not altogether conform to the principles of 'systematic distortion' established by its protagonist. The same is true of the later definitions of the *esperpento*, formulated by Valle after the publication of *Los cuernos de don Friolera* (1921). These stress as the central characteristic the incongruity between life's essential tragedies and the inadequate contemporary actors who are called upon to perform the roles. They are like "cardboard men without passions or ideals who appear ludicrous decked out in their heroic trappings"[59] or "knock-kneed clowns playing out a tragedy".[60] The descriptions may be well-suited to *Don Friolera*, but appear oversimplified when applied to *Lights of Bohemia*, because they take no account of the ambiguity surrounding Max's 'tragic role' or of the influence of external historical factors in our perception of that role. The play obstinately refuses to be pinned down by any definition of the genre to which it allegedly belongs. What gives the play its unique identity within the context of the *esperpentos* is the degree of self-determination granted to the central character and the degree of empathy Valle allows his audience. *Lights of Bohemia* is the only play of this group in which there is a moral distinction between the protagonist and the social forces which alienate him. In *Don Friolera* the protagonist has no genuine self-awareness or values of his own to oppose the social myths that manipulate him. In *Las galas del difunto*, the one-time victim turns into an unprincipled rebel, indistinguishable from the self-interested context around him. In *La hija del capitán*, the victim turns exploiter. It is true of course that Max's acceptance of the slush money degrades him both in his own eyes and those of the audience. But the transformation which follows this is prompted by a recognition of that degradation and aimed at preserving whatever integrity the situation allows him. The reader or spectator is still able to see him as 'tragic' and possibly even 'heroic'. Once the the plays lose the contrast between the values and perspective of a self-aware protagonist and those of the society, they lose their capacity to evoke conflicting emotional responses in the audience. *Lights of Bohemia*, on the other hand, engages us in a constant tug-of-war between conflicting feelings and ideas: tragedy and the grotesque, absurdity and pathos, detachment and empathy, freedom and determinism, authenticity and histrionics. The capacity to provoke a richly ambivalent response may not feature in the canon of *esperpento* theory, but it constitutes one of the play's most original and enduring characteristics.

---

59    F.Madrid, p.345.
60    From G.Martínez Sierra, 'Hablando con Valle-Inclán: de él y su obra', *ABC*, 7 December 1928 (reprinted in Dougherty, *Un Valle-Inclán olvidado*, pp. 173-9).

# Selected Bibliography

## Plays by Valle-Inclán in English translation

*Divine Words (Divinas palabras)*, trans. Edwin Williams in *Modern Spanish Theatre*, George Wellwarth and Michael Benedikt (eds.). New York: Dutton, 1968, 1-78.

*Luces de bohemia / Bohemian Lights*, trans. A. Zahareas and G. Gillespie. Introduction and Notes by A. Zahareas. Edinburgh: Edinburgh University Press, 1976.

*Los cuernos de don Friolera / The Grotesque Farce of Mr Punch the Cuckold*, translated and edited by Dominic Keown and Robin Warner. Warminster: Aris and Phillips, 1991.

## Selected works of criticism

Buero Vallejo, A., 'De rodillas, de pie, en el aire' in *Tres maestros ante el público*. Madrid: Alianza, 1973.

Cardona, R., Greenfield, S. and Zahareas, A. (eds.), *Ramón del Valle-Inclán. An Appraisal of his Life and Works*. New York: Las Americas, 1968.

Cardona, R. and Zahareas, A., *Visión del esperpento. Teoría y práctica en los esperpentos de Valle-Inclán*. 2a edición corregida y ampliada. Madrid: Castalia, 1982.

Hormigón, J. A. (ed.), *Busca y rebusca de Valle-Inclán: Simposio internacional sobre Valle-Inclán 1986*, 2 vols. Madrid: Ministerio de Cultura, 1989.

Greenfield, S., *Valle-Inclán: anatomía de un teatro problemático*. Madrid: Fundamentos, 1972.

Lyon, J., *The Theatre of Valle-Inclán*. Cambridge: Cambridge University Press, 1983.

——'Valle-Inclán and the Art of the Theatre', *Bulletin of Hispanic Studies*, 46 (1969), 132-52.

Ruiz Ramón, F., *Historia del teatro español*, vol. 2. *Siglo XX*. Madrid: Alianza, 1971.

Smith, V., *Ramón del Valle-Inclán*. New York: Twayne, 1973.

Weber, F.W., *Luces de bohemia* and the Impossibility of Art', *Modern Language Notes*, 82 (1967), 575-89.

Zahareas, A., Introduction to R. del Valle-Inclán, *Luces de bohemia / Bohemian Lights*. Edinburgh: Edinburgh University Press, 1976, 1-81

——'The *Esperpento* and the Aesthetics of Commitment', *Modern Language Notes*, 81 (1966), 159-73.

Zamora Vicente, A., *La realidad esperpéntica: Aproximación a 'Luces de bohemia.'* Madrid: Gredos, 1969.

——Introduction to R. del Valle-Inclán, *Luces de bohemia*. Madrid: Clásicos Castellanos, 1973.

## Books on the historical background

Baroja, R., *Gente del '98*. Madrid: Cátedra, 1989.

Brenan, G., *The Spanish Labyrinth*. Cambridge: Cambridge University Press, 1967.

Carr, R., *Spain: 1808-1975*, 2nd edn. Oxford: Oxford University Press, 1982.

——*Modern Spain: 1875-1980*. Oxford: Oxford University Press, 1980.

**Interviews, letters, lectures, etc.**

Dougherty, Dru, *Un Valle-Inclán olvidado: entrevistas y conferencias.* Madrid:
Fundamentos, 1983.

Hormigón, J. A., *Valle-Inclán: cronología, escritos dispersos, epistolario.* Madrid:
Fundación Banco Exterior, 1988.

*Caricature of Valle-Inclán by Ernesto García Cabral from* Buen Humor, 22 January
*1922*

*Max Estrella and Don Latino in a scene from Lluis Pascual's 1984 production.*

# Ramón María del Valle-Inclán
# LIGHTS OF BOHEMIA *(Luces de bohemia)*

*Drawing by John Lyon based on a painting by Francisco Sancha.*

# DRAMATIS PERSONAE

Max Estrella
*Su mujer*, Madame Collet
*Su hija*, Claudinita
Don Latino de Hispalis
Zaratustra
Don Gay
Un Pelón
La Chica de la portera
Pica Lagartos
Un Coime de taberna
Enriqueta la Pisa-Bien
El Rey de Portugal
Un Borracho
Dorio de Gadex, Rafael de los Vélez, Lucio Vero,     *Jóvenes*
Mínguez, Gálvez, Clarinito y Pérez     *Modernistas*
Pitito, *capitán de los équites municipales*
Un Sereno
La voz de un Vecino
Dos Guardias del Orden
Serafín el Bonito
Un Celador
Un Preso
El Portero de una redacción
Don Filiberto, *redactor en jefe*
El Ministro de la Gobernación
Dieguito, *secretario de Su Excelencia*
Un Ujier
Una Vieja Pintada
La Lunares
Un Jóven Desconocido
La Madre del Niño Muerto, El Empeñista, El Guardia,     *Todos*
La Portera, Un Albañil, Una Vieja, La Trapera, y El Retirado     *del Barrio*
Otra Portera
Una Vecina
Basilio Soulinake
Un Cochero de la funeraria
Dos Sepultureros
Rubén Darío
El Marqués de Bradomín
El Pollo del Pay-Pay
La Periodista
Turbas, Guardias, Perros, Gatos, un Loro

**La acción en un Madrid absurdo, brillante y hambriento.**

# CHARACTERS

Max Estrella,
Madame Collet, *his wife*
Claudinita, *his daughter*
Don Latino de Hispalis
Zarathustra
Don Gay
Boy
Concierge's daughter
Lizard-Slicer
Pot Boy
Henrietta the Hoofer
A Drunk
Dorio de Gadex, Rafael de los Vélez, Lucio Vero,          *Young*
Mínguez, Gálvez, Clarinito and Pérez          *Modernist Poets*
Pitito, *Captain of the Municipal Mounted Police*
A Nightwatchman
A Neighbour's Voice
Two Civil Guards
Serafin the Paint
A Jailer
A Prisoner
Doorman of a Newspaper Office
Don Filiberto, *Editor*
Minister of the Interior
Dieguito, *Secretary to His Excellency*
An Usher
Painted Tart
Lunares
Anonymous Young Man
Mother of Dead Child, Pawnbroker, Policeman, Concierge,          *Local*
Bricklayer, Old Woman, Rag-and-Bone Woman, Retired Officer          *Residents*
Another Concierge
A Neighbour
Basilio Soulinake
Hearse Driver
Two Gravediggers
Rubén Darío
The Marquis de Bradomín
Fantail the Pimp
Newspaper Seller
Crowds, Policemen, Dogs, Cats and a Parrot

**The action takes place in Madrid: a city of grotesque farce, sparkling wits and empty stomachs.**

# Escena Primera

*Hora crepuscular. Un guardillón con ventano angosto, lleno de sol. Retratos, grabados, autógrafos repartidos por las paredes, sujetos con chinches de dibujante. Conversación lánguida de un hombre ciego y una mujer pelirrubia, triste y fatigada. El hombre ciego es un hiperbólico andaluz, poeta de odas y madrigales, Máximo Estrella. A la pelirrubia, por ser francesa, le dicen en la vecindad Madama Collet.*

MAX          Vuelve a leerme la carta del Buey Apis.

MADAMA COLLET  Ten paciencia, Max.

MAX          Pudo esperar a que me enterrasen.

MADAMA COLLET  Le toca ir delante.

MAX          ¡Collet, mal vamos a vernos sin esas cuatro crónicas! ¿Dónde gano yo veinte duros, Collet?

MADAMA COLLET  Otra puerta se abrirá.

MAX          La de la muerte. Podemos suicidarnos colectivamente.

MADAMA COLLET  A mí la muerte no me asusta. ¡Pero tenemos una hija, Max!

MAX          ¿Y si Claudinita estuviese conforme con mi proyecto de suicidio colectivo?

MADAMA COLLET  ¡Es muy joven!

MAX          También se matan los jóvenes, Collet.

MADAMA COLLET  No por cansancio de la vida. Los jóvenes se matan por romanticismo.

MAX          Entonces, se matan por amar demasiado la vida. Es una lástima la obcecación de Claudinita. Con cuatro perras de carbón, podíamos hacer el viaje eterno.

MADAMA COLLET  No desesperes. Otra puerta se abrirá.

MAX          ¿En qué redacción me admiten ciego?

MADAMA COLLET  Escribes una novela.

MAX          Y no hallo editor.

MADAMA COLLET  ¡Oh! No te pongas a gatas, Max. Todos reconocen tu talento.

MAX          ¡Estoy olvidado! Léeme la carta del Buey Apis.

MADAMA COLLET  No tomes ese caso por ejemplo.

MAX          Lee.

MADAMA COLLET  Es un infierno de letra.

MAX          Lee despacio.

*Madama Collet, el gesto abatido y resignado, deletrea en voz baja la carta. Se oye fuera una escoba retozona. Suena la campanilla de la escalera.*

MADAMA COLLET  Claudinita, deja quieta la escoba, y mira quién ha llamado.

# Scene One

*The twilight hour.[1]  A garret with a small window lit by the setting sun. Photographic portraits, engravings, autograph poems, held by drawing-pins, dotted around the walls.[2]  Desultory conversation between a blind man and a fair-haired woman of sad and listless appearance.  The blind man is an Andalusian poet, Máximo Estrella, composer of odes and madrigals and master of hyperbole.[3]  The fair-haired woman is French and is known in the neighbourhood as Madama Collet.*

MAX  Read me Bull Apis's letter again.[4]

MADAMA COLLET  Have patience, Max.

MAX  He might have waited till they buried me.

MADAMA COLLET  They will bury him first.

MAX  Collet, without those articles,[5] we're in trouble.  How else do I earn a hundred pesetas, Collet?

MADAMA COLLET  Another door will open.

MAX  Ay, death's door!  We could all commit suicide.

MADAMA COLLET  I'm not afraid of dying.  But we have a daughter, Max.

MAX  Supposing she agreed to my plan for a suicide pact?

MADAMA COLLET  She's too young!

MAX  The young kill themselves too, Collet.

MADAMA COLLET  Not because they are tired of living.  The young kill themselves for romantic reasons.

MAX  Because they love life too much.  Most regrettable blindness on Claudinita's part.  For fourpenn'orth of charcoal,[6] we could all go on the eternal journey.

MADAMA COLLET  Don't lose hope.  Another door will open.

MAX  What newspaper would take on a blind man?

MADAMA COLLET  You could write a novel.

MAX  And not find a publisher.

MADAMA COLLET  Oh, don't put yourself on your knees, Max!  Everybody recognises your talent.

MAX  I'm a forgotten man!  Just read Bull Apis's letter.

MADAMA COLLET  Don't take that as an example.

MAX  Read it.

MADAMA COLLET  His writing is diabolical.

MAX  Take your time and read.

*With dejected and resigned expression, Madama Collet reads out the letter syllable by syllable in a soft and halting voice.  The sound of a briskly-sweeping broom is heard outside.  The bell on the staircase rings.*

MADAMA COLLET  Claudinita, stop sweeping and see who's ringing.

LA VOZ DE CLAUDINITA  Siempre será Don Latino.
MADAMA COLLET  ¡Válgame Dios!
LA VOZ DE CLAUDINITA  ¿Le doy con la puerta en las narices?
MADAMA COLLET  A tu padre le distrae.
LA VOZ DE CLAUDINITA  ¡Ya se siente el olor del aguardiente!

*Máximo Estrella se incorpora con un gesto animoso, esparcida sobre el pecho la hermosa barba con mechones de canas. Su cabeza rizada y ciega, de un gran carácter clásico-arcaico, recuerda los Hermes.*

MAX                    ¡Espera, Collet! ¡He recobrado la vista! ¡Veo! ¡Oh, cómo
                       veo! ¡Magníficamente! ¡Está hermosa la Moncloa! ¡El único
                       rincón francés en este páramo madrileño! ¡Hay que volver a
                       París, Collet! ¡Hay que volver allá, Collet! ¡Hay que renovar
                       aquellos tiempos!
MADAMA COLLET  Estás alucinado, Max.
MAX                    ¡Veo, y veo magníficamente!
MADAMA COLLET  ¿Pero qué ves?
MAX                    ¡El mundo!
MADAMA COLLET  ¿A mí me ves?
MAX                    ¡Las cosas que toco, para qué necesito verlas!
MADAMA COLLET  Siéntate. Voy a cerrar la ventana. Procura adormecerte.
MAX                    ¡No puedo!
MADAMA COLLET  ¡Pobre cabeza!
MAX                    ¡Estoy muerto! Otra vez de noche.

*Se reclina en el respaldo del sillón. La mujer cierra la ventana, y la guardilla queda en una penumbra rayada de sol poniente. El ciego se adormece, y la mujer, sombra triste, se sienta en una silleta, haciendo pliegues a la carta del Buey Apis. Una mano cautelosa empuja la puerta, que se abre con largo chirrido. Entra un vejete asmático, quepis, anteojos, un perrillo y una cartera con revistas ilustradas. Es Don Latino de Hispalis. Detrás, despeinada, en chancletas, la falda pingona, aparece una mozuela: Claudinita.*

DON LATINO  ¿Cómo están los ánimos del genio?
CLAUDINITA  Esperando los cuartos de unos libros que se ha llevado un
                       vivales para vender.
DON LATINO  ¿Niña, no conoces otro vocabulario más escogido para referirte
                       al compañero fraternal de tu padre, de ese hombre grande que
                       me llama hermano? ¡Qué lenguaje, Claudinita!
MADAMA COLLET  ¿Trae usted el dinero, Don Latino?

VOICE OF CLAUDINITA  It'll be Don Latino, as usual.
MADAMA COLLET  Oh, Lord!
VOICE OF CLAUDINITA  Shall I slam the door in his face?
MADAMA COLLET  No, he seems to amuse your father.
VOICE OF CLAUDINITA  I can smell the booze on his breath from here!

*Máximo Estrella suddenly sits up with an animated expression, his magnificent beard, streaked with grey hairs, spilling over his chest. His tousled head and sightless eyes give him a classical-archaic air reminiscent of the busts of Hermes.[7]*

MAX                 Wait, Collet! I've recovered my sight! I can see! Oh, how I
                    can see! Magnificently! The Moncloa[8] is looking marvellous!
                    An oasis of France in this wilderness of Madrid! We must go
                    back to Paris, Collet! We must go back, Collet! We must
                    relive those old times!
MADAMA COLLET  You're getting your hallucinations, Max.
MAX                 I tell you I can see and see magnificently!
MADAMA COLLET  But what can you see?
MAX                 The world!
MADAMA COLLET  Can you see me?
MAX                 Why do I need to see the things I can touch!
MADAMA COLLET  Sit down. I'll close the shutters. Try and get some sleep.
MAX                 I can't.
MADAMA COLLET  That poor dear head!
MAX                 I'm dead! It's all black night again.

*He slumps back in the armchair. The woman closes the shutters and the garret is left in semi-darkness, streaked with the last rays of the setting sun. The blind man dozes off and the dejected figure of the woman sits down on a small kitchen chair, folding the letter as she does so. A hand gingerly pushes at the door, which opens with a prolonged creak. A doddery old man with an asthmatic cough enters wearing spectacles and a military-style peaked cap. He is carrying a satchel full of illustrated magazines and is accompanied by a small dog. It is Don Latino de Hispalis.[9] Behind him appears a young girl with dishevelled hair, slippers and a tattered skirt: Claudinita.*

DON LATINO  And how are our genius's spirits today?
CLAUDINITA  Our genius is waiting for the cash from the books that some old
                    leech was supposed to sell for him.
DON LATINO  My dear child, can you think of no more suitable form of
                    address for a bosom companion of your father, that great man
                    who honours me with the name of 'brother'? Such language,
                    Claudinita!
MADAMA COLLET  Have you brought the money, Don Latino?

DON LATINO     Madama Collet, la desconozco, porque siempre ha sido usted
               una inteligencia razonadora. Max había dispuesto noblemente
               de ese dinero.
MADAMA COLLET  ¿Es verdad, Max? ¿Es posible?
DON LATINO     ¡No le saque usted de los brazos de Morfeo!
CLAUDINITA     Papá, ¿tú qué dices?
MAX            ¡Idos todos al diablo!
MADAMA COLLET  ¡Oh, querido, con tus generosidades nos has dejado sin
               cena!
MAX            Latino, eres un cínico.
CLAUDINITA     Don Latino, si usted no apoquina, le araño.
DON LATINO     Córtate las uñas, Claudinita.
CLAUDINITA     Le arranco los ojos.
DON LATINO     ¡Claudinita!
CLAUDINITA     ¡Golfo!
DON LATINO     Max, interpón tu autoridad.
MAX            ¿Qué sacaste por los libros, Latino?
DON LATINO     ¡Tres pesetas, Max! ¡Tres cochinas pesetas! ¡Una indignidad!
               ¡Un robo!
CLAUDINITA     ¡No haberlos dejado!
DON LATINO     Claudinita, en ese respecto te concedo toda la razón. Me han
               cogido de pipi. Pero aún se puede deshacer el trato.
MADAMA COLLET  ¡Oh, sería bien!
DON LATINO     Max, si te presentas ahora conmigo en la tienda de ese granuja
               y le armas un escándalo, le sacas hasta dos duros. Tú tienes
               otro empaque.
MAX            Habría que devolver el dinero recibido.
DON LATINO     Basta con hacer el ademán. Se juega de boquilla, maestro.
MAX            ¿Tú crees?...
DON LATINO     ¡Naturalmente!
MADAMA COLLET  Max, no debes salir.
MAX            El aire me refrescará. Aquí hace un calor de horno.
DON LATINO     Pues en la calle corre fresco.
MADAMA COLLET  ¡Vas a tomarte un disgusto sin conseguir nada, Max!
CLAUDINITA     ¡Papá, no salgas!
MADAMA COLLET  Max, yo buscaré alguna cosa que empeñar.
MAX            No quiero tolerar ese robo. ¿A quién le has llevado los libros,
               Latino?
DON LATINO     A Zaratustra.
MAX            ¡Claudina, mi palo y mi sombrero!
CLAUDINITA     ¿Se los doy, mamá?
MADAMA COLLET  ¡Dáselos!
DON LATINO     Madama Collet, verá usted qué faena.
CLAUDINITA     ¡Golfo!
DON LATINO     ¡Todo en tu boca es canción, Claudinita!

DON LATINO   Madama Collet, I'm surprised at you. I've always considered
you a rational and intelligent woman. Max had already disposed
of that money in a noble cause.

MADAMA COLLET   Is that true, Max? Is it possible?

DON LATINO   Tear him not from the arms of Morpheus![10]

CLAUDINITA   Papa, what have you got to say?

MAX   To hell with the lot of you!

MADAMA COLLET   Oh, my dear, you and your generosity! You've left us
without supper again.

MAX   Latino, you're a barefaced liar.

CLAUDINITA   Don Latino, cough up or I'll claw you to shreds!

DON LATINO   You cut your fingernails, Claudinita!

CLAUDINITA   I'll scratch your eyes out!

DON LATINO   Claudinita!

CLAUDINITA   Parasite!

DON LATINO   Max, exercise your authority!

MAX   What did you get for the books, Latino?

DON LATINO   Three pesetas, Max. Three miserable pesetas. An insult!
Daylight robbery!

CLAUDINITA   You shouldn't have left them!

DON LATINO   Claudinita, on that point I grant you are right. They diddled me
like a novice! But we can still cancel the deal.

MADAMA COLLET   That would be good.[11]

DON LATINO   Max, come with me now to that scoundrel's bookshop and kick
up a rumpus and you could get as much as ten pesetas. You've
got more of a way with you.

MAX   We'd have to return the money he's given us.

DON LATINO   The gesture would suffice. Bluff, my dear maestro!

MAX   You think so...?

DON LATINO   But, of course.

MADAMA COLLET   Max, you shouldn't go out.

MAX   A breath of air will do me good. It's like an oven in here.

DON LATINO   There's a cool breeze in the street.

MADAMA COLLET   You will only upset yourself for nothing, Max.

CLAUDINITA   Papa, don't go out!

MADAMA COLLET   Max, I'll find something to pawn.

MAX   No, I'm not standing for this robbery! Who did you take the
books to, Latino?

DON LATINO   To Zarathustra.[12]

MAX   Claudinita, my hat and walking stick!

CLAUDINITA   Shall I give them to him, Mama?

MADAMA COLLET   Give them to him.

DON LATINO   Now we'll see some real fancy cape-work,[13] Madama Collet!

CLAUDINITA   Leech! Parasite!

DON LATINO   Everything is music on your lips, Claudinita!

*Máximo Estrella sale apoyado en el hombro de Don Latino. Madama Collet suspira apocada, y la hija, toda nervios, comienza a quitarse las horquillas del pelo.*
CLAUDINITA ¿Sabes cómo acaba todo esto? ¡En la taberna de Pica Lagartos!

## Escena Segunda

*La cueva de Zaratustra en el Pretil de los Consejos. Rimeros de libros hacen escombro y cubren las paredes. Empapelan los cuatro vidrios de una puerta cuatro cromos espeluznantes de un novelón por entregas. En la cueva hacen tertulia el gato, el loro, el can y el librero. Zaratustra, abichado y giboso, la cara de tocino rancio y la bufanda de verde serpiente, promueve, con su caracterización de fantoche, una aguda y dolorosa disonancia muy emotiva y muy moderna. Encogido en el roto pelote de una silla enana, con los pies entrapados y cepones en la tarima del brasero, guarda la tienda. Un ratón saca el hocico intrigante por un agujero.*

ZARATUSTRA ¡No pienses que no te veo, ladrón!
EL GATO ¡Fu! ¡Fu! ¡Fu!
EL CAN ¡Guau!
EL LORO ¡Viva España!

*Están en la puerta Max Estrella y Don Latino de Hispalis. El poeta saca el brazo por entre los pliegues de su capa, y lo alza majestuoso, en un ritmo con su clásica cabeza ciega.*

MAX ¡Mal Polonia recibe a un extranjero!
ZARATUSTRA ¿Qué se ofrece?
MAX Saludarte, y decirte que tus tratos no me convienen.
ZARATUSTRA Yo nada he tratado con usted.
MAX Cierto. Pero has tratado con mi intendente, Don Latino de Hispalis.
ZARATUSTRA ¿Y ese sujeto de qué se queja? ¿Era mala la moneda?

*Don Latino interviene con ese matiz del perro cobarde, que da su ladrido entre las piernas del dueño.*

DON LATINO El maestro no está conforme con la tasa, y deshace el trato.
ZARATUSTRA El trato no puede deshacerse. Un momento antes que hubieran llegado... Pero ahora es imposible. Todo el atadijo, conforme estaba, acabo de venderlo ganando dos perras. Salir el comprador, y entrar ustedes.

*Máximo Estrella goes out, leaning on Don Latino's shoulder. Madama Collet heaves a sigh of resignation and the daughter, in a state of nervous agitation, starts removing the hairpins from her hair.*

CLAUDINITA   You know where all this will end up, don't you? In Lizard-Slicer's bar![14]

# Scene Two

*Zarathustra's cave[15] on Pretil de los Consejos. Disordered heaps of books litter the floor and cover the walls. The four glass panes of the door are papered over with four blood-curdling colour plates from a cheap serialized novel. Inside the cave are gathered the cat, the parrot, the dog and the bookseller. Zarathustra, beetle-like, hunchbacked, with his face the colour of rancid bacon fat and his scarf of serpent green, strikes a poignantly discordant and contemporary note with his grotesque puppet-like appearance. Sitting hunched up on the torn goat-hair stuffing of a stunted chair, with his stubby feet wrapped in rags and resting on the framework of the brazier, he minds the shop. A mouse pokes its inquisitive snout out of its hole.*

ZARATHUSTRA   Don't think I can't see you, you little thief!
*The cat hisses. The dog barks.*
PARROT         Viva España! Long live Spain!

*Max Estrella and Don Latino de Hispalis are standing in the doorway. The poet takes his arm from beneath the folds of his cape and raises it in a majestic gesture, lifting his classical blind head as he does so.*

MAX            'Most rudely Poland doth receive a stranger!'[16]
ZARATHUSTRA   What do you want?
MAX            First to greet you, then to tell you I don't like the way you do business.
ZARATHUSTRA   I've done no business with you.
MAX            True. But you have with my business manager, Don Latino de Hispalis.
ZARATHUSTRA   And what's he complaining about? Wasn't the money good?

*Don Latino intervenes like a cowardly dog snapping from between its master's legs.*

DON LATINO   The maestro doesn't agree to the price and is calling the deal off.
ZARATHUSTRA   Can't be done. If only you'd arrived a minute sooner... but it's impossible now. I've sold the whole bundle, just as you brought it in, for a few pennies profit. The buyer just left as you came in.

*El librero, al tiempo que habla, recoge el atadijo que aún está encima del mostrador, y penetra en la lóbrega trastienda, cambiando una seña con Don Latino. Reaparece.*

DON LATINO Hemos perdido el viaje. Este zorro sabe más que nosotros, maestro.
MAX Zaratustra, eres un bandido.
ZARATUSTRA Ésas, Don Max, no son apreciaciones convenientes.
MAX Voy a romperte la cabeza.
ZARATUSTRA Don Max, respete usted sus laureles.
MAX ¡Majadero!

*Ha entrado en la cueva un hombre alto, flaco, tostado del sol. Viste un traje de antiguo voluntario cubano, calza alpargates abiertos de caminante, y se cubre con una gorra inglesa. Es el extraño Don Peregrino Gay, que ha escrito la crónica de su vida andariega en un rancio y animado castellano, trastocándose el nombre en Don Gay Peregrino. Sin pasar de la puerta, saluda jovial y circunspecto.*

DON GAY ¡Salutem plúrimam!
ZARATUSTRA ¿Cómo le ha ido por esos mundos, Don Gay?
DON GAY Tan guapamente.
DON LATINO ¿Por dónde has andado?
DON GAY De Londres vengo.
MAX ¿Y viene usted de tan lejos a que lo desuelle Zaratustra?
DON GAY Zaratustra es un buen amigo.
ZARATUSTRA ¿Ha podido usted hacer el trabajo que deseaba?
DON GAY Cumplidamente. Ilustres amigos, en dos meses me he copiado en la Biblioteca Real el único ejemplar existente del Palmerín de Constantinopla.
MAX ¿Pero, ciertamente, viene usted de Londres?
DON GAY Allí estuve dos meses.
DON LATINO ¿Cómo queda la familia Real?
DON GAY No los he visto en el muelle. Maestro, ¿usted conoce la Babilonia Londinense?
MAX Sí, Don Gay.

*Zaratustra entra y sale en la trastienda, con una vela encendida. La palmatoria pringosa tiembla en la mano del fantoche. Camina sin ruido, con andar entrapado. La mano, calzada con mitón negro, pasea la luz por los estantes de libros. Media cara en reflejo y media en sombra. Parece que la nariz se le dobla sobre una oreja. El loro ha puesto el pico bajo el ala. Un retén de polizontes pasa con un hombre maniatado. Sale alborotando el barrio un chico pelón montado en una caña, con una bandera.*

EL PELÓN ¡Vi-va-Es-pa-ña!

*As he speaks, the bookseller picks up the bundle which is still on the counter and slides into the dark recesses behind the shop, exchanging signs with Don Latino. He reappears.*

DON LATINO  A wasted journey, maestro. The old fox has outsmarted us.
MAX             Zarathustra, you're a swindler!
ZARATHUSTRA  That is not very becoming language, Don Max.
MAX             I'll break your neck!
ZARATHUSTRA  Now, now, Don Max, have some regard for your poetic laurels!
MAX             Miserable clown!

*A tall, thin, sun-tanned individual has entered the cave. He is wearing the uniform of the old Cuban militia,[17] the open rope-soled sandals of a tramp on his feet and an English cap on his head. It is the eccentric Don Peregrino Gay,[18] who, changing his name to Don Gay Peregrino, has written a chronicle of his wayfaring life in quaint and racy Castilian prose. Without crossing the threshold, he waves a cheerful and circumspect greeting.*

DON GAY       Salutem plurimam![19] Health and prosperity to all!
ZARATHUSTRA  Ah, Don Gay! How did you get on in those foreign parts?
DON GAY       Splendidly! Splendidly!
DON LATINO  And where have you been?
DON GAY       Just arrived from London.
MAX             You've come all that way just to be fleeced by Zarathustra?
DON GAY       Zarathustra is my good friend.
ZARATHUSTRA  Did you manage to do all the work you wanted to?
DON GAY       Absolutely. In two months, my illustrious friends, I transcribed the only existing copy of *Palmerin, Knight of Constantinople* in the Royal Library.[20]
MAX             But, have you really come from London?
DON GAY       Two months I was there.
DON LATINO  And how was the Royal Family?
DON GAY       I didn't see them on the quayside. Are you acquainted with the Modern Babylon,[21] maestro?
MAX             I am, Don Gay.

*Zarathustra potters in and out of the back room with a lighted candle, the greasy sconce trembling in his hand. Moving noiselessly on rag-bound feet, the black-mittened hand directs the flame along the bookshelves. With half his face lit up and half in shadow, his nose appears to be bent back on his ear. The parrot has tucked its beak under its wing. A police patrol passes by with a man in handcuffs.[22] A shaven-headed boy, riding a cane like a hobby-horse and waving a flag, disturbs the neighbourhood peace.*

BOY             Viva España! Long live Spain!

EL CAN         ¡Guau! ¡Guau!
ZARATUSTRA ¡Está buena España!

*Ante el mostrador, los tres visitantes, reunidos como tres pájaros en una rama,*
*ilusionados y tristes, divierten sus penas en un coloquio de motivos literarios.*
*Divagan ajenos al tropel de polizontes, al viva del pelón, al gañido del perro, y*
*al comentario apesadumbrado del fantoche que los explota. Eran intelectuales*
*sin dos pesetas.*

DON GAY        Es preciso reconocerlo. No hay país comparable a Inglaterra.
               Allí el sentimiento religioso tiene tal decoro, tal dignidad, que
               indudablemente las más honorables familias son las más
               religiosas. Si España alcanzase un más alto concepto religioso,
               se salvaba.
MAX            ¡Recémosle un Réquiem! Aquí los puritanos de conducta son
               los demagogos de la extrema izquierda. Acaso nuevos
               cristianos, pero todavía sin saberlo.
DON GAY        Señores míos, en Inglaterra me he convertido al dogma
               iconoclasta, al cristianismo de oraciones y cánticos, limpio de
               imágenes milagreras. ¡Y ver la idolatría de este pueblo!
MAX            España, en su concepción religiosa, es una tribu del Centro de
               África.
DON GAY        Maestro, tenemos que rehacer el concepto religioso, en el
               arquetipo del Hombre-Dios. Hacer la Revolución Cristiana,
               con todas las exageraciones del Evangelio.
DON LATINO  Son más que las del compañero Lenin.
ZARATUSTRA Sin religión no puede haber buena fe en el comercio.
DON GAY        Maestro, hay que fundar la Iglesia Española Independiente.
MAX            Y la Sede Vaticana, El Escorial.
DON GAY        ¡Magnífica Sede!
MAX            Berroqueña.
DON LATINO  Ustedes acabarán profesando en la Gran Secta Teosófica.
               Haciéndose iniciados de la sublime doctrina.
MAX            Hay que resucitar a Cristo.
DON GAY        He caminado por todos los caminos del mundo, y he aprendido
               que los pueblos más grandes no se constituyeron sin una Iglesia
               Nacional. La creación política es ineficaz si falta una
               conciencia religiosa con su ética superior a las leyes que
               escriben los hombres.
MAX            Ilustre Don Gay, de acuerdo. La miseria del pueblo español, la
               gran miseria moral, está en su chabacana sensibilidad ante los
               enigmas de la vida y de la muerte. La Vida es un magro
               puchero; la Muerte, una carantoña ensabanada que enseña los
               dientes; el Infierno, un calderón de aceite albando donde los

*The Dog barks.*

ZARATHUSTRA  And a fine mess we're in too!

*Standing in front of the counter like three birds perched on a branch, the visitors, with a mixture of hope and sadness, beguile their troubles with an esoteric, literary discussion. They ramble on, oblivious of the crowd of policemen, the cries of the boy, the growling of the dog and the doleful comment of the grotesque character who exploits them. Intellectuals without a penny to their name.*

| | |
|---|---|
| DON GAY | You've got to hand it to them. There's no country like England. There, religious feeling is so closely identified with dignity and decorum that, undoubtedly, the most respectable families are also the most religious. If Spain could achieve a more elevated concept of religion, there might be some hope for us. |
| MAX | Then we might as well say a Requiem Mass for ourselves! Here the only people who behave with any principles are the puritan demagogues of the far left.[23]  Maybe they are the new Christians, but they certainly don't know it yet. |
| DON GAY | I tell you, gentlemen, in England I became a convert to the dogma of iconoclasm, a Christianity of prayers and hymns, divested of miracle-working images. When I see the sheer idolatry of this country...! |
| MAX | In its concept of religion Spain is a tribe from Central Africa. |
| DON GAY | Maestro, we must rebuild that concept of religion on the foundation of the God-made-Man archetype. The Christian Revolution with all the exaggerations of the Gospels. |
| DON LATINO | Which are greater than those of Comrade Lenin. |
| ZARATHUSTRA | Without a basis of religion, there can be no good faith in business. |
| DON GAY | Maestro, we must establish the National Church of Spain. |
| MAX | With the Escorial[24] as its Holy See! |
| DON GAY | A magnificent seat! |
| MAX | And hard as granite.[25] |
| DON LATINO | You'll all end up joining the Grand Theosophical Society[26] and being initiated into the sublime doctrine. |
| MAX | We must resurrect the living Christ. |
| DON GAY | I have travelled to the four corners of the earth and if there is one thing I have learned it is that no nation can be great without the foundation of a National Church. Political initiative is futile if there is no overriding religious ethos over and above man-made laws. |
| MAX | Agreed, my illustrious friend. The indigence, the great moral indigence, of the Spanish people is in the coarseness of its sensibilities to the great enigmas of life and death. Life is a bowl of watery stew; Death is a gargoyle wrapped in a white |

pecadores se achicharran como boquerones; el Cielo, una kermés sin obscenidades, a donde, con permiso del párroco, pueden asistir las Hijas de María. Este pueblo miserable transforma todos los grandes conceptos en un cuento de beatas costureras. Su religión es una chochez de viejas que disecan al gato cuando se les muere.

ZARATUSTRA  Don Gay, y qué nos cuenta usted de esos marimachos que llaman sufragistas.

DON GAY  Que no todas son marimachos. Ilustres amigos, ¿saben ustedes cuánto me costaba la vida en Londres? Tres peniques, una equivalencia de cuatro perras. Y estaba muy bien, mejor que aquí en una casa de tres pesetas.

DON LATINO  Max, vámonos a morir a Inglaterra. Apúnteme usted las señas de ese Gran Hotel, Don Gay.

DON GAY  Saint James Square. ¿No caen ustedes? El Asilo de Reina Elisabeth. Muy decente. Ya digo, mejor que aquí una casa de tres pesetas. Por la mañana té con leche, pan untado de mantequilla. El azúcar, algo escaso. Después, en la comida, un potaje de carne. Alguna vez arenques. Queso, té... Yo solía pedir un boc de cerveza, y me costaba diez céntimos. Todo muy limpio. Jabón y agua caliente para lavatorios, sin tasa.

ZARATUSTRA  Es verdad que se lavan mucho los ingleses. Lo tengo advertido. Por aquí entran algunos, y se les ve muy refregados. Gente de otros países, que no sienten el frío como nosotros, los naturales de España.

DON LATINO  Lo dicho. Me traslado a Inglaterra. Don Gay, ¿cómo no te has quedado tú en ese Paraíso?

DON GAY  Porque soy reumático, y me hace falta el sol de España.

ZARATUSTRA  Nuestro sol es la envidia de los extranjeros.

MAX  ¿Qué sería de este corral nublado? ¿Qué seríamos los españoles? Acaso más tristes y menos coléricos... Quizá un poco más tontos... Aunque no lo creo.

*Asoma la chica de una portera. Trenza en perico, caídas calcetas, cara de hambre.*

LA CHICA  ¿Ha salido esta semana entrega d'*El Hijo de la Difunta*?

ZARATUSTRA  Se está repartiendo.

LA CHICA  ¿Sabe usted si al fin se casa Alfredo?

DON GAY  ¿Tú qué deseas, pimpollo?

LA CHICA  A mí, plin. Es doña Loreta la del coronel quien lo pregunta.

ZARATUSTRA  Niña, dile a esa señora que es un secreto lo que hacen los personajes de las novelas. Sobre todo en punto de muertes y casamientos.

sheet and baring its teeth; Hell, a cauldron of boiling oil where sinners are deep-fried like anchovies; Heaven, a church fête with no hanky-panky which the Children of Mary[27] may attend with the permission of the parish priest. This miserable nation transforms all the great mysteries of life and religion into the tittle-tattle of bigoted old crones doting over a stuffed cat.

ZARATHUSTRA  And what can you tell us, Don Gay, about those battle-axes they call suffragettes?[28]

DON GAY  That they are not all battle-axes. But I ask my distinguished friends here, how much do you think it cost me to live in London? Three pence a day, the equivalent of forty centimes. And very well too. Better than a three-peseta doss house here.

DON LATINO  Max, we must go and end our days in England. Make a note of the address of that Grand Hotel, Don Gay.

DON GAY  Saint James's Square. See the connection?[29]  The Queen Elizabeth Hostel.[30]  Very respectable. As I said, better than a three-peseta place here. In the mornings tea with milk, bread and butter. Not much sugar. Then for dinner, hotpot. Occasionally, herrings. Cheese, more tea – I used to ask for a glass of beer – and all for ten centimes. Very clean. Soap provided and unlimited hot water for washing.

ZARATHUSTRA  The English wash a great deal. I've noticed that. I get some of them in here and you can tell they're well scrubbed. People from other countries don't feel the cold like we do in Spain.

DON LATINO  I repeat. I'm emigrating to England. Why didn't you stay there, Don Gay? It sounds like paradise.

DON GAY  Because I've got rheumatism. I need the Spanish sun.

ZARATHUSTRA  Our sun is the envy of all foreigners.

MAX  What would this farmyard be like under a permanently overcast sky? What would *we* be like? A little gloomier perhaps, less hot-tempered. Perhaps a little more stupid... though I doubt that's possible.

*A little girl, a concierge's daughter, pokes her head round the door. Plaits done up in a bun, stockings round her ankles, under-nourished appearance.*

GIRL  Has this week's episode of *The Dead Woman's Son*[31] come out yet?

ZARATHUSTRA  It's being delivered now.

GIRL  Do you know if Alfredo gets married in the end?

DON GAY  Would you like him to, sunshine?

GIRL  Me? Why should I care? It's Doña Loreta, the colonel's wife,[32] who's asking.

ZARATHUSTRA  Well, now. You tell the lady that what characters do in serials is a secret. Especially in matters of death and marriage.

MAX                Zaratustra, ándate con cuidado, que te lo van a preguntar de
                   Real Orden.
ZARATUSTRA   Estaría bueno que se divulgase el misterio. Pues no habría
                   novela.

*Escapa la chica salvando los charcos con sus patas de caña. El Peregrino
Ilusionado en un rincón conferencia con Zaratustra. Máximo Estrella y Don
Latino se orientan a la taberna de Pica Lagartos, que tiene su clásico laurel en
la calle de la Montera.*

# Escena Tercera

*La Taberna de Pica Lagartos: Luz de acetileno: Mostrador de cinc: Zaguán
oscuro con mesas y banquillos: Jugadores de mus: Borrosos diálogos. Máximo
Estrella y Don Latino de Hispalis, sombras en las sombras de un rincón, se
regalan con sendos quinces de morapio.*

EL CHICO DE LA TABERNA   Don Max, ha venido buscándole la Marquesa
                   del Tango.
UN BORRACHO     ¡Miau!
MAX                No conozco a esa dama.
EL CHICO DE LA TABERNA   Enriqueta la Pisa-Bien.
DON LATINO    ¿Y desde cuándo titula esa golfa?
EL CHICO DE LA TABERNA   Desde que heredó del finado difunto de su papá,
                   que entodavía vive.
DON LATINO    ¡Mala sombra!
MAX                ¿Ha dicho si volvería?
EL CHICO DE LA TABERNA   Entró, miró, preguntó y se fue rebotada,
                   torciendo la gaita. ¡Ya la tiene usted en la puerta!

*Enriqueta la Pisa-Bien, una mozuela golfa, revenida de un ojo, periodista y
florista, levantaba el cortinillo de verde sarga, sobre su endrina cabeza,
adornada de peines gitanos.*

LA PISA-BIEN  ¡La vara de nardos! ¡La vara de nardos! Don Max, traigo para
                   usted un memorial de mi mamá: Está enferma y necesita la luz
                   del décimo que le ha fiado.
MAX                Le devuelves el décimo y le dices que se vaya al infierno.
LA PISA-BIEN  De su parte, caballero. ¿Manda usted algo más?

*El ciego saca una vieja cartera, y tanteando los papeles con aire vago, extrae el
décimo de la lotería y lo arroja sobre la mesa: Queda abierto entre los vasos de*

MAX                    Have a care, Zarathustra. They'll get it out of you by Royal
                       Decree.[33]
ZARATHUSTRA  You can't go giving secrets away like that. There'd be no
                       mystery. There'd be no serials.

*The girl runs off, jumping over the puddles on her spindly legs. Don Gay, the*
*ever-optimistic globetrotter, confers with Zarathustra in a corner. Máximo*
*Estrella and Don Latino move off in the direction of Lizard-Slicer's tavern which*
*displays its traditional bay tree on Montera Street.*

# Scene Three

*Lizard-Slicer's tavern: light from acetylene lamps, zinc-covered bar, dark*
*recesses with tables and benches, card players and a confused hubbub of*
*conversation. Máximo Estrella and Don Latino de Hispalis, shadows amongst*
*the shadows, regale themselves with glasses of cheap red wine in a corner of the*
*bar.*

POT BOY          Don Max, the Tango queen was here looking for you.
DRUNK            Bah!
MAX              I'm not acquainted with the lady.
POT BOY          Henrietta the Hoofer.
DON LATINO   And since when does that strumpet go around with a royal
                       title?
POT BOY          Since she inherited it from her long-lost and recently-deceased
                       old man, who, in fact, turns out to be still alive![34]
DON LATINO   Very funny!
MAX              Did she say if she'd be back?
POT BOY          She came in, she looked, she asked and bounced out again,
                       twisting and craning her neck. Look, there she is at the door!

*Henrietta the Hoofer, a young whore with a shrivelled-up eye socket, street*
*vendor of flowers and newspapers,[35] raises the green serge curtain above her*
*raven-black hair, adorned with gypsy combs.*

HENRIETTA    Flowers, lovely flowers! Flowers for your button-hole![36] Don
                       Max, I've got a message for you from my old Mum. She's sick
                       and needs the cash for that lottery ticket she let you have on
                       credit.
MAX              Then give her the ticket and tell her to go to hell.
HENRIETTA    Much obliged, I'm sure, kind sir. Anything else I can do for
                       you?

*The blind man takes out an ancient wallet and, after fumbling uncertainly*
*through the papers, pulls out the lottery ticket and throws it on the table. It lies*

*vino, mostrando el número bajo el parpadeo azul del acetileno. La Pisa-Bien se*
*apresura a echarle la zarpa.*

DON LATINO    ¡Ese número sale premiado!
LA PISA-BIEN  Don Max desprecia el dinero.
EL CHICO DE LA TABERNA  No le deje usted irse, Don Max.
MAX           Niño, yo hago lo que me da la gana. Pídele para mí la petaca al
              amo.
EL CHICO DE LA TABERNA  Don Max, es un capicúa de sietes y cincos.
LA PISA-BIEN  ¡Que tiene premio, no falla! Pero es menester apoquinar tres
              melopeas, y este caballero está afónico. Caballero, me retiro
              saludándole. si quiere usted un nardo, se lo regalo.
MAX           Estáte ahí.
LA PISA-BIEN  Me espera un cabrito viudo.
MAX           Que se aguante. Niño, ve a colgarme la capa.
LA PISA-BIEN  Por esa pañosa no dan ni los buenos días. Pídale usted las tres
              beatas a Pica Lagartos.
EL CHICO DE LA TABERNA  Si usted le da coba, las tiene en la mano. Dice
              que es usted segundo Castelar.
MAX           Dobla la capa, y ahueca.
EL CHICO DE LA TABERNA  ¿Qué pido?
MAX           Toma lo que quieran darte.
LA PISA-BIEN  ¡Si no la reciben!
DON LATINO    Calla, mala sombra.
MAX           Niño, huye veloz.
EL CHICO DE LA TABERNA  Como la corza herida, Don Max.
MAX           Eres un clásico.
LA PISA-BIEN  Si no te admiten la prenda, dices que es de un poeta.
DON LATINO    El primer poeta de España.
EL BORRACHO   ¡Cráneo previlegiado!
MAX           Yo nunca tuve talento.   ¡He vivido siempre de un modo
              absurdo!
DON LATINO    No has tenido el talento de saber vivir.
MAX           Mañana me muero, y mi mujer y mi hija se quedan haciendo
              cruces en la boca.

*Tosió cavernoso, con las barbas estremecidas, y en los ojos ciegos un vidriado*
*triste, de alcohol y de fiebre.*

DON LATINO    No has debido quedarte sin capa.
LA PISA-BIEN  Y ese trasto ya no parece. Siquiera, convide usted, Don Max.
MAX           Tome usted lo que guste, Marquesa.
LA PISA-BIEN  Una copa de Rute.
DON LATINO    Es la bebida elegante.
LA PISA-BIEN  ¡Ay! Don Latino, por algo es una la morganática del Rey de
              Portugal.  Don Max, no puedo detenerme, que mi esposo me

*spread out amongst the wine glasses, revealing its number under the flickering blue light of the acetylene lamps. Henrietta snaps it up with her claw.*

| | |
|---|---|
| DON LATINO | Hey, that number's a winner! |
| HENRIETTA | Don Max despises money. |
| POT BOY | Don't let her get away, Don Max! |
| MAX | Boy, I'll do as I damn well please. Go and ask the guv'nor for the loan of his tobacco pouch. |
| POT BOY | But Don Max, it's a lucky number – sevens and fives.[37] |
| HENRIETTA | It'll get a prize all right. Can't fail. But you've got to sing for your supper and this gentleman's lost his voice! Sir, with your permission I'll take my leave. If you want a button-hole, it's on the house. |
| MAX | Stay where you are. |
| HENRIETTA | I've got my billy goat waiting outside. |
| MAX | Let him wait. Boy, go and pawn my cape. |
| HENRIETTA | They wouldn't give you the time of day for that old rag. Ask Lizard-Slicer for the three pesetas. |
| POT BOY | Butter him up a bit and the money's as good as yours. He says you talk like the great Castelar.[38] |
| MAX | Just fold the cape and push off. |
| POT BOY | How much shall I ask for it? |
| MAX | Take whatever they want to give you. |
| HENRIETTA | They won't touch it with a barge-pole! |
| DON LATINO | Silence, Jonah! |
| MAX | Boy, fly like the wind! |
| POT BOY | Like the wounded stag,[39] Don Max! |
| MAX | The boy's a classicist! |
| HENRIETTA | If they won't take the cape, tell 'em it belongs to a poet. |
| DON LATINO | The greatest poet in Spain. |
| DRUNK | A privileged mind! |
| MAX | I never had any talent. My life has been an absurdity! |
| DON LATINO | You never had much talent for living. |
| MAX | I shall die tomorrow, and my wife and daughter will be left yawning with hunger and making crosses over their mouths.[40] |

*A cavernous cough shakes Max's beard and his blind eyes appear glazed over with fever and alcohol.*

| | |
|---|---|
| DON LATINO | You shouldn't have got rid of your cape. |
| HENRIETTA | And it's probably the last we've seen of that little bastard. So how about buying us a drink, Don Max? |
| MAX | State your pleasure, duchess. |
| HENRIETTA | A glass of anis from Rute.[41] |
| DON LATINO | That's high-class hooch. |
| HENRIETTA | I'm not the morganatic wife[42] of the King of Portugal for nothing, you know, Don Latino. Sorry, Don Max, I can't stop |

hace señas desde la acera.

MAX Invítale a pasar.

*Un golfo largo y astroso, que vende periódicos, ríe asomado a la puerta, y como perro que se espulga, se sacude con jaleo de hombros, la cara en una gran risa de viruelas. Es el Rey de Portugal, que hace las bellaquerías con Enriqueta La Pisa-Bien, Marquesa del Tango.*

LA PISA-BIEN ¡Pasa, Manolo!

EL REY DE PORTUGAL Sal tú fuera.

LA PISA-BIEN ¿Es que temes perder la corona? ¡Entra de incógnito, so pelma!

EL REY DE PORTUGAL Enriqueta, a ver si te despeino.

LA PISA-BIEN ¡Filfa!

EL REY DE PORTUGAL ¡Consideren ustedes que me llama Rey de Portugal para significar que no valgo un chavo! Argumentos de esta golfa desde que fue a Lisboa, y se ha enterado del valor de la moneda. Yo, para servir a ustedes, soy Gorito, y no está medio bien que mi morganática me señale por el alias.

LA PISA-BIEN ¡Calla, chalado!

EL REY DE PORTUGAL ¿Te caminas?

LA PISA-BIEN Aguarda que me beba una copa de Rute. Don Max me la paga.

EL REY DE PORTUGAL ¿Y qué tienes que ver con ese poeta?

LA PISA-BIEN Colaboramos.

EL REY DE PORTUGAL Pues despacha.

LA PISA-BIEN En cuanto me la mida Pica Lagartos.

PICA LAGARTOS ¿Qué has dicho tú, so golfa?

LA PISA-BIEN ¡Perdona, rico!

PICA LAGARTOS Venancio me llamo.

LA PISA-BIEN ¡Tienes un nombre de novela! Anda, mídeme una copa de Rute, y dale a mi esposo un vaso de agua, que está muy acalorado.

MAX Venancio, no vuelvas a compararme con Castelar. ¡Castelar era un idiota! Dame otro quince.

DON LATINO Me adhiero a lo del quince y a lo de Castelar.

PICA LAGARTOS Son ustedes unos doctrinarios. Castelar representa una gloria nacional de España. Ustedes acaso no sepan que mi padre lo sacaba diputado.

LA PISA-BIEN ¡Hay que ver!

PICA LAGARTOS Mi padre era el barbero de Don Manuel Camo. ¡Una gloria nacional de Huesca!

EL BORRACHO ¡Cráneo previlegiado!

PICA LAGARTOS Cállate la boca, Zacarías.

now.  My regal spouse is making signs at me from the
pavement.

MAX             Invite him to step this way.

*A lanky individual of beggarly appearance, a newsvendor by trade, appears in
the doorway, twitching his shoulders and scratching like a dog de-fleaing itself,
his face split in a huge pock-marked grin.  It is the King of Portugal who has
shady dealings with Henrietta, the Hoofer, Queen of the Tango.*

HENRIETTA    Come on in, Manolo.[43]
KING OF PORTUGAL  You come outside.
HENRIETTA    Why?  Are you scared of losing your crown?[44]  Take it off and
                enter incognito then, you great oaf!
KING OF PORTUGAL  Just watch yourself, Henrietta, or I might ruffle your
                hair-do.
HENRIETTA    Bullshit!
KING OF PORTUGAL  King of Portugal she calls me.  That's supposed to
                mean that I'm nothing, a nobody.  From the time that this
                whore was on the beat in Lisbon and discovered the money
                wasn't worth the paper the king's head was printed on![45]  My
                name is Gorito at your service, gentlemen, and she's got no
                right pinning aliases on me.
HENRIETTA    Oh, shut up, muttonhead!
KING OF PORTUGAL  Come on, get moving.
HENRIETTA    Wait till I've had my drink.  Don Max is buying.
KING OF PORTUGAL  What are you doing with a poet like him?
HENRIETTA    We're working together.
KING OF PORTUGAL  Well, get it over with.
HENRIETTA    As soon as Lizard-Slicer pours my drink.
LIZARD-SLICER  What was that you said, you little slut!
HENRIETTA    Sorry, my precious!
LIZARD-SLICER  My name is Venancio.
HENRIETTA    Now there's a name straight out of a romantic novel!  Pour me
                a glass of Rute, there's a dear, and give my consort a glass of
                water, he's overheating.
MAX             Venancio, don't ever compare me to Castelar.  Castelar was an
                idiot.  And give me a glass of red.
DON LATINO  I second both motions: Castelar and the glass of red.
LIZARD-SLICER  Doctrinaires, that's what you are.  Doctrinaires.  Castelar
                represents one of Spain's national glories.  I don't suppose you
                are aware that my father helped to get him elected.
HENRIETTA    You don't say!
LIZARD-SLICER  My father was barber to Don Manuel Camo,[46] election-rigger
                extraordinary.  A national glory from the province of Huesca!
DRUNK        A privileged mind!
LIZARD-SLICER  Button your lip, Zacharias.

EL BORRACHO  ¿Acaso falto?

PICA LAGARTOS  ¡Pudieras!

EL BORRACHO  Tiene mucha educación servidorcito.

LA PISA-BIEN  ¡Como que ha salido usted del Colegio de los Escolapios!  ¡Se
    educó usted con mi papá!

EL BORRACHO  ¿Quién es tu papá?

LA PISA-BIEN  Un diputado.

EL BORRACHO  Yo he recibido educación en el extranjero.

LA PISA-BIEN  ¿Viaja usted de incógnito?  ¿Por un casual, será usted Don
    Jaime?

EL BORRACHO  ¡Me has sacado por la fotografía!

LA PISA-BIEN  ¡Naturaca!  ¿Y va usted sin una flor en la solapa?

EL BORRACHO  Ven tú a ponérmela.

LA PISA-BIEN  Se la pongo a usted y le obsequio con ella.

EL REY DE PORTUGAL  ¡Hay que ser caballero, Zacarías!  ¡Y hay que
    mirarse mucho, soleche, antes de meter mano!  La Enriqueta es
    cosa mía.

LA PISA-BIEN  ¡Calla, bocón!

EL REY DE PORTUGAL  ¡Soleche, no seas tú provocativa!

LA PISA-BIEN  No introduzcas tú la pata, pelmazo.

*El Chico de la Taberna entra con azorado sofoco, atado a la frente un pañuelo
con roeles de sangre. Una ráfaga de emoción mueve caras y actitudes; todas las
figuras, en su diversidad, pautan una misma norma.*

EL CHICO DE LA TABERNA  ¡Hay carreras por las calles!

EL REY DE PORTUGAL  ¡Viva la huelga de proletarios!

EL BORRACHO  ¡Chócala!  Anoche lo hemos decidido por votación en la Casa
    del Pueblo.

LA PISA-BIEN  ¡Crispín, te alcanzó un cate!

EL CHICO DE LA TABERNA  ¡Un marica de la Acción Ciudadana!

PICA LAGARTOS  ¡Niño, sé bien hablado!  El propio republicanismo reconoce
    que la propiedad es sagrada.  La Acción Ciudadana está
    integrada por patronos de todas circunstancias, y por los
    miembros varones de sus familias.  ¡Hay que saber lo que se
    dice!

*Grupos vocingleros corren por el centro de la calle, con banderas enarboladas.
Entran en la taberna obreros golfantes – blusa, bufanda y alpargata – y
mujeronas encendidas, de arañada greña.*

EL REY DE PORTUGAL  ¡Enriqueta, me hierve la sangre!  Si tú no sientes la
    política, puedes quedarte.

DRUNK        Did I say something wrong?

LIZARD-SLICER  You might.

DRUNK        I've got very good manners, I'll have you know.

HENRIETTA    From an ex-pupil of the College of Christian Brothers,[47] one would expect no less. You must have been educated with my papa.

DRUNK        Who is your papa?

HENRIETTA    A member of Parliament.

DRUNK        I got my education abroad.

HENRIETTA    Are you travelling incognito? You wouldn't be the royal prince Don Jaime,[48] pretender to the throne, by any chance?

DRUNK        You recognized me by my photo!

HENRIETTA    But, of course! And you going around with no flower in your lapel!

DRUNK        Come and stick it in yourself.

HENRIETTA    There you are, with my compliments.

KING OF PORTUGAL  Your good breeding is slipping, Zacharias! You'd better watch it before laying your paws on her! Henrietta's my property.

HENRIETTA    You keep your big mouth shut!

KING OF PORTUGAL  You stop being provocative, slut!

HENRIETTA    And you stop inserting your great oar, cabbage-head!

*The Pot Boy, dazed and out of breath, enters with a blood-stained handkerchief tied round his forehead. A shock-wave of excitement changes attitudes and expressions, all the faces, in their diversity, registering a uniform emotion.*

POT BOY      They're running wild in the streets!

KING OF PORTUGAL  Up with the proletarian strike!

DRUNK        Put it there! We voted in favour of it last night at the union meeting.[49]

HENRIETTA    Crispin, that's a nasty clout you've caught there!

POT BOY      Some poofter from the Citizens' Action Group!

LIZARD-SLICER  You watch your language, boy! Even the Republicans recognise the sanctity of private property. The Citizens' Action Group[50] is constituted by business employers, great and small, and the male members of their families. So just watch what you're saying!

*Slogan-shouting groups run down the middle of the road with flags and banners aloft. A number of down-and-out workers in smocks, mufflers and rope-soled sandals and flushed, dishevelled women come into the tavern.*

KING OF PORTUGAL  Henrietta, my blood's boiling! If you don't feel the fire of political passion in your veins, you can stay where you are.

LA PISA-BIEN  So pelma, yo te sigo a todas partes. ¡Enfermera Honoraria de la Cruz Colorada!
PICA LAGARTOS  ¡Chico, baja el cierre! Se invita a salir al que quiera jaleo.

*La florista y el coime salen empujándose, revueltos con otros parroquianos.*
*Corren por la calle tropeles de obreros. Resuena el golpe de muchos cierres*
*metálicos.*

EL BORRACHO  ¡Vivan los héroes del Dos de Mayo!
DON LATINO  Niño, ¿qué dinero te han dado?
EL CHICO DE LA TABERNA  ¡Nueve pesetas!
MAX        Cóbrate, Venancio. ¡Y tú, trae el décimo, Marquesa!
DON LATINO  ¡Voló esa pájara!
MAX        ¡Se lleva el sueño de mi fortuna! ¿Dónde daríamos con esa golfa?
PICA LAGARTOS  Ésa ya no se aparta del tumulto.
EL CHICO DE LA TABERNA  Recala en la Modernista.
MAX        Latino, préstame tus ojos para buscar a la Marquesa del Tango.
DON LATINO  Max, dame la mano.
EL BORRACHO  ¡Cráneo privilegiado!
UNA VOZ        ¡Mueran los maricas de la Acción Ciudadana! ¡Abajo los ladrones!

## Escena Cuarta

*Noche. Máximo Estrella y Don Latino de Hispalis se tambalean asidos del*
*brazo por una calle enarenada y solitaria. Faroles rotos, cerradas todas,*
*ventanas y puertas. En la llama de los faroles un igual temblor verde y*
*macilento. La luna sobre el alero de las casas, partiendo la calle por medio. De*
*tarde en tarde, el asfalto sonoro. Un trote épico. Soldados Romanos. Sombras*
*de Guardias. Se extingue el eco de la patrulla. La Buñolería Modernista*
*entreabre su puerta, y una banda de luz parte la acera. Max y Don Latino,*
*borrachos lunáticos, filósofos peripatéticos, bajo la línea luminosa de los*
*faroles, caminan y tambalean.*

MAX        ¿Dónde estamos?
DON LATINO  Esta calle no tiene letrero.
MAX        Yo voy pisando vidrios rotos.
DON LATINO  No ha hecho mala cachiza el honrado pueblo.
MAX        ¿Qué rumbo consagramos?

HENRIETTA    What d'you mean, you great oaf! I'll follow you anywhere.
                   I'm not an honorary Red Cross nurse[51] for nothing, you know!
LIZARD-SLICER  Boy, lower the shutters.  Anybody looking for trouble is
                   invited to leave now.

*Mingling with other customers, the flower girl and her pimp push and shove each other to the door. Groups of workers run amok in the streets. The crash of metallic shutters coming down.*

DRUNK           Long live the heroes of the second of May![52]
DON LATINO   Boy, how much did they give you for the cape?
POT BOY       Nine pesetas!
MAX             Here's for the drinks, Venancio!  And you, duchess, hand over
                   the lottery ticket!
DON LATINO   The bird has flown!
MAX             And taken the dream of my fortune with her.  Where would we
                   find the little tramp now?
DON LATINO   She'll stick with the crowds.
POT BOY       She usually ends up in the Modernist Café.
MAX             Latino, lend me your eyes to look for our Queen of the Tango.
DON LATINO   Give me your hand, Max.
DRUNK           A privileged mind!
A VOICE         Death to the bastards of Citizens' Action! Down with the
                   exploiters!

# Scene Four

*Night. Máximo Estrella and Don Latino de Hispalis stagger arm in arm along a deserted, sand-covered street.[53] Broken streetlamps, all doors locked, windows shuttered. The lights burn with a regular, pulsating, pale-green glow. Moonlight picks out the eaves of the houses and divides the street down the middle. From time to time the asphalt reverberates to the epic trot of the so-called 'Roman Guard'.[54] Shadows of civil guards. Then the echo of the night patrol dies away. The door of the Modernist Café stands ajar; a shaft of light cuts across the pavement. Max and Don Latino, drunkenly eccentric, peripatetic philosophers, stumble along under the luminous row of streetlamps.*

MAX             Where are we?
DON LATINO   This street hasn't got a name.
MAX             I'm treading on broken glass.
DON LATINO   The honest proletariat has smashed the place up a bit.
MAX             Which direction are we honouring?

| | |
|---|---|
| DON LATINO | Déjate guiar. |
| MAX | Condúceme a casa. |
| DON LATINO | Tenemos abierta La Buñolería Modernista. |
| MAX | De rodar y de beber estoy muerto. |
| DON LATINO | Un café de recuelo te integra. |
| MAX | Hace frío, Latino. |
| DON LATINO | ¡Corre un cierto gris!... |
| MAX | Préstame tu macferlán. |
| DON LATINO | ¡Te ha dado el delirio poético! |
| MAX | ¡Me quedé sin capa, sin dinero y sin lotería! |
| DON LATINO | Aquí hacemos la captura de la niña Pisa-Bien. |

*La Niña Pisa-Bien, despintada, pingona, marchita, se materializa bajo un farol con su pregón de golfa madrileña.*

| | |
|---|---|
| LA PISA-BIEN | ¡5775! ¡El número de la suerte! ¡Mañana sale! ¡Lo vendo! ¡Lo vendo! ¡5775! |
| DON LATINO | ¡Acudes al reclamo! |
| LA PISA-BIEN | Y le convido a usted a un café de recuelo. |
| DON LATINO | Gracias, preciosidad. |
| LA PISA-BIEN | Y a Don Max, a lo que guste. ¡Ya nos ajuntamos los tres tristes trogloditas! Don Max, yo por usted hago la jarra, y muy honrada. |
| MAX | Dame el décimo y vete al infierno. |
| LA PISA-BIEN | Don Max, por adelantado decláreme en secreto si cameló las tres beatas y si las lleva en el portamonedas. |
| MAX | ¡Pareces hermana de Romanones! |
| LA PISA-BIEN | ¡Quién tuviera los miles de ese pirante! |
| DON LATINO | ¡Con sólo la renta de un día, yo me contentaba! |
| MAX | La Revolución es aquí tan fatal como en Rusia. |
| DON LATINO | ¡Nos moriremos sin verla! |
| MAX | Pues viviremos muy poco. |
| LA PISA-BIEN | ¿Ustedes bajaron hasta la Cibeles? Allí ha sido la faena entre los manifestantes, y los Polis Honorarios. A alguno le hemos dado mulé. |
| DON LATINO | Todos los amarillos debían ser arrastrados. |
| LA PISA-BIEN | ¡Conforme! Y aquel momento que usted no tenga ocupaciones urgentes, nos ponemos a ello, Don Latino. |
| MAX | Dame ese capicúa, Enriqueta. |
| LA PISA-BIEN | Venga el parné, y tenga usted su suerte. |
| MAX | La propina, cuando cobre el premio. |
| LA PISA-BIEN | ¡No mira eso la Enriqueta! |

DON LATINO    Just be guided by me.
MAX           Guide me home.
DON LATINO    I see the Modernist Café is open.
MAX           I'm dead on my feet with drinking and roaming the streets.
DON LATINO    A cup of recycled coffee will revive you.
MAX           It's cold, Latino.
DON LATINO    There's a nip in the air.
MAX           Lend me your Macfarlane overcoat.[55]
DON LATINO    You've got the poetic D.Ts again!
MAX           Here I am with no cape, no money and no lottery ticket!
DON LATINO    We should capture our nymph Henrietta around here.

*Pasty-faced, jaded and bedraggled, the Nymph Henrietta materializes under a lamp-post with her street-vendor's cry on her lips.*

HENRIETTA     Five, seven seven, five!  Get your lucky number!  Out
              tomorrow!  Selling now and selling cheap!  Five, seven seven,
              five!
DON LATINO    The answer to our mating call!
HENRIETTA     What's more, I invite you to a cup of coffee.
DON LATINO    Thank you, my precious.
HENRIETTA     And for Don Max, whatever may be his pleasure!  Well, once
              more we flock together, the three dismal dodos![56]  It would be
              an honour to spend my last cent on a man like you, Don Max.
MAX           Just give me the ticket and go to hell.
HENRIETTA     Don Max, first whisper in my ear if you wangled the three
              pesetas and if you've got 'em in your purse.
MAX           You sound like a sister of that Shylock, Romanones.[57]
HENRIETTA     I wish I had his millions, the old shark.
DON LATINO    I'd settle for what he earns in one day.
MAX           There'll be a revolution in this country, as surely as there was
              in Russia.[58]
DON LATINO    But we'll be dead before we see it.
MAX           Then we haven't got long to live.
HENRIETTA     Have you been down to Cibeles?[59]  There was a dust-up
              between the demonstrators and the vigilantes from Citizens'
              Action. We did one or two of 'em in.
DON LATINO    All bourgeois liberals[60] should be dragged to the guillotine!
HENRIETTA     Quite right.  And when you can tear yourself away from your
              pressing engagements, we'll do something about it, eh, Don
              Latino?
MAX           Give me that reversible number, Henrietta.
HENRIETTA     Let's see the colour of your money... and here's your fortune.
MAX           You'll get your tip when I collect the prize.
HENRIETTA     Henrietta doesn't consider such things!

*La Buñolería entreabre su puerta, y del antro apestoso de aceite van saliendo
deshilados, uno a uno, en fila india, los Epígonos del Parnaso Modernista:
Rafael de los Vélez, Dorio de Gadex, Lucio Vero, Mínguez, Gálvez, Clarinito y
Pérez. Unos son largos, tristes y flacos, otros vivaces, chaparros y carillenos.
Dorio de Gadex, jovial como un trasgo, irónico como un ateniense, ceceoso
como un cañí, mima su saludo versallesco y grotesco.*

DORIO DE GADEX ¡Padre y Maestro Mágico, salud!
MAX            ¡Salud, Don Dorio!
DORIO DE GADEX ¡Maestro, usted no ha temido el rebuzno libertario del
               honrado pueblo!
MAX            ¡El épico rugido del mar! ¡Yo me siento pueblo!
DORIO DE GADEX ¡Yo, no!
MAX            ¡Porque eres un botarate!
DORIO DE GADEX ¡Maestro, pongámonos el traje de luces de la cortesía!
               ¡Maestro, usted tampoco se siente pueblo! Usted es un poeta, y
               los poetas somos aristocracia. Como dice Ibsen, las multitudes
               y las montañas se unen siempre por la base.
MAX            ¡No me aburras con Ibsen!
PÉREZ          ¿Se ha hecho usted crítico de teatros, Don Max?
DORIO DE GADEX ¡Calla, Pérez!
DON LATINO     Aquí sólo hablan los genios.
MAX            Yo me siento pueblo. Yo había nacido para ser tribuno de la
               plebe, y me acanallé perpetrando traducciones y haciendo
               versos. ¡Eso sí, mejores que los hacéis los modernistas!
DORIO DE GADEX Maestro, preséntese usted a un sillón de la Academia.
MAX            No lo digas en burla, idiota. ¡Me sobran méritos! Pero esa
               prensa miserable me boicotea. Odian mi rebeldía y odian mi
               talento. Para medrar hay que ser agradador de todos los
               Segismundos. ¡El Buey Apis me despide como a un criado!
               ¡La Academia me ignora! ¡Y soy el primer poeta de España!
               ¡El primero! ¡El primero! ¡Y ayuno! ¡Y no me humillo
               pidiendo limosna! ¡Y no me parte un rayo! ¡Yo soy el
               verdadero immortal, y no esos cabrones del cotarro académico!
               ¡Muera Maura!
LOS MODERNISTAS ¡Muera! ¡Muera! ¡Muera!
CLARINITO      Maestro, nosotros los jóvenes impondremos la candidatura de
               usted para un sillón de la Academia.
DORIO DE GADEX Precisamente ahora está vacante el sillón de Don Benito el
               Garbancero.
MAX            Nombrarán al Sargento Basallo.

*The café door swings open and from the cavernous interior, heavy with the reek of oil, issue in ragged single file the Epigones of the Modernist Parnassus:*[61] *Rafael de los Vélez, Dorio de Gadex, Lucio Vero, Mínguez, Gávez, Clarinito and Pérez. Some are long, lugubrious and thin, others squat, vivacious and chubby-cheeked. Dorio de Gadex, jaunty as a leprechaun, ironic as an Athenian and lisping like a Romany, stages his grotesque and Versaillesque greeting.*

DORIO DE GADEX  All hail, oh magic maestro and father of us all![62]
MAX  Greetings, Don Dorio!
DORIO DE GADEX  Maestro, you have braved the righteous wrath of the freedom-braying masses!
MAX  The epic roar of the sea! I am a man of the people!
DORIO DE GADEX  Not I, Don Max.
MAX  Because you are a buffoon!
DORIO DE GADEX  Maestro, let us don the shining armour of courtesy! Maestro, you are no more a man of the people than I am. You are a poet and we poets are aristocracy. As Ibsen says, the masses and the mountain peaks are always joined at their base.[63]
MAX  Don't bore me with Ibsen!
PEREZ  Have you turned drama critic, Don Max?
DORIO DE GADEX  Silence, Pérez!
DON LATINO  Only geniuses have leave to speak here.
MAX  I am a man of the people. I was born to be tribune of the plebs, but I prostituted myself by perpetrating translations and writing verse. Admittedly, better than the trash you Modernists turn out!
DORIO DE GADEX  Maestro, you should apply for a seat in the Spanish Academy.
MAX  Speak not in jest, my good buffoon. I have qualifications to spare. But I am boycotted by the lackeys of the press. They hate my rebellion and detest my talent. To succeed, you have to lick the arse of every petty tyrant.[64] My editor, the great Bull Apis, dismisses me like a servant! The Academy ignores me! And I am the greatest poet in Spain! I say the greatest! The greatest! And I'm dying of hunger. But I will not grovel for the crumbs of charity! I'll be damned if I will! I am the true immortal and not those bastards from the academic spelling bee! Death to president Maura![65]
THE MODERNISTS  Death to Maura! Death to Maura! Death to Maura!
CLARINITO  Maestro, we of the younger generation will press your claim for a chair in the Academy.
DORIO DE GADEX  As a matter of fact, there's a vacancy at the moment: the chair of Don Benito Pérez Galdós, novelist and corn merchant.[66]
MAX  They'll probably elect Sergeant Basallo for his heroic memoirs of the Moroccan campaign.[67]

DORIO DE GADEX  Maestro, ¿usted conoce los Nuevos Gozos del Enano de la
Venta? ¡Un Jefe de Obra! Ayer de madrugada los cantamos en
la Puerta del Sol. ¡El éxito de la temporada!
CLARINITO      ¡Con decir que salió el retén de Gobernación!
LA PISA-BIEN  ¡Ni Rafael el Gallo!
DON LATINO  Deben ustedes ofrecerle una audición al Maestro.
DORIO DE GADEX  Don Latino, ni una palabra más.
PÉREZ      Usted cantará con nosotros, Don Latino.
DON LATINO  Yo doy una nota más baja que el cerdo.
DORIO DE GADEX  Usted es un clásico.
DON LATINO  ¿Y qué hace un clásico en el tropel de ruiseñores modernistas?
Niños, ¡a ello!

*Dorio de Gadex, feo, burlesco y chepudo, abre los brazos, que son como alones
sin pluma, en el claro lunero.*

DORIO DE GADEX  El Enano de la Venta.
CORO DE MODERNISTAS  ¡Cuenta! ¡Cuenta! ¡Cuenta!
DORIO DE GADEX  Con bravatas de valiente.
CORO DE MODERNISTAS  ¡Miente! ¡Miente! ¡Miente!
DORIO DE GADEX  Quiere gobernar la Harca.
CORO DE MODERNISTAS  ¡Charca! ¡Charca! ¡Charca!
DORIO DE GADEX  Y es un Tartufo Malsín.
CORO DE MODERNISTAS  ¡Sin! ¡Sin! ¡Sin!
DORIO DE GADEX  Sin un adarme de seso.
CORO DE MODERNISTAS  ¡Eso! ¡Eso! ¡Eso!
DORIO DE GADEX  Pues tiene hueca la bola.
CORO DE MODERNISTAS  ¡Chola! ¡Chola! ¡Chola!
DORIO DE GADEX  Pues tiene la chola hueca.
CORO DE MODERNISTAS  ¡Eureka! ¡Eureka! ¡Eureka!

*Gran interrupción. Un trote épico, y la patrulla de soldados romanos
desemboca por una calle traviesa. Traen la luna sobre los cascos y en los
charrascos. Suena un toque de atención, y se cierra con golpe pronto la puerta
de la Buñolería. Pitito, capitán de los équites municipales, se levanta sobre los
estribos.*

EL CAPITÁN PITITO  ¡Mentira parece que sean ustedes intelectuales y que
promuevan estos escándalos! ¿Qué dejan ustedes para los
analfabetos?
MAX      ¡Eureka! ¡Eureka! ¡Eureka! ¡Pico de Oro! En griego, para
mayor claridad, Crisóstomo. Señor Centurión, ¡usted hablará
el griego en sus cuatro dialectos!
EL CAPITÁN PITITO  ¡Por borrachín, a la Delega!
MAX      ¡Y más chulo que un ocho! Señor Centurión, ¡yo también
chanelo el sermo vulgaris!

DORIO DE GADEX  Maestro, have you heard the latest limericks on Maura, the mighty midget?[68] A *chef d'oeuvre*! We gave a rendition in the early hours of yesterday morning in the Puerta del Sol.[69] The success of the season!

CLARINITO  They even called out the police reserve!

HENRIETTA  Really! You get more police protection than a bullfighter![70]

DON LATINO  You should give a special performance for the maestro!

DORIO DE GADEX  Don Latino, say no more.

PEREZ  You must sing with us, Don Latino.

DON LATINO  I've got a voice lower than a pig's grunt.

DORIO DE GADEX  You are a classical performer.

DON LATINO  And what's a classicist doing in a flock of modernist songbirds? Go to it, lads!

*Dorio de Gadex, hunchbacked, ugly and grotesque, raises his arms like the plucked wings of a chicken in the clear moonlight.*

DORIO DE GADEX  There once was a midget so 'loco'
with a head both enormous and hollow.

CHORUS OF MODERNIST POETS  Hollow!

DORIO DE GADEX  With bluster and blarney
he called on his army
to conquer the whole of Morocco!

CHORUS OF MODERNIST POETS  Conquer the whole of Morocco!

DORIO DE GADEX  You're a fraud and a fake they declare.
We suspect you are not quite all there.

CHORUS OF MODERNIST POETS  All there!

DORIO DE GADEX  You're a bit of a loon;
your head's a balloon.
It's empty and full of hot air!

CHORUS OF MODERNIST POETS  Empty and full of hot air!

*Violent interruption. With a heroic clatter of hooves, the night patrol of 'Roman' soldiers emerges from a side street. Moonlight glinting on helmets and swords. There is a bugle call and the café door is promptly slammed to. Pitito, Captain of the Municipal Mounted Police, stands up in his stirrups.*

CAPTAIN PITITO  It is quite incredible that intellectuals like you should be creating a disturbance like this! If this is how you behave, what can we expect from the illiterates?

MAX  Ah, eureka! The man with the golden voice! St John Chrysostom,[71] I presume. In Greek, for greater clarity, I beg of you, Mr Centurion, sir! I assume you speak Greek in all its four dialects.

CAPTAIN PITITO  Pissed as a newt. Take him to the slammer!

MAX  And cocky as a figure eight! Fortunately I also understand the common vernacular, the *sermo vulgaris*, Mr Centurion,[72] sir!

EL CAPITÁN PITITO  ¡Serenooo!... ¡Serenooo!...
EL SERENO       ¡Vaaa!...
EL CAPITÁN PITITO  ¡Encárguese usted de este curda!


*Llega El Sereno, meciendo a compás el farol y el chuzo. Jadeos y vahos de
aguardiente. El Capitán Pitito revuelve el caballo. Vuelan chispas de las
herraduras. Resuena el trote sonoro de la patrulla que se aleja.*

EL CAPITÁN PITITO  ¡Me responde usted de ese hombre, Sereno!
EL SERENO       ¿Habrá que darle amoniaco?
EL CAPITÁN PITITO  Habrá que darle para el pelo.
EL SERENO       ¡Está bien!
DON LATINO  Max, convídale a una copa.  Hay que domesticar a este
            troglodita asturiano.
MAX         Estoy apré.
DON LATINO  ¿No te queda nada?
MAX         ¡Ni una perra!
EL SERENO   Camine usted.
MAX         Soy ciego.
EL SERENO   ¿Quiere usted que un servidor le vuelva la vista?
MAX         ¿Eres Santa Lucía?
EL SERENO   ¡Soy autoridad!
MAX         No es lo mismo.
EL SERENO   Pudiera serlo.  Camine usted.
MAX         Ya he dicho que soy ciego.
EL SERENO   Usted es un anárquico y estos sujetos de las melenas: ¡Viento!
            ¡Viento! ¡Viento! ¡Mucho viento!
DON LATINO  ¡Una galerna!
EL SERENO   ¡Atrás!
VOCES DE LOS MODERNISTAS       ¡Acompañamos al Maestro!
            ¡Acompañamos al Maestro!
UN VECINO   ¡Pepeee! ¡Pepeee!
EL SERENO   ¡Vaaa! Retírense ustedes sin manifestación.


*Golpea con el chuzo en la puerta de la Buñolería. Asoma el buñolero, un
hombre gordo con delantal blanco: Se informa, se retira musitando, y a poco
salen adormilados, ciñéndose el correaje dos guardias municipales.*

UN GUARDIA  ¿Qué hay?
EL SERENO   Este punto para la Delega.
EL OTRO GUARDIA  Nosotros vamos al relevo.  Lo entregaremos en
            Gobernación.
EL SERENO   Donde la duerma.
EL VECINO   ¡Pepeee! ¡Pepeee!

CAPTAIN PITTO  Watchmaan! Watchmaan!
NIGHT-WATCHMAN  Co—ming!
CAPTAIN PITTO  Take charge of this wino!

*Rhythmically swinging staff and lantern, the Night-Watchman arrives. Heavy breathing and alcoholic vapours. Captain Pitito turns his horse around. Sparks fly from the horseshoes. The hollow clatter of hooves is heard as the night patrol departs.*

CAPTAIN PITITO  Watchman, I'm holding you responsible for this man!
NIGHT-WATCHMAN  Shall we have to give him a dose of ammonia?
CAPTAIN PITITO  A good hiding, more like.
NIGHT-WATCHMAN  Right!
DON LATINO  Max, invite him for a drink.  We must tame this Asturian troglodyte.[73]
MAX  I'm flat broke.
DON LATINO  Haven't you got anything left?
MAX  Not a cent.
NIGHT-WATCHMAN  Get moving!
MAX  I'm blind.
NIGHT-WATCHMAN  I'll soon make you see something, if you like!
MAX  Why, are you Saint Lucy?[74]
NIGHT-WATCHMAN  I'm the municipal authority!
MAX  It's not quite the same thing.
NIGHT-WATCHMAN  It could be. Now, get moving!
MAX  I already told you I'm blind.
NIGHT-WATCHMAN  What you are is an anarchist, you and the whole lot of this long-haired crew. All wind and hot air, that's what you are. Wind! Wind! Wind!
DON LATINO  A positive hurricane.
NIGHT-WATCHMAN  Stand back!
VOICES OF MODERNISTS  We shall accompany our leader!  We shall accompany the maestro!
NEIGHBOUR'S VOICE  Pepeee! Pepeee!
NIGHT-WATCHMAN  Co—ming!  I advise you to withdraw without causing an affray.

*He pounds on the café door with his staff. The owner, a fat man in a white apron, appears; he listens to the night-watchman and retires, muttering under his breath. Shortly afterwards, two municipal policemen come out, bleary-eyed, adjusting their belts.*

1st POLICEMAN  What's up?
NIGHT-WATCHMAN  This joker's for the lock-up.
2nd POLICEMAN  We're on relief duty. We'll drop him at headquarters.
NIGHT-WATCHMAN  Anywhere he can sleep it off.
NEIGHBOUR'S VOICE  Pepeee! Pepeee!

EL SERENO     ¡Otro curda! ¡Vaaa! Sus lo entrego.

LOS DOS GUARDIAS  Ustedes, caballeros, retírense.

DORIO DE GADEX  Acompañamos al Maestro.

UN GUARDIA  ¡Ni que se llamase este curda Don Mariano de Cavia! ¡Ése sí
          que es cabeza! ¡Y cuanto más curda, mejor lo saca!

EL OTRO GUARDIA  ¡Por veces también se pone pelma!

DON LATINO  ¡Y faltón!

UN GUARDIA  Usted, por lo que habla, ¿le conoce?

DON LATINO  Y le tuteo.

EL OTRO GUARDIA  ¿Son ustedes periodistas?

DORIO DE GADEX  ¡Lagarto! ¡Lagarto!

LA PISA-BIEN  Son banqueros.

UN GUARDIA  Si quieren acompañar a su amigo, no se oponen las leyes, y
          hasta lo permiten; pero deberán guardar moderación ustedes.
          Yo respeto mucho el talento.

EL OTRO GUARDIA  Caminemos.

MAX           Latino, dame la mano.   ¡Señores guardias, ustedes me
          perdonarán que sea ciego!

UN GUARDIA  Sobra tanta política.

DON LATINO  ¿Qué ruta consagramos?

UN GUARDIA  Al Ministerio de la Gobernación.

EL OTRO GUARDIA  ¡Vivo! ¡Vivo!

MAX           ¡Muera Maura! ¡Muera el Gran Fariseo!

CORO DE MODERNISTAS  ¡Muera! ¡Muera! ¡Muera!

MAX           Muera el judío y toda su execrable parentela.

UN GUARDIA  ¡Basta de voces! ¡Cuidado con el poeta curda! ¡Se la está
          ganando, me caso en Sevilla!

EL OTRO GUARDIA  A éste habrá que darle para el pelo.  Lo cual que sería
          lástima, porque debe ser hombre de mérito.

NIGHT-WATCHMAN  Another drunk!  Coming!  I'll leave him to you then.

BOTH POLICEMEN  Now, if you gentlemen would move along please...

DORIO DE GADEX  We are accompanying the maestro!

1st POLICEMAN  Anybody would think he was Don Mariano de Cavia,[75] the dipso who writes for the papers.  Now there's a real brain!  And the drunker he is, the better he writes!

2nd POLICEMAN  Sometimes goes too far though.

DON LATINO  Too near the knuckle.

1st POLICEMAN  The way you talk, you seem to know him.

DON LATINO  Like a brother.

2nd POLICEMAN  You from the papers?  Journalists?

DORIO DE GADEX  Don't mention that word!

HENRIETTA  They're financial speculators.

1st POLICEMAN  If you want to keep your friend company, there's no law against it.  It's even allowed provided you behave with due moderation.  I have a great respect for talent.

2nd POLICEMAN  Let's move.

MAX  Latino, give me your hand.  Officers, you must forgive me for being blind!

1st POLICEMAN  You can dispense with the diplomacy.

DON LATINO  Which direction shall we honour?

1st POLICEMAN  To Police Headquarters.

2nd POLICEMAN  Come on, look lively!

MAX  Death to Maura!  Death to the Great Humbug!

CHORUS OF MODERNISTS  Death to Maura!  Death to Maura!  Death to Maura!

MAX  Death to the Pharisee and his execrable tribe![76]

1st POLICEMAN  That's enough of the shouting!  Just listen to the drunken poet, will you.  He's asking for it, for Christ's sake!

2nd POLICEMAN  We may have to get rough with this one.  Pity, though.  He seems to be a man of talent.

# Escena Quinta

*Zaguán en el Ministerio de la Gobernación. Estantería con legajos. Bancos al filo de la pared. Mesa con carpetas de badana mugrienta. Aire de cueva y olor frío de tabaco rancio. Guardias soñolientos. Policías de la Secreta. Hongos, garrotes, cuellos de celuloide, grandes sortijas, lunares rizosos y flamencos. Hay un viejo chabacano, bisoñé y manguitos de percalina, que escibe, y un pollo chulapón de peinado reluciente, con brisas de perfumería, que se pasea y dicta humeando un veguero. Don Serafín, le dicen sus obligados, y la voz de la calle, Serafín el Bonito. Leve tumulto. Dando voces, la cabeza desnuda, humorista y lunático, irrumpe Max Estrella. Don Latino le guía por la manga, implorante y suspirante. Detrás asoman los cascos de los Guardias. Y en el corredor se agrupan, bajo la luz de una candileja, pipas, chalinas y melenas del modernismo.*

MAX          ¡Traigo detenida una pareja de guindillas! Estaban emborrachándose en una tasca y los hice salir a darme escolta.

SERAFÍN EL BONITO  Corrección, señor mío.

MAX          No falto a ella, señor Delegado.

SERAFÍN EL BONITO  Inspector.

MAX          Todo es uno y lo mismo.

SERAFÍN EL BONITO  ¿Cómo se llama usted?

MAX          Mi nombre es Máximo Estrella. Mi seudónimo, Mala Estrella. Tengo el honor de no ser Académico.

SERAFÍN EL BONITO  Está usted propasándose. Guardias, ¿por qué viene detenido?

UN GUARDIA  Por escándalo en la vía pública y gritos internacionales. ¡Está algo briago!

SERAFÍN EL BONITO  ¿Su profesión?

MAX          Cesante.

SERAFÍN EL BONITO  ¿En qué oficina ha servido usted?

MAX          En ninguna.

SERAFÍN EL BONITO  ¿No ha dicho usted que cesante?

MAX          Cesante de hombre libre y pájaro cantor. ¿No me veo vejado, vilipendiado, encarcelado, cacheado e interrogado?

SERAFÍN EL BONITO  ¿Dónde vive usted?

MAX          Bastardillos. Esquina a San Cosme. Palacio.

# Scene Five

*Anteroom at Police Headquarters in the Ministry of the Interior.*[77] *Shelves stuffed with files and dossiers. Benches alongside the walls. A table covered with grimy, leather-bound portfolios. Dank, fetid atmosphere of a cellar with a stench of stale tobacco. Somnolent officials. Members of the Secret Police in plain clothes: bowler hats, truncheons, celluloid collars, large signet rings and extravagant, curly-haired moles. An uncouth-looking old man with toupée and percaline oversleeves writes at the dictation of a young dandy with brilliantined hair, who paces up and down puffing at a cheroot, leaving a waft of eau de cologne on the air. The latter is known as Don Serafín to his subordinates, but, to the man in the street, as Serafín the Paint. There is some disturbance as the bare-headed figure of Max Estrella bursts upon the scene with cries of humorous eccentricity. Don Latino guides him by the sleeve, imploring silence and heaving sighs of impatience. Behind them can be seen the helmets of the policemen. Outside in the corridor, gathered round the light of an oil lamp, are the pipes, cravats and long manes of the Modernists.*

MAX                  I am placing these two flatfoots under arrest.  They were drinking themselves under the table in a common tavern and I obliged them to escort me to the station.

SERAFIN THE PAINT  A little more respect, my dear sir.

MAX                  I was not aware that I was displaying any lack of it, Commissioner.

SERAFIN THE PAINT  Inspector.

MAX                  It's all one and the same.

SERAFIN THE PAINT  What is your name?

MAX                  My name is Máximo Estrella.  I go under the pseudonym of Ill-starred Max.  I have the honour not to be a member of the Spanish Academy.

SERAFIN THE PAINT  You're overstepping the mark, sir.  Officers, why was this man arrested?

1st POLICEMAN  For disturbing the peace and shouting internationalist slogans in the street.  He is somewhat inebriated.

SERAFIN THE PAINT  Your profession?

MAX                  Redundant.[78]

SERAFIN THE PAINT  Where did you last work?

MAX                  I didn't.

SERAFIN THE PAINT  Did you not say you'd been made redundant?

MAX                  And what is more redundant than an ex-songbird?  Or an ex-free man who finds himself harassed, vilified, frisked, interrogated and imprisoned?

SERAFIN THE PAINT  Where do you live?

MAX                  The palace on the corner of Bastardillos Street and San Cosme.

UN GUINDILLA  Diga usted casa de vecinos. Mi señora, cuando aún no lo era,
           habitó un sotabanco de esa susodicha finca.
MAX          Donde yo vivo, siempre es un palacio.
EL GUINDILLA  No lo sabía.
MAX          Porque tú, gusano burocrático, no sabes nada. ¡Ni soñar!
SERAFÍN EL BONITO  ¡Queda usted detenido!
MAX          ¡Bueno! Latino, ¿hay algún banco donde pueda echarme a
           dormir?
SERAFÍN EL BONITO  Aquí no se viene a dormir.
MAX          ¡Pues yo tengo sueño!
SERAFÍN EL BONITO  ¡Está usted desacatando mi autoridad! ¿Sabe usted
           quién soy yo?
MAX          ¡Serafín el Bonito!
SERAFÍN EL BONITO  ¡Como usted repita esa gracia, de una bofetada, le
           doblo!
MAX          ¡Ya se guardará usted del intento! ¡Soy el primer poeta de
           España! ¡Tengo influencia en todos los periódicos! ¡Conozco
           al Ministro! ¡Hemos sido compañeros!
SERAFÍN EL BONITO  El Señor Ministro no es un golfo.
MAX          Usted desconoce la Historia Moderna.
SERAFÍN EL BONITO  ¡En mi presencia no se ofende a Don Paco! Eso no lo
           tolero. ¡Sepa usted que Don Paco es mi padre!
MAX          No lo creo. Permítame usted que se lo pregunte por teléfono.
SERAFÍN EL BONITO  Se lo va usted a preguntar desde el calabozo.
DON LATINO  Señor Inspector, ¡tenga usted alguna consideración! ¡Se trata
           de una gloria nacional! ¡El Víctor Hugo de España!
SERAFÍN EL BONITO  Cállese usted.
DON LATINO  Perdone usted mi entrometimiento.
SERAFÍN EL BONITO  ¡Si usted quiere acompañarle, también hay para usted
           alojamiento!
DON LATINO  ¡Gracias, Señor Inspector!
SERAFÍN EL BONITO  Guardias, conduzcan ustedes ese curda al Número 2.
UN GUARDIA  ¡Camine usted!
MAX          No quiero.
SERAFÍN EL BONITO  Llévenle ustedes a rastras.
OTRO GUARDIA  ¡So golfo!
MAX          ¡Que me asesinan! ¡Que me asesinan!
UNA VOZ MODERNISTA  ¡Bárbaros!
DON LATINO  ¡Que es una gloria nacional!
SERAFÍN EL BONITO  Aquí no se protesta. Retírense ustedes.
OTRA VOZ MODERNISTA  ¡Viva la Inquisición!
SERAFÍN EL BONITO  ¡Silencio, o todos quedan detenidos!
MAX          ¡Que me asesinan! ¡Que me asesinan!
LOS GUARDIAS  ¡Borracho! ¡Golfo!
EL GRUPO MODERNISTA  ¡Hay que visitar las Redacciones!

A POLICEMAN  Better put tenement. My missus, before we was married, once
          lived in the attic of that aforementioned property.

MAX          Where I live is always a palace.

A POLICEMAN  I wouldn't know about that.

MAX          Because you, bureaucratic worm, wouldn't know about
          anything. Not even how to dream!

SERAFIN THE PAINT  You are under arrest!

MAX          Fine! Latino, is there a bench around here where I can lie
          down and sleep?

SERAFIN THE PAINT  You don't come here to sleep!

MAX          Well, I'm tired!

SERAFIN THE PAINT  Sir, you are challenging my authority! Do you realize
          who I am?

MAX          Serafin the Paint!

SERAFIN THE PAINT  Say that once more and I'll knock the wind out of you!

MAX          You'd better not try! I am Spain's greatest living poet! I have
          influence in all the newspapers! And I am a personal friend of
          the Minister!

SERAFIN THE PAINT  His Excellency the Minister is no tramp!

MAX          You display a lamentable ignorance of contemporary history!

SERAFIN THE PAINT  No one insults Don Paco in my presence! That I will
          not tolerate! I'll have you know that Don Paco has been a
          father to me!

MAX          I don't believe it. Allow me to ask him on the telephone.

SERAFIN THE PAINT  You can ask him from a prison cell!

DON LATINO  Inspector, sir, you must make some allowances. This man is
          one of our national glories. The Victor Hugo of Spain![79]

SERAFIN THE PAINT  You hold your tongue!

DON LATINO  Please forgive the intrusion.

SERAFIN THE PAINT  If you wish to keep him company, we always have
          room for one more!

DON LATINO  Thank you, Inspector.

SERAFIN THE PAINT  Officers, take this drunk to cell two.

A POLICEMAN  Move!

MAX          I will not!

SERAFIN THE PAINT  Then drag him!

ANOTHER POLICEMAN  Move, you drunken bastard!

MAX          They're murdering me! Help! Murder!

A MODERNIST VOICE  Barbarians!

DON LATINO  But he's one of our great national figures.

SERAFIN THE PAINT  I will not have protests in here! Kindly withdraw!

ANOTHER MODERNIST VOICE  Three cheers for the Inquisition!

SERAFIN THE PAINT  Silence, or I'll have you all arrested!

MAX          Murderers! Assassins!

POLICEMEN  Drunken flea-bag! Tramp!

GROUP OF MODERNISTS  To the newspapers! We must go to the
          newspapers!

*Sale en tropel el grupo. Chalinas flotantes, pipas apagadas, románticas greñas.*
*Se oyen estallar las bofetadas y las voces tras la puerta del calabozo.*

SERAFÍN EL BONITO  ¡Creerán esos niños modernistas que aquí se reparten
      caramelos!

# Escena Sexta

*El calabozo. Sótano mal alumbrado por una candileja. En la sombra se mueve*
*el bulto de un hombre. Blusa, tapabocas y alpargatas. Pasea hablando solo.*
*Repentinamente se abre la puerta. Max Estrella, empujado y trompicando,*
*rueda al fondo del calabozo. Se cierra de golpe la puerta.*

MAX           ¡Canallas! ¡Asalariados! ¡Cobardes!
VOZ FUERA   ¡Aún vas a llevar mancuerna!
MAX           ¡Esbirro!

*Sale de la tiniebla el bulto del hombre morador del calabozo. Bajo la luz se le*
*ve esposado, con la cara llena de sangre.*

EL PRESO     ¡Buenas noches!
MAX           ¿No estoy solo?
EL PRESO     Así parece.
MAX           ¿Quién eres, compañero?
EL PRESO     Un paria.
MAX           ¿Catalán?
EL PRESO     De todas partes.
MAX           ¡Paria!... Solamente los obreros catalanes aguijan su rebeldía
      con ese denigrante epíteto. Paria, en bocas como la tuya, es
      una espuela. Pronto llegará vuestra hora.
EL PRESO     Tiene usted luces que no todos tienen. Barcelona alimenta una
      hoguera de odio, soy obrero barcelonés, y a orgullo lo tengo.
MAX           ¿Eres anarquista?
EL PRESO     Soy lo que me han hecho las Leyes.
MAX           Pertenecemos a la misma Iglesia.
EL PRESO     Usted lleva chalina.
MAX           ¡El dogal de la más horrible servidumbre! Me lo arrancaré,
      para que hablemos.
EL PRESO     Usted no es proletario.
MAX           Yo soy el dolor de un mal sueño.
EL PRESO     Parece usted hombre de luces. Su hablar es como de otros
      tiempos.

*The group exits in disarray. A flurry of cravats, unlit pipes and long, romantic locks. The sounds of blows and cries can be heard behind the door leading to the cells.*

SERAFIN THE PAINT  These arty-farty types must think we're handing out free sweeties in here.

# Scene Six

*Prison cell in a basement dimly lit by an oil lamp. A human form – smock, muffler and rope-soled sandals – stirs in the shadows. He paces about muttering to himself. Suddenly the door opens. Max Estrella is pushed through, stumbles and rolls to the back of the cell. The door is slammed shut.*

MAX                Mercenary scum! Cowards!
VOICE FROM OUTSIDE  And there's more of that to come!
MAX                Minion!

*The human form occupying the cell emerges from the darkness. In the light, it can be seen that he is handcuffed and has bloodstains on his face.*

PRISONER     Good evening!
MAX          I'm not alone then?
PRISONER     So it seems.
MAX          Who are you, friend?
PRISONER     A pariah.
MAX          From Catalonia?
PRISONER     From everywhere... and anywhere.
MAX          Pariah!... Only a Catalan worker would use that degrading epithet as a rallying call to rebellion. Pariah, on lips like yours, is a spur. Your time will come, and soon.
PRISONER     You can see further than most. Barcelona is a bonfire, smouldering with hate and ready to burst into flames.[80] Yes, I'm a worker from Barcelona – and proud of it.
MAX          Are you an anarchist?
PRISONER     I am what the law has made me.[81]
MAX          Then we belong to the same Church.
PRISONER     But you wear an artist's cravat.
MAX          The yoke of the most abject servitude! I'll tear it off, so that we can talk.
PRISONER     You're no proletarian.
MAX          I'm the pain from a waking nightmare.
PRISONER     You sound like an educated man. You talk like someone from the old days.

MAX          Yo soy un poeta ciego.

EL PRESO     ¡No es pequeña desgracia!... En España el trabajo y la
             inteligencia siempre se han visto menospreciados. Aquí todo lo
             manda el dinero.

MAX          Hay que establecer la guillotina eléctrica en la Puerta del Sol.

EL PRESO     No basta. El ideal revolucionario tiene que ser la destrucción
             de la riqueza, como en Rusia. No es suficiente la degollación
             de todos los ricos. Siempre aparecerá un heredero, y aun
             cuando se suprima la herencia, no podrá evitarse que los
             despojados conspiren para recobrarla. Hay que hacer
             imposible el orden anterior, y eso sólo se consigue destruyendo
             la riqueza. Barcelona industrial tiene que hundirse para renacer
             de sus escombros con otro concepto de la propiedad y del
             trabajo. En Europa, el patrono de más negra entraña es el
             catalán, y no digo del mundo porque existen las Colonias
             Españolas de América. ¡Barcelona solamente se salva
             pereciendo!

MAX          ¡Barcelona es cara a mi corazón!

EL PRESO     ¡Yo también la recuerdo!

MAX          Yo le debo los únicos goces en la lobreguez de mi ceguera
             Todos los días, un patrono muerto, algunas veces, dos... Eso
             consuela.

EL PRESO     No cuenta usted los obreros que caen...

MAX          Los obreros se reproducen populosamente, de un modo
             comparable a las moscas. En cambio, los patronos, como los
             elefantes, como todas las bestias poderosas y prehistóricas,
             procrean lentamente. Saulo, hay que difundir por el mundo la
             religión nueva.

EL PRESO     Mi nombre es Mateo.

MAX          Yo te bautizo Saulo. Soy poeta y tengo el derecho al alfabeto.
             Escucha para cuando seas libre, Saulo. Una buena cacería
             puede encarecer la piel de patrono catalán por encima del
             marfil de Calcuta.

EL PRESO     En ello laboramos.

MAX          Y en último consuelo, aun cabe pensar que exterminando al
             proletario también se extermina al patrón.

EL PRESO     Acabando con la ciudad, acabaremos con el judaísmo
             barcelonés.

MAX          No me opongo. Barcelona semita sea destruida, como Cartago
             y Jerusalén. ¡Alea jacta est! Dame la mano.

EL PRESO     Estoy esposado.

MAX          ¿Eres joven? No puedo verte.

EL PRESO     Soy joven. Treinta años.

MAX          ¿De qué te acusan?

EL PRESO     Es cuento largo. Soy tachado de rebelde... No quise dejar el
             telar por ir a la guerra y levanté un motín en la fábrica. Me

MAX            I'm a blind poet.
PRISONER       Then you've got problems too! In Spain, work and the intellect
               have always been despised. Everything is ruled by money
               here.
MAX            We must set up an electric guillotine in the Puerta del Sol.
PRISONER       It wouldn't be enough. The revolutionary ideal should be the
               destruction of wealth, as it was in Russia. It's not enough to
               chop the heads off all the rich people. Somebody'll always
               turn up to inherit and even if you do away with inheritance, you
               won't stop all the disinherited from plotting to get it back. No.
               We've got to make the old order impossible and you can only
               do that by destroying money. The whole of industrial
               Barcelona must be destroyed and rise from its ashes with an
               entirely new concept of labour and property ownership.[82] The
               Catalan is the blackest bastard of an employer in Europe. I say
               Europe because there are always the Spanish colonies in Latin
               America.[83] The only hope for Barcelona lies in its destruction!
MAX            And yet Barcelona is dear to my heart!
PRISONER       I remember it too.
MAX            The only moments of joy in my hours of darkness I owe to her.
               Every day a dead capitalist, sometimes two... That comforts
               me.
PRISONER       You don't count the workers who fall...
MAX            The workers multiply like flies, in their thousands. Whereas
               the bosses are more like elephants and all powerful, prehistoric
               beasts. They procreate slowly. Saul, we must preach the new
               gospel throughout the world.
PRISONER       My name is Matthew.[84]
MAX            I baptize thee Saul.[85] I'm a poet and the alphabet is my
               prerogative. Listen and remember for when you're free again,
               Saul: a really good bag could raise the price of Catalan boss-
               hide higher than that of Calcutta ivory.
PRISONER       We're working on it.
MAX            And if it's any consolation, by exterminating the workers,
               they're also helping to exterminate the employers.
PRISONER       And by destroying the city, we shall destroy the Judaic spirit of
               commercialism that goes with it.[86]
MAX            I have no objection. Let Semitic Barcelona perish, like
               Carthage and Jerusalem! *Alea iacta est!*[87] Give me your hand.
PRISONER       I'm handcuffed.
MAX            Are you young? I can't see you.
PRISONER       I'm young. Thirty years old.
MAX            What are they accusing you of?
PRISONER       It's a long story. I'm branded as a rebel... I refused to leave my
               job at the mill to go to war and started a riot in the factory.[88]

denunció el patrón, cumplí condena, recorrí el mundo buscando trabajo, y ahora voy por tránsitos, reclamado de no sé qué jueces. Conozco la suerte que me espera: cuatro tiros por intento de fuga. Bueno. Si no es más que eso...

| | |
|---|---|
| MAX | ¿Pues qué temes? |
| EL PRESO | Que se diviertan dándome tormento. |
| MAX | ¡Bárbaros! |
| EL PRESO | Hay que conocerlos. |
| MAX | Canallas. ¡Y ésos son los que protestan de la leyenda negra! |
| EL PRESO | Por siete pesetas, al cruzar un lugar solitario, me sacarán la vida los que tienen a su cargo la defensa del pueblo. ¡Y a esto llaman justicia los ricos canallas! |
| MAX | Los ricos y los pobres, la barbarie ibérica es unánime. |
| EL PRESO | ¡Todos! |
| MAX | ¡Todos! Mateo, ¿dónde está la bomba que destripe el terrón maldito de España? |
| EL PRESO | ¡Señor poeta!, que tanto adivina, ¿no ha visto usted una mano levantada? |

*Se abre la puerta del calabozo, y El Llavero, con jactancia de rufo ordena al preso maniatado que le acompañe.*

| | |
|---|---|
| EL LLAVERO | Tú, catalán, ¡disponte! |
| EL PRESO | Estoy dispuesto. |
| EL LLAVERO | Pues andando. Gachó, vas a salir en viaje de recreo. |

*El esposado, con resignada entereza, se acerca al ciego y le toca el hombro con la barba. Se despide hablando a media voz.*

| | |
|---|---|
| EL PRESO | Llegó la mía... Creo que no volveremos a vernos... |
| MAX | ¡Es horrible! |
| EL PRESO | Van a matarme... ¿Qué dirá mañana esa prensa canalla? |
| MAX | Lo que le manden. |
| EL PRESO | ¿Está usted llorando? |
| MAX | De impotencia y de rabia. Abracémonos, hermano. |

*Se abrazan. El Carcelero y el esposado salen. Vuelve a cerrarse la puerta. Max Estrella tantea buscando la pared, y se sienta con las piernas cruzadas, en una actitud religiosa, de meditación asiática. Exprime un gran dolor taciturno el bulto del poeta ciego. Llega de fuera tumulto de voces y galopar de caballos.*

I was shopped by the boss, did my time and then tramped the country looking for work. Now I'm being shifted from one court to another, summoned by some judge or other. I know how it will all end: a couple of shots in the back for 'attempting to escape'.[89] Well, it wouldn't be so bad, if that was all...

MAX        Why, what are you afraid of?

PRISONER   That they might amuse themselves by torturing me.

MAX        Barbarians!

PRISONER   That's how they are.

MAX        Miserable vermin! And they are the ones who protest against the Black Legend of Spain![90]

PRISONER   So, for a handful of pesetas, in some deserted spot, they'll finish me off. That's the defenders of the people for you! And that's what the rich bastards call justice!

MAX        The rich and the poor. The barbarism of Iberia is unanimous.

PRISONER   All of them.

MAX        All of them, Matthew. Where is the bomb that will blow this Spanish shit-heap to hell?

PRISONER   You are a poet, sir, and can see many things. Have you not seen a raised fist in the darkness?

*The cell door opens and the Jailer, with thug-like arrogance, orders the handcuffed prisoner to follow him.*

JAILER     Hey, you, Catalan! Get yourself ready!

PRISONER   I am ready.

JAILER     Get a move on then. You're going on a little joy ride, my friend.

*With resigned fortitude, the prisoner comes over to the blind man and touches him on the shoulder with his chin. He makes his farewell in a whisper.*

PRISONER   My time has come... I don't think we shall meet again...

MAX        This is horrible!

PRISONER   They'll kill me... and then what will that bastard press say tomorrow?

MAX        Whatever they're told to print.

PRISONER   Are you crying?

MAX        With impotence and rage. Let us embrace, brother.

*They embrace. The Jailer and the Prisoner go out. The door closes again. Max Estrella gropes about him feeling for the wall and sits down with his legs crossed in an attitude of oriental religious meditation. The shadowy form of the blind poet is an expression of unspoken grief. From outside comes the sound of confused cries and galloping horses.*

# Escena Séptima

*La Redacción de «El Popular»: Sala baja con piso de baldosas. En el centro,*
*una mesa larga y negra, rodeada de sillas vacías, que marcan los puestos, ante*
*roídas carpetas, y rimeros de cuartillas, que destacan su blancura en el círculo*
*luminoso y verdoso de una lámpara con enagüillas. Al extremo, fuma y escribe*
*un hombre calvo, el eterno redactor del perfil triste, el gabán con flecos, los*
*dedos de gancho y las uñas entintadas. El hombre lógico y mítico enciende el*
*cigarro apagado. Se abre la mampara, y el grillo de un timbre rasga el silencio.*
*Asoma El Conserje, vejete renegado, bigotudo, tripón, parejo de aquellos*
*bizarros coroneles que en las procesiones se caen del caballo. Un enorme*
*parecido que extravaga.*

EL CONSERJE Ahí está Don Latino de Hispalis, con otros capitalistas de su
          cuerda. Vienen preguntando por el Señor Director. Les he
          dicho que solamente estaba usted en la casa. ¿Los recibe usted
          Don Filiberto?
DON FILIBERTO Que pasen.

*Sigue escribiendo. El Conserje sale, y queda batiente la verde mampara, que*
*proyecta un recuerdo de garitos y naipes. Entra el cotarro modernista, greñas,*
*pipas, gabanes repelados, y alguna capa. El periodista calvo levanta los*
*anteojos a la frente, requiere el cigarro y se da importancia.*

DON FILIBERTO ¡Caballeros y hombres buenos, adelante! ¿Ustedes me dirán
          lo que desean de mí y del Journal?
DON LATINO ¡Venimos a protestar contra un indigno atropello de la Policía!
          Max Estrella, el gran poeta, aun cuando muchos se nieguen a
          reconocerlo, acaba de ser detenido y maltratado brutalmente en
          un sótano del Ministerio de la Desgobernación.
DORIO DE GADEX En España sigue reinando Carlos II.
DON FILIBERTO ¡Válgame un santo de palo! ¿Nuestro gran poeta estaría
          curda?
DON LATINO Una copa de más no justifica esa violación de los derechos
          individuales.
DON FILIBERTO Max Estrella también es amigo nuestro. ¡Válgame un santo
          de palo! El Señor Director, cuando a esta hora falta, ya no
          viene... Ustedes conocen cómo se hace un periódico. ¡El
          Director es siempre un tirano!... Yo, sin consultarle, no me
          decido a recoger en nuestras columnas la protesta de ustedes.

# Scene Seven

*Editorial Offices of the 'The People'.[91] A low-ceilinged room with a tiled floor. In the centre, a long, black table surrounded by empty chairs marking the places of the editorial staff. In front of these, ragged-edged folders and piles of paper gleaming white under the bright green circle of light projected by a frilly lampshade. At one end, a bald-headed man is smoking and writing, the archetypal editor of gaunt and lugubrious features, frayed overcoat, hook-like fingers with inkstained nails. The archetype of logical analysis re-lights his extinguished cigar. The partition door opens and the cricket of an electric bell perforates the silence. The figure of the Doorman appears – a cantankerous, mustachioed, pot-bellied old man, exactly like those gallant colonels who fall off their horses in military processions. An extraordinary, mind-boggling resemblance.*

DOORMAN    It's Don Latino de Hispalis and a few others of his capitalist crew. They're asking for the Editor, but I told them you were the only one in the office. Will you see them, Don Filiberto?

DON FILIBERTO   Show them in.

*He continues writing. The Concierge goes out and the green partition door swings to and fro behind him, evoking images of gambling dens and card tables. The crew of Modernists files in, all hair, pipes, threadbare overcoats and the occasional cape. The bald-headed journalist pushes up his glasses on to his forehead, reaches for his cigar and assumes an air of importance.*

DON FILIBERTO   Ah, gentlemen and my very good friends, do come in! Tell me, what can I and our *Journal*[92] do for you?

DON LATINO   We have come to protest about a disgraceful abuse of police power! Max Estrella, our great poet, though some refuse to recognize him as such, has just been arrested and brutally manhandled in the cellars of the Ministry of Misgovernment!

DORIO DE GADEX   In Spain, we are still in the reign of Charles the Bewitched![93]

DON FILIBERTO   The saints preserve us! I imagine our great poet would be... well oiled?

DON LATINO   A glass or two over the odds does not justify this violation of individual rights.

DON FILIBERTO   Max Estrella is our friend as well. My goodness, yes. The Managing Editor isn't back yet, and if he's not here by now, it means he won't be coming in... You gentlemen know how a newspaper is run. The Editor is always a dictator!... Without prior consultation with him, I cannot take it upon myself to publish your protest in our columns. I don't

Desconozco la política del periódico con la Dirección de Seguridad... Y el relato de ustedes, francamente, me parece un poco exagerado.

DORIO DE GADEX  ¡Es pálido, Don Filiberto!

CLARINITO        ¡Una cobardía!

PÉREZ            ¡Una vergüenza!

DON LATINO       ¡Una canallada!

DORIO DE GADEX  ¡En España reina siempre Felipe II!

DON LATINO  ¡Dorio, hijo mío, no nos anonades!

DON FILIBERTO  ¡Juventud! ¡Noble apasionamiento! ¡Divino tesoro, como dijo el vate de Nicaragua! ¡Juventud, divino tesoro! Yo también leo, y algunas veces admiro a los genios del modernismo. El Director bromea que estoy contagiado. ¿Alguno de ustedes ha leído el cuento que publiqué en *Los Orbes*?

CLARINITO  ¡Yo, Don Filiberto! Leído y admirado.

DON FILIBERTO  ¿Y usted, amigo Dorio?

DORIO DE GADEX  Yo nunca leo a mis contemporáneos, Don Filiberto.

DON FILIBERTO  ¡Amigo Dorio, no quiero replicarle que también ignora a los clásicos!

DORIO DE GADEX  A usted y a mí nos rezuma el ingenio, Don Filiberto. En el cuello del gabán llevamos las señales.

DON FILIBERTO  Con esa alusión a la estética de mi indumentaria, se me ha revelado usted como un joven esteta.

DORIO DE GADEX  ¡Es usted corrosivo, Don Filiberto!

DON FILIBERTO  ¡Usted me ha buscado la lengua!

DORIO DE GADEX  ¡A eso no llego!

CLARINITO  Dorio, no hagas chistes de primero de latín.

DON FILIBERTO  Amigo Dorio, tengo alguna costumbre de estas cañas y lanzas del ingenio. Son las justas del periodismo. No me refiero al periodismo de ahora. Con Silvela he discreteado en un banquete, cuando me premiaron en los Juegos Florales de Málaga la Bella. Narciso Díaz aún recordaba poco hace aquel torneo en una crónica suya de *El Heraldo*. Una crónica deliciosa como todas las suyas, y reconocía que no había yo llevado la peor parte. Citaba mi definición del periodismo. ¿Ustedes la conocen? Se la diré, sin embargo. El periodista es el plumífero parlamentario. El Congreso es una gran redacción, y cada redacción, un pequeño Congreso. El periodismo es travesura, lo mismo que la política. Son el mismo círculo en diferentes espacios. Teosóficamente podría explicárselo a ustedes, si estuviesen ustedes iniciados en la noble Doctrina del Karma.

DORIO DE GADEX  Nosotros no estamos iniciados, pero quien chanela algo es Don Latino.

quite know what the paper's policy is concerning matters of
law and order... And, in any case, frankly, your account does
sound a trifle exaggerated.

DORIO DE GADEX  A pale reflection of the truth, Don Filiberto!

CLARINITO       A dastardly act!

PEREZ           An outrage!

DON LATINO      A despicable crime!

DORIO DE GADEX  In Spain we are still in the reign of Philip II![94]

DON LATINO  Dorio, my boy, don't overwhelm us with your erudition!

DON FILIBERTO  Ah, the noble passion of youth! 'Divine treasure', as Rubén
                Darío, the Bard of Nicaragua,[95] had it! 'Youth, divine
                treasure!' Ah, yes, I too read and even admire the geniuses of
                Modernism. The Director even jokes that I'm becoming
                contaminated. Did any of you read the story I published in *The
                Spheres*?

CLARINITO       I did, Don Filiberto! Read it and admired it!

DON FILIBERTO  And you, friend Dorio?

DORIO DE GADEX  I never read my contemporaries, Don Filiberto.

DON FILIBERTO  My dear Dorio, I could reply that you are equally ignorant of
                the classics.

DORIO DE GADEX  You and I simply ooze intelligence and wit, Don Filiberto.
                We carry the evidence all over our coat collars.[96]

DON FILIBERTO  That allusion to my personal attire reveals the depth of your
                aesthetic sensibility.

DORIO DE GADEX  I am seared by your irony, Don Filiberto!

DON FILIBERTO  It was you who goaded me into it.[97]

DORIO DE GADEX  I wouldn't go that far!

CLARINITO       Dorio, let's not descend to school-boy humour.

DON FILIBERTO  My dear Dorio, I am tolerably familiar with the cut-and-
                thrust of repartee. These are the jousts of journalism. I'm not,
                of course, referring to the journalism of today. I once did battle
                with the great politician Silvela[98] at a banquet, when I won the
                trophy at the Floral Games[99] in the fair city of Malaga. Matter
                of fact, there was an article by Narciso Díaz[100] recalling that
                encounter not so long ago in the *Herald*.[101] Delightful account,
                like everything he writes. And he admitted that I didn't get the
                worst of it. He quoted my definition of journalism. Do you
                know it? I'll repeat it for you, even so. The journalist is a
                plumiferous politician. Parliament is a vast newspaper office
                and every newspaper office a parliament in miniature.
                Journalism, like politics, is the art of mischief. They are the
                same circle in different spheres. I could explain it to you
                theosophically, if you gentlemen were initiated into the noble
                doctrine of Karma.[102]

DORIO DE GADEX  We are not initiates ourselves, but Don Latino has a
                smattering, I believe.

DON LATINO  ¡Más que algo, niño, más que algo! Ustedes no conocen la cabalatrina de mi seudónimo: soy Latino por las aguas del bautismo, soy Latino por mi nacimiento en la bética Hispalis, y Latino por dar mis murgas en el Barrio Latino de París. Latino, en lectura cabalística, se resuelve en una de las palabras mágicas: Onital. Usted, Don Filiberto, también toca algo en el magismo y la cábala.

DON FILIBERTO  No confundamos. Eso es muy serio, Don Latino. ¡Yo soy teósofo!

DON LATINO  ¡Yo no sé lo que soy!

DON FILIBERTO  Lo creo.

DORIO DE GADEX  Un golfo madrileño.

DON LATINO  Dorio, no malgastes el ingenio, que todo se acaba. Entre amigos basta con sacar la petaca, se queda mejor. ¡Vaya, dame un pito!

DORIO DE GADEX  No fumo.

DON FILIBERTO  ¡Otro vicio tendrá usted!

DORIO DE GADEX  Estupro criadas.

DON FILIBERTO  ¿Es agradable?

DORIO DE GADEX  Tiene sus encantos, Don Filiberto.

DON FILIBERTO  ¿Será usted padre innúmero?

DORIO DE GADEX  Las hago abortar.

DON FILIBERTO  ¡También infanticida!

PÉREZ            Un cajón de sastre.

DORIO DE GADEX  ¡Pérez, no metas la pata! Don Filiberto, un servidor es neo-maltusiano.

DON FILIBERTO  ¿Lo pone usted en las tarjetas?

DORIO DE GADEX  Y tengo un anuncio luminoso en casa.

DON LATINO  Y así, revertiéndonos la olla vacía, los españoles nos consolamos del hambre y de los malos gobernantes.

DORIO DE GADEX  Y de los malos cómicos, y de las malas comedias, y del servicio de tranvías, y del adoquinado.

PÉREZ            ¡Eres un iconoclasta!

DORIO DE GADEX  Pérez, escucha respetuosamente y calla.

DON FILIBERTO  En España podrá faltar el pan, pero el ingenio y el buen humor no se acaban.

DORIO DE GADEX  ¿Sabe usted quién es nuestro primer humorista, Don Filiberto?

DON FILIBERTO  Ustedes los iconoclastas dirán, quizá, que Don Miguel de Unamuno.

DORIO DE GADEX  ¡No, señor! El primer humorista es Don Alfonso XIII.

DON FILIBERTO  Tiene la viveza madrileña y borbónica.

DON LATINO  More than a smattering, my boy, more than a smattering! You are probably not aware of the cabalistic origins of my pseudonym. I am Latino by the waters of baptism; I am Latino by virtue of being born in the Roman city of Hispalis in the Roman province of Baetica and Latino because of my binges in the Latin Quarter of Paris. A cabalistic transmutation of Latino gives you Onital, one of the great magical words. You also dabble in the Cabala[103] and the occult sciences, I gather, Don Filiberto.

DON FILIBERTO  Let us not confuse the issue. This is very serious, Don Latino. I am a theosophist!

DON LATINO  And I have no idea what I am!

DON FILIBERTO  That I can well believe.

DORIO DE GADEX  The biggest loafer in Madrid.

DON LATINO  Don't overtax your wit, Dorio. There's a limit to everything. You would be more popular with your friends if you reached for your tobacco. Come on, let's have a smoke!

DORIO DE GADEX  I don't smoke.

DON FILIBERTO  You must have some vices!

DORIO DE GADEX  I ravish chambermaids.

DON FILIBERTO  Is it agreeable?

DORIO DE GADEX  It has its moments, Don Filiberto.

DON FILIBERTO  You must be father to thousands.

DORIO DE GADEX  I also arrange abortions.

DON FILIBERTO  Infanticide to boot!

PEREZ  A jack of all trades!

DORIO DE GADEX  Pérez, don't interrupt. Actually, Don Filiberto, I'm a Neo-Malthusian. I believe in population control.[104]

DON FILIBERTO  Do you put it on your visiting cards?

DORIO DE GADEX  And in lights outside my house.

DON LATINO  And when the food runs out, this is how we Spaniards beguile our hunger and console ourselves against bad governments.

DORIO DE GADEX  And against bad actors, and bad plays, the bad tram service and the bad state of the pavements.

PEREZ  You're an iconoclast![105]

DORIO DE GADEX  Pérez, just listen respectfully and keep quiet.

DON FILIBERTO  In Spain, we may be short of bread, but we never run out of wit and good humour!

DORIO DE GADEX  Do you know who our number one humorist is, Don Filiberto?

DON FILIBERTO  I imagine you iconoclasts would say Don Miguel de Unamuno.[106]

DORIO DE GADEX  No, sir! Our number one humorist is His Majesty Alfonso XIII.[107]

DON FILIBERTO  He has the ready wit of the capital and of the Bourbon line.

DORIO DE GADEX  El primer humorista, Don Filiberto. ¡El primero! Don
        Alfonso ha batido el récord haciendo presidente del Consejo a
        García Prieto.
DON FILIBERTO  Aquí, joven amigo, no se pueden proferir esas blasfemias.
        Nuestro periódico sale inspirado por Don Manuel García
        Prieto. Reconozco que no es un hombre brillante, que no es un
        orador, pero es un político serio. En fin, volvamos al caso de
        nuestro amigo Mala-Estrella. Yo podría telefonear a la
        secretaría particular del Ministro. Está en ella un muchacho
        que hizo aquí tribunales. Voy a pedir comunicación.
        ¡Válgame un santo de palo! Mala-Estrella es uno de los
        maestros y merece alguna consideración. ¿Qué dejan esos
        caballeros para los chulos y los guapos? ¡La gentuza de
        navaja! ¿Mala-Estrella se hallaría como de costumbre?...
DON LATINO  Iluminado.
DON FILIBERTO  ¡Es deplorable!
DON LATINO  Hoy no pasaba de lo justo. Yo le acompañaba. ¡Cuente usted!
        ¡Amigos desde París! ¿Usted conoce París? Yo fui a París con
        la Reina Doña Isabel. Escribí entonces en defensa de la
        Señora. Traduje algunos libros para la Casa Garnier. Fui
        redactor financiero de *La Lira Hispano-Americana:* ¡Una gran
        revista! Y siempre mi seudónimo Latino de Hispalis.

*Suena el timbre del teléfono. Don Filiberto, el periodista calvo y catarroso, el
hombre lógico y mítico de todas las redacciones, pide comunicación con el
Ministerio de Gobernación, Secretaría Particular. Hay un silencio. Luego
murmullos, leves risas, algún chiste en voz baja. Dorio de Gadex se sienta en el
sillón del Director, pone sobre la mesa sus botas rotas y lanza un suspiro.*

DORIO DE GADEX  Voy a escribir el artículo de fondo, glosando el discurso
        de nuestro jefe: «¡Todas las fuerzas vivas del país están
        muertas!», exclamaba aún ayer en un magnífico arranque
        oratorio nuestro amigo el ilustre Marqués de Alhucemas. Y la
        Cámara, completamente subyugada, aplaudía la profundidad
        del concepto, no más profundo que aquel otro: «Ya se van
        alejando los escollos.» Todos los cuales se resumen en el
        supremo apóstrofe: «Santiago y abre España, a la libertad y al
        progreso.»

*Don Filiberto suelta la trompetilla del teléfono y viene al centro de la sala,
cubriéndose la calva con las manos amarillas y entintadas. ¡Manos de
esqueleto memorialista en el día bíblico del Juicio Final!*

DORIO DE GADEX Our number one humourist, Don Filiberto. The number one! Our King Alfonso has just broken all known records by making García Prieto Prime Minister. [108]

DON FILIBERTO We do not allow that kind of blasphemy in here, my young friend. Our newspaper is published under the auspices of Don Manuel García Prieto. He is not a brilliant man, I grant you, and he is no orator. But he is a serious politician. Well now, to return to the case of our friend Ill-starred Max. I could ring the Minister's private office. There's a lad there who used to cover the law reports for the paper. I'll go and ask for a line. My goodness, yes. Max Estrella is one of the greats and surely deserves some sort of consideration! What can people expect from the pimps and the thugs, if that is how these gentlemen behave? The rabble with knives? You say Max was in his usual condition...?

DON LATINO Illuminated.

DON FILIBERTO Most deplorable!

DON LATINO Today was within reason. I was with him. I've been with him since our days in Paris together! Do you know Paris? I went to Paris in '68 with Queen Isabel II[109] when she went into exile. In fact I wrote a few articles in defence of that lady. Translated a few books for the publishers Garnier.[110] Financial editor for the *Spanish-American Lyre*.[111] A great review, that. All under my pseudonym, Latino de Hispalis.

*The telephone bell pings as the bald-headed, catarrh-ridden Don Filiberto, archetypal newspaper man, asks to be connected with the private secretary's office of the Ministry of the Interior. There is a silence. Then murmuring, titters and a whispered joke. Dorio de Gadex sits down in the Editor's chair, puts his worn-out boots up on the table and heaves a sigh.*

DORIO DE GADEX I shall write the leading article by paraphrasing the speech of our illustrious leader: "All the vital forces of our country are dead!" exclaimed our illustrious colleague, the Marquis of Alhucemas,[112] yesterday in a magnificent oratorical outburst. And a packed, spell-bound house applauded the profundity of the concept, a concept no less profound than that other which ran: "The menacing reefs which beset us are receding into the distance." All of which culminated in the final superb call to arms: "God for Spaniards and Saint James, and open our ranks to liberty and progress!"

*Don Filiberto puts down the receiver and returns to the middle of the room, clasping his bald pate with yellowing, ink-stained hands. The hands of a skeletal amanuensis on the Day of Judgement!*

DON FILIBERTO  ¡Esa broma es intolerable!  ¡Baje usted los pies!  ¡Dónde se
       ha visto igual grosería!
DORIO DE GADEX  En el Senado Yanqui.
DON FILIBERTO  ¡Me ha llenado usted la carpeta de tierra!
DORIO DE GADEX  Es mi lección de filosofía.  ¡Polvo eres, y en polvo te
       convertirás!
DON FILIBERTO  ¡Ni siquiera sabe usted decirlo en latín!  ¡Son ustedes unos
       niños procaces!
CLARINITO     Don Filiberto, nosotros no hemos faltado.
DON FILIBERTO  Ustedes han celebrado la gracia, y la risa en este caso es otra
       procacidad.  ¡La risa de lo que está muy por encima de ustedes!
       Para ustedes no hay nada respetable: ¡Maura es un charlatán!
DORIO DE GADEX  ¡El Rey del Camelo!
DON FILIBERTO  ¡Benlliure un santi boni barati!
DORIO DE GADEX  Dicho en valenciano.
DON FILIBERTO  Cavestany, el gran poeta, un coplero.
DORIO DE GADEX  Professor de guitarra por cifra.
DON FILIBERTO  ¡Qué de extraño tiene que mi ilustre jefe les parezca un
       mamarracho!
DORIO DE GADEX  Un yerno más.
DON FILIBERTO  Para ustedes en nuestra tierra no hay nada grande, nada
       digno de admiración.  ¡Les compadezco!  ¡Son ustedes bien
       desgraciados!  ¡Ustedes no sienten la Patria!
DORIO DE GADEX  Es un lujo que no podemos permitirnos.  Espere usted que
       tengamos automóvil, Don Filiberto.
DON FILIBERTO  ¡Ni siquiera pueden ustedes hablar en serio!  Hay alguno de
       ustedes, de los que ustedes llaman maestros, que se atreve a
       gritar viva la bagatela.  ¡Y eso no en el café, no en la tertulia de
       amigos, sino en la tribuna de la Docta Casa!  ¡Y eso no puede
       ser, caballeros!  Ustedes no creen en nada.  Son iconoclastas y
       son cínicos.  Afortunadamente hay una juventud que no son
       ustedes, una juventud estudiosa, una juventud preocupada, una
       juventud llena de civismo.
DON LATINO    Protesto, si se refiere usted a los niños de la Acción Ciudadana.
       Siquiera estos modernistas, llamémosles golfos distinguidos,
       no han llegado a ser policías honorarios.  A cada cual lo suyo.
       ¿Y parece ser que esta tarde mataron a uno de esos pollos de
       gabardina?  ¿Usted tendrá noticias?
DON FILIBERTO  Era un pollo relativo.  Sesenta años.
DON LATINO    Bueno, pues que lo entierren.  ¡Que haya un cadáver más, sólo
       importa a la funeraria!

DON FILIBERTO  This is beyond a joke! Take your feet off the desk! I've never seen such uncouth behaviour!

DORIO DE GADEX  I suggest you try the American Senate.

DON FILIBERTO  You've got dirt all over my folder!

DORIO DE GADEX  My lesson in philosophy for today. 'Dust thou art and unto dust shalt thou return!'

DON FILIBERTO  You can't even say it in Latin! You're all a crowd of impudent street urchins!

CLARINITO  Don Filiberto, *we* haven't shown any disrespect.

DON FILIBERTO  You laughed at the joke and, in this case, that's just the same as impudence. You laugh at things that are way beyond your understanding! For you there is nothing worthy of your respect. That great statesman, Maura, for instance, is a charlatan!

DORIO DE GADEX  King of the con men!

DON FILIBERTO  The great sculptor Benlliure[113] a pedlar of plaster saints!

DORIO DE GADEX  Saints for sale! Very good, very cheap![114]

DON FILIBERTO  The great poet Cavestany[115] a doggerel merchant.

DORIO DE GADEX  Also a teacher of the guitar by numbers.

DON FILIBERTO  Small wonder that my distinguished superior seems a clown to you!

DORIO DE GADEX  Just one more link in the old boy network.[116]

DON FILIBERTO  As far as you are concerned, there's nothing great in our country, nothing worthy of admiration. I pity you! You must be very unhappy! You have no feeling of national pride!

DORIO DE GADEX  It's a luxury we can't afford. Wait until we own a motor car, Don Filiberto.

DON FILIBERTO  You are incapable of talking seriously. There's even one of you, one of those you call 'maestro', who dares to proclaim 'Long live the trivial!'[117] Not in the café, mind you, or amongst a group of friends, but from the gallery of the Atheneum, the House of Learning itself! And that cannot be tolerated, gentlemen! You don't believe in anything. You are cynics and iconoclasts. Fortunately, there is a younger generation – not yourselves – a hard-working, socially-conscious generation with a sense of social responsibility.

DON LATINO  If you are referrring to the youth of the Citizens' Action Group, I must protest. At least these Modernists – call them high-class layabouts if you like – have not sunk so low as to become honorary policemen. Credit where credit's due. Apparently one of your gabardine-clad youths was killed this afternoon. I expect you've heard.

DON FILIBERTO  Youth? Only relatively speaking. Sixty years old.

DON LATINO  Ah, well, put him in the ground. As the poet says, one more corpse for the graveyard, who cares but the undertaker?[118]

*Rompe a sonar el timbre del teléfono. Don Filiberto toma la trompetilla y comienza una pantomima de cabeceos, apartes y gritos. Mientras escucha con el cuello torcido y la trompetilla en la oreja, esparce la mirada por la sala, vigilando a los jóvenes modernistas. Al colgar la trompetilla tiene una expresión candorosa de conciencia honrada. Reaparece el teósofo, en su sonrisa plácida, en el marfil de sus sienes, en toda la ancha redondez de su calva.*

DON FILIBERTO   Ya está transmitida la orden de poner en libertad a nuestro amigo Estrella. Aconséjenle ustedes que no beba. Tiene talento. Puede hacer mucho más de lo que hace. Y ahora váyanse y déjenme trabajar. Tengo que hacerme solo todo el periódico.

# Escena Octava

*Secretaría particular de Su Excelencia. Olor de brevas habanas, malos cuadros, lujo aparente y provinciano. La estancia tiene un recuerdo partido por medio, de oficina y sala de círculo con timba. De repente el grillo del teléfono se orina en el gran regazo burocrático. Y Dieguito García – Don Diego del Corral, en la «Revista de Tribunales y Estrados» – pega tres brincos y se planta la trompetilla en la oreja.*

DIEGUITO   ¿Con quién hablo?... Ya he transmitido la orden para que se le ponga en libertad... ¡De nada! ¡De nada!... ¡Un alcohólico!... Sí... Conozco su obra.... ¡Una desgracia!... No podrá ser. ¡Aquí estamos sin un cuarto!... Se lo diré. Tomo nota. ...¡De nada! ¡De nada!

*Max Estrella aparece en la puerta, pálido, arañado, la corbata torcida, la expresión altanera y alocada. Detrás, abotonándose los calzones, aparece El Ujier.*

EL UJIER     Deténgase usted, caballero.
MAX          No me ponga usted la mano encima.
EL UJIER     Salga usted sin hacer desacato.
MAX          Anúncieme usted al Ministro.
EL UJIER     No está visible.
MAX          ¡Ah! Es usted un gran lógico. Pero estará audible.
EL UJIER     Retírese, caballero. Éstas no son horas de audiencia.
MAX          Anúncieme usted.
EL UJIER     Es la orden... Y no vale ponerse pelmazo, caballero.
DIEGUITO     Fernández, deje usted a ese caballero que pase.
MAX          ¡Al fin doy con un indígena civilizado!

*The telephone shrills. Don Filiberto takes up the receiver and begins a pantomime of nods, muttered asides and indignant shouts. As he listens with the receiver to his ear, with his neck twisted round he scans the room keeping watch on the young Modernists. On hanging up the receiver, he wears the guileless expression of a satisfied conscience. The theosophist re-emerges in the beatific smile, in the serenity of his ivory temples and the ample curvature of his bald pate.*

DON FILIBERTO  The order for our friend Estrella's release has already been given. Advise him not to drink so much. He has talent. But he could produce much more than he does. And now, gentlemen, you must leave and let me work. I've got to get the whole paper out by myself.

# Scene Eight

*Office of His Excellency's private secretary.*[119] *The aroma of good havana cigars, bad paintings, flash provincial luxury. The room suggests a cross between an office and a gambling club. Suddenly the cricket of the telephone urinates in the great bureaucratic lap and Dieguito García – Don Diego del Corral to the readers of the Law Reports – makes three loping strides and claps the receiver to his ear.*

DIEGUITO  Who's that speaking, please?... I've already issued the order for his release... Not at all! Not at all!... An alcoholic!... Yes.. I know his work. An absolute tragedy! Impossible, I'm afraid. We haven't got a bean here!... I'll tell him. I'll make a note of it... Not at all! Not at all!

*Max Estrella appears in the doorway, his face drawn and scratched, his cravat awry and a wild, arrogant look on his face. Behind him appears the Usher, buttoning his breeches.*

| | |
|---|---|
| USHER | That's far enough, sir! |
| MAX | Don't lay your hand on me. |
| USHER | Kindly leave this room, sir, and don't make any trouble. |
| MAX | Announce me to the Minister. |
| USHER | You can't see him. |
| MAX | A very logical observation. But I can hear him. |
| USHER | Have the goodness to withdraw, sir. It's outside visiting hours. |
| MAX | Announce me. |
| USHER | Those are my orders... It's no good making a nuisance of yourself, sir. |
| DIEGUITO | Fernández, let the gentleman come in. |
| MAX | At last, a civilized native! |

| | |
|---|---|
| DIEGUITO | Amigo Mala-Estrella, usted perdonará que sólo un momento me ponga a sus órdenes. Me habló por usted la Redacción de *El Popular*. Allí le quieren a usted. A usted le quieren y el admiran en todas partes. Usted me deja mandado aquí y donde sea. No me olvide... ¡Quién sabe!... Yo tengo la nostalgia del periodismo... Pienso hacer algo... Hace tiempo acaricio la idea de una hoja volandera, un periódico ligero, festivo, espuma de champaña, fuego de virutas. Cuento con usted. Adiós, maestro. ¡Deploro que la ocasión de conocernos haya venido de suceso tan desagradable! |
| MAX | De eso vengo a protestar. ¡Tienen ustedes una policía reclutada entre la canalla más canalla! |
| DIEGUITO | Hay de todo, maestro. |
| MAX | No discutamos. Quiero que el Ministro me oiga, y al mismo tiempo darle las gracias por mi libertad. |
| DIEGUITO | El Señor Ministro no sabe nada. |
| MAX | Lo sabrá por mí. |
| DIEGUITO | El Señor Ministro ahora trabaja. Sin embargo, voy a entrar. |
| MAX | Y yo con usted. |
| DIEGUITO | ¡Imposible! |
| MAX | ¡Daré un escándalo! |
| DIEGUITO | ¡Está usted loco! |
| MAX | Loco de verme desconocido y negado. El Ministro es amigo mío, amigo de los tiempos heroicos. ¡Quiero oírle decir que no me conoce! ¡Paco! ¡Paco! |
| DIEGUITO | Le anunciaré a usted. |
| MAX | Yo me basto. ¡Paco! ¡Paco! ¡Soy un espectro del pasado! |

*Su Excelencia abre la puerta de su despacho y asoma en mangas de camisa, la bragueta desabrochada, el chaleco suelto, y los quevedos pendientes de un cordón, como dos ojos absurdos bailándole sobre la panza.*

| | |
|---|---|
| EL MINISTRO | ¿Qué escándalo es éste, Dieguito? |
| DIEGUITO | Señor Ministro, no he podido evitarlo. |
| EL MINISTRO | ¿Y ese hombre quién es? |
| MAX | ¡Un amigo de los tiempos heroicos! ¡No me reconoces, Paco! ¡Tanto me ha cambiado la vida! ¡No me reconoces! ¡Soy Máximo Estrella! |
| EL MINISTRO | ¡Claro! ¡Claro! ¡Claro! ¿Pero estás ciego? |
| MAX | Como Homero y como Belisario. |
| EL MINISTRO | Una ceguera accidental, supongo... |

| | |
|---|---|
| DIEGUITO | Well, my dear friend Ill-starred Max! You must forgive me if I can only spare you a moment. The editorial office of *The People* has just been on the phone to me about you. They're very fond of you down there. You are loved and admired everywhere, my dear fellow. And you will find me at your service now and at any time. Keep in touch now... Who knows!... I miss the world of journalism... Some day I mean to do something... I've been toying with the idea for some time now... a sort of broadsheet, a light, festive paper with the sparkle of champagne and the crackle of a bonfire.[120] I'm counting on your collaboration. Well, goodbye, maestro. I deeply regret that the occasion of our meeting should have been such an unfortunate occurrence! |
| MAX | That is precisely what I have come to protest about. You've got a police force recruited from the lowest rabble, the scum de la scum! |
| DIEGUITO | There's a bit of everything, maestro. |
| MAX | I'm not here to argue. I want the Minister to hear me. I want to thank him personally for my freedom. |
| DIEGUITO | His Excellency knows nothing of this. |
| MAX | He will, when I've finished with him. |
| DIEGUITO | His Excellency is working at the moment. However, I'll go in and see. |
| MAX | And I'll go with you. |
| DIEGUITO | That's impossible! |
| MAX | I'll make a scene! |
| DIEGUITO | You're mad! |
| MAX | Yes, mad from being forgotten, ignored and denied! The Minister is a friend of mine, a friend from the heroic days. I want to hear him say that he doesn't know who I am! Paco! Paco! |
| DIEGUITO | I'll announce you. |
| MAX | I'll announce myself. Paco! I am a ghost from times past! |

*His Excellency opens the door of his office and appears in his shirt sleeves, his flies and waistcoat unbuttoned and his pince-nez dangling on a ribbon like two grotesque eyeballs dancing on his paunch.*

| | |
|---|---|
| MINISTER | What's the meaning of this uproar, Dieguito? |
| DIEGUITO | I couldn't prevent it, Minister. |
| MINISTER | And who is this man? |
| MAX | A friend from the old days! Don't you recognize me, Paco? Has life changed me that much? You don't recognize me. I am Máximo Estrella! |
| MINISTER | Why, of course, of course, of course... But... are you blind? |
| MAX | Blind like Homer and like Belisarius.[121] |
| MINISTER | Temporarily, I trust... |

MAX                Definitiva e irrevocable. Es el regalo de Venus.
EL MINISTRO        Válgate Dios. ¿Y cómo no te has acordado de venir a verme
                   antes de ahora? Apenas leo tu firma en los periódicos.
MAX                ¡Vivo olvidado! Tú has sido más vidente dejando las letras por
                   hacernos felices gobernando. Paco, las letras no dan para
                   comer. ¡Las letras son colorín, pingajo y hambre!
EL MINISTRO        Las letras, ciertamente, no tienen la consideración que
                   debieran, pero son ya un valor que se cotiza. Amigo Max, yo
                   voy a continuar trabajando. A este pollo le dejas una nota de lo
                   que deseas... Llegas ya un poco tarde.
MAX                Llego en mi hora. No vengo a pedir nada. Vengo a exigir una
                   satisfacción y un castigo. Soy ciego, me llaman poeta, vivo de
                   hacer versos y vivo miserable. Estás pensando que soy un
                   borracho. ¡Afortunadamente! Si no fuese un borracho ya me
                   hubiera pegado un tiro. ¡Paco, tus sicarios no tienen derecho a
                   escupirme y abofetearme, y vengo a pedir un castigo para esa
                   turba de miserables, y un desagravio a la Diosa Minerva!
EL MINISTRO        Amigo Max, yo no estoy enterado de nada. ¿Qué ha pasado,
                   Dieguito?
DIEGUITO           Como hay un poco de tumulto callejero, y no se consienten
                   grupos, y estaba algo excitado el maestro...
MAX                He sido injustamente detenido, inquisitorialmente torturado.
                   En las muñecas tengo las señales.
EL MINISTRO        ¿Qué parte han dado los guardias, Dieguito?
DIEGUITO           En puridad, lo que acabo de resumir al Señor Ministro.
MAX                ¡Pues es mentira! He sido detenido por la arbitrariedad de un
                   legionario, a quien pregunté, ingenuo, si sabía los cuatro
                   dialectos griegos.
EL MINISTRO        Real y verdaderamente la pregunta es arbitraria. ¡Suponerle a
                   un guardia tan altas Humanidades!
MAX                Era un teniente.
EL MINISTRO        Como si fuese un Capitán General. ¡No estás sin ninguna
                   culpa! ¡Eres siempre el mismo calvatrueno! ¡Para ti no pasan
                   los años! ¡Ay, cómo envidio tu eterno buen humor!
MAX                ¡Para mí, siempre es de noche! Hace un año que estoy ciego.
                   Dicto y mi mujer escribe, pero no es posible.
EL MINISTRO        ¿Tu mujer es francesa?

| | |
|---|---|
| MAX | Definitively and irrevocably.  A gift from the goddess Venus.[122] |
| MINISTER | Good Heavens!  And why didn't you think of coming to see me before now?  I scarcely see your name in the papers these days. |
| MAX | I live in oblivion!  You had more foresight when you abandoned the Arts to make us all happier by governing.  You can't eat Art, Paco.  Under the tinsel, Art is all rags and starvation. |
| MINISTER | The Arts don't get the consideration they deserve, that's true, but nonetheless they are becoming a marketable commodity. Max, my friend, I must get back to my work.  Just leave a note of what you want with this young man... though you have come a little late. |
| MAX | I have come when I had to.  I'm not here to ask for favours.  I have come to demand satisfaction and justice.  I am blind. They call me a poet.  I live by making verses and I live like a pauper.  You may think that I'm a drunk.  It's just as well, because if I weren't a drunk, I'd have blown my brains out long ago.  But Paco, your hirelings have no right to spit on me and slap me around and I have come to demand punishment for the whole miserable gang of them and redress for the Goddess Minerva![123] |
| MINISTER | Max, my friend, I know nothing about this.  What has happened, Dieguito? |
| DIEGUITO | As there is a certain amount of unrest in the streets and public gatherings are not allowed, and as the maestro here was somewhat excited... |
| MAX | I have been unjustly arrested and inquisitorially tortured.  I've got the marks on my wrists. |
| MINISTER | What did the police say in their report, Dieguito? |
| DIEGUITO | In essence, what I have just outlined to your Excellency. |
| MAX | Then it's a lie!  I was arrested by the arbitrary action of a legionary, of whom I inquired, in all innocence, whether he was familiar with the four Greek dialects. |
| MINISTER | Really and truly, it is the question that is arbitrary.  To assume such a knowledge of the Humanities on the part of a policeman! |
| MAX | He was an officer. |
| MINISTER | I don't care if he was a Captain General.  You're not entirely blameless, are you?  Still the same old tearaway!  The years make no impression on you, do they, Max?  I really envy that eternal good humour of yours! |
| MAX | For me the only eternal thing is the dark!  I have been blind for a year now.  I try to dictate and my wife writes, but it's no good. |
| MINISTER | Your wife is French, isn't she? |

MAX        Una santa del Cielo, que escribe el español con una ortografía del Infierno. Tengo que dictarle letra por letra. Las ideas se me desvanecen. ¡Un tormento! Si hubiera pan en mi casa, maldito si me apenaba la ceguera. El ciego se entera mejor de las cosas del mundo, los ojos son unos ilusionados embusteros. ¡Adiós, Paco! Conste que no he venido a pedirte ningún favor. Max Estrella no es el pobrete molesto.

EL MINISTRO Espera, no te vayas, Máximo. Ya que has venido, hablemos. Tú resucitas toda una época de mi vida, acaso la mejor. ¡Qué lejana! Estudiábamos juntos. Vivíais en la calle del Recuerdo. Tenías una hermana. De tu hermana anduve yo enamorado. ¡Por ella hice versos!

MAX        ¡Calle del Recuerdo,
           ventana de Helena,
           la niña morena
           que asomada vi!
           ¡Calle del Recuerdo,
           rondalla de tuna,
           y escala de luna
           que en ella prendí!

EL MINISTRO ¡Qué memoria la tuya! ¡Me dejas maravillado! ¿Qué fue de tu hermana?

MAX        Entró en un convento.

EL MINISTRO ¿Y tu hermano Alex?

MAX        ¡Murió!

EL MINISTRO ¿Y los otros? ¡Érais muchos!

MAX        ¡Creo que todos han muerto!

EL MINISTRO ¡No has cambiado!... Max, yo no quiero herir tu delicadeza, pero en tanto dure aquí, puedo darte un sueldo.

MAX        ¡Gracias!

EL MINISTRO ¿Aceptas?

MAX        ¡Qué remedio!

EL MINISTRO Tome usted nota, Dieguito. ¿Dónde vives, Max?

MAX        Dispóngase usted a escribir largo, joven maestro: — Bastardillos, veintitrés, duplicado, Escalera interior, Guardilla B—. Nota. Si en este laberinto hiciese falta un hilo para guiarse, no se le pida a la portera, porque muerde.

EL MINISTRO ¡Cómo te envidio el humor!

MAX        El mundo es mío, todo me sonríe, soy un hombre sin penas.

EL MINISTRO ¡Te envidio!

MAX        ¡Paco, no seas majadero!

EL MINISTRO Max, todos los meses te llevarán el haber a tu casa. ¡Ahora, adiós! ¡Dame un abrazo!

| | |
|---|---|
| MAX | My wife is a saint from Heaven, but her spelling in Spanish is diabolical.[124] I have to dictate to her letter by letter. I lose the thread of my ideas. It's agony! If there were bread in my house, damned if I would worry about being blind. The blind man discovers more about the things of the world, the eyes only flatter to deceive. Goodbye, Paco! Remember, I didn't come to ask you for a handout. Max Estrella is no importunate beggar. |
| MINISTER | Wait, don't go, Máximo. Now that you're here, let's talk a while. You bring back a whole chapter of my life, perhaps the best one. How distant it all seems now! We used to study together. You lived in the Calle del Recuerdo – Memory Lane. You had a sister. In fact I was rather keen on your sister for a time. I even wrote poetry to her! |
| MAX | Helena's window[125] Down Memory Lane, The dark-eyed girl That there I did see. Oh, night serenade Down Memory Lane! A stairway of moonlight That brings her to me.[126] |
| MINISTER | What a fantastic memory! I'm flabbergasted! Whatever happened to your sister? |
| MAX | She went into a convent. |
| MINISTER | And what about your brother Alex?[127] |
| MAX | He died. |
| MINISTER | And the others? There were so many of you. |
| MAX | I think they're all dead. |
| MINISTER | You haven't changed a bit! ...Max, I don't want to hurt your feelings, but as long as I last in this job,[128] I could arrange a small income for you. |
| MAX | Thanks! |
| MINISTER | You accept? |
| MAX | What choice have I got? |
| MINISTER | Make a note of this, Dieguito. Where do you live, Max? |
| MAX | Prepare to write at length, young maestro: Bastardillos, twenty-three, A, Interior staircase, Attic Flat, B. Footnote: If in this labyrinth you should need a thread to guide you, don't ask the concierge for one, she bites.[129] |
| MINISTER | How I envy your humour! |
| MAX | The world is mine, fortune smiles upon me, I'm a man without cares. |
| MINISTER | I envy you! |
| MAX | Paco, don't be a clown! |
| MINISTER | Max, the cash will be delivered to your house every month. And now, farewell! Give me your arms. |

| MAX | Toma un dedo, y no te enternezcas. |
|---|---|
| EL MINISTRO | ¡Adiós, Genio y Desorden! |
| MAX | Conste que he venido a pedir un desagravio para mi dignidad, y un castigo para unos canallas. Conste que no alcanzo ninguna de las dos cosas, y que me das dinero, y que lo acepto porque soy un canalla. No me estaba permitido irme del mundo sin haber tocado alguna vez el fondo de los Reptiles. ¡Me he ganado los brazos de Su Excelencia! |

*Máximo Estrella, con los brazos abiertos en cruz, la cabeza erguida, los ojos parados, trágicos en su ciega quietud, avanza como un fantasma. Su Excelencia, trípudo, repintado, mantecoso, responde con un arranque de cómico viejo, en el buen melodrama francés. Se abrazan los dos. Su Excelencia, al separarse, tiene una lágrima detenida en los párpados. Estrecha la mano del bohemio, y deja en ella algunos billetes.*

| EL MINISTRO | ¡Adiós! ¡Adiós! Créeme que no olvidaré este momento. |
|---|---|
| MAX | ¡Adiós, Paco! ¡Gracias en nombre de dos pobres mujeres! |

*Su Excelencia toca un timbre. El Ujier acude soñoliento. Máximo Estrella, tanteando con el palo, va derecho hacia el fondo de la estancia, donde hay un balcón.*

| EL MINISTRO | Fernández, acompañe usted a ese caballero, y déjele en un coche. |
|---|---|
| MAX | Seguramente que me espera en la puerta mi perro. |
| EL UJIER | Quien le espera a usted es un sujeto de edad, en la antesala. |
| MAX | Don Latino de Hispalis: mi perro. |

*El Ujier toma de la manga al bohemio. Con aire torpón le saca del despacho, y guipa al soslayo el gesto de Su Excelencia. Aquel gesto manido de actor de carácter en la gran escena del reconocimiento.*

| EL MINISTRO | ¡Querido Dieguito, ahí tiene usted un hombre a quien le ha faltado el resorte de la voluntad! Lo tuvo todo, figura, palabra, gracejo. Su charla cambiaba de colores como las llamas de un ponche. |
|---|---|
| DIEGUITO | ¡Qué imagen soberbia! |
| EL MINISTRO | ¡Sin duda, era el que más valía entre los de mi tiempo! |
| DIEGUITO | Pues véalo usted ahora en medio del arroyo, oliendo a aguardiente, y saludando en francés a las proxenetas. |
| EL MINISTRO | ¡Veinte años! ¡Una vida! ¡E, inopinadamente, reaparece ese espectro de la bohemia! Yo me salvé del desastre renunciando |

| MAX | Here's a finger, and spare me the tears. |
|---|---|
| MINISTER | Farewell, Genius and Anarchy! |
| MAX | Remember I came here to demand redress for an offence to my dignity and a punishment for the blackguards responsible. I want it on record that I achieved neither of these objectives, that you offered me money instead and that I accepted, because I too am a blackguard. It was not in my stars that I should leave this world without drawing on the Reptiles' slush fund.[130] I have indeed earned Your Excellency's embrace! |

*Máximo Estrella, with arms flung wide, his head high, his dead eyes tragic in their stillness, advances like a zombie. His Excellency, pot-bellied and larded with greasepaint, responds with the effusive alacrity of a ham actor in a French melodrama. The two embrace. When they separate, a tear has welled in His Excellency's eye. He clasps the bohemian's hand and presses some banknotes into it.*

| MINISTER | Farewell! Farewell! Believe me I shall never forget this moment! |
|---|---|
| MAX | Goodbye, Paco. And thanks, in the name of two poor, unfortunate women! |

*His Excellency presses a bell. The Usher arrives heavy-eyed. Máximo Estrella, groping with his stick, makes straight for the back of the room, where there is a balcony.*

| MINISTER | Fernández, accompany this gentleman and put him in a cab. |
|---|---|
| MAX | My pet dog is bound to be waiting outside the door. |
| USHER | Don't know about a dog, but some old codger's waiting for you in the anteroom. |
| MAX | Don Latino de Hispalis: my dog.[131] |

*The Usher takes the bohemian by the sleeve and guides him awkwardly out of the office, stealing a sidelong glance at His Excellency's expression, as he does so: the played-out expression of a bad character actor in his big recognition scene.*

| MINISTER | Dieguito, dear boy, there goes a man who lacked nothing but strength of will. He had everything else: looks, wit, charm. His conversation changed colour like the flames on a bowl of punch. |
|---|---|
| DIEGUITO | What a superb image! |
| MINISTER | He was undoubtedly the most talented of my contemporaries. |
| DIEGUITO | And now look at him, wallowing in the gutter, reeking of alcohol and greeting all the brothel-keepers in French. |
| MINISTER | Twenty years! It's a lifetime! And then, out of the blue, this ghost from bohemia comes back to haunt me! I averted disaster by giving up the pleasure of writing poetry. You, |

|  | al goce de hacer versos. Dieguito, usted de esto no sabe nada, porque usted no ha nacido poeta. |
| --- | --- |
| DIEGUITO | ¡Lagarto! ¡Lagarto! |
| EL MINISTRO | ¡Ay, Dieguito, usted no alcanzará nunca lo que son ilusión y bohemia! Usted ha nacido institucionista, usted no es un renegado del mundo del ensueño. ¡Yo, sí! |
| DIEGUITO | ¿Lo lamenta usted, Don Francisco? |
| EL MINISTRO | Creo que lo lamento. |
| DIEGUITO | ¿El Excelentísimo Señor Ministro de la Gobernación, se cambiaría por el poeta Mala-Estrella? |
| EL MINISTRO | ¡Ya se ha puesto la toga y los vuelillos el Señor Licenciado Don Diego del Corral! Suspenda un momento el interrogatorio su señoria, y vaya pensando cómo se justifican las pesetas que hemos de darle a Máximo Estrella. |
| DIEGUITO | Las tomaremos de los fondos de Policía. |
| EL MINISTRO | ¡Eironeia! |

*Su Excelencia se hunde en una poltrona, ante la chimenea que aventa sobre la alfombra una claridad trémula. Enciende un cigarro con sortija, y pide La Gaceta. Cabálgase los lentes, le pasa la vista, se hace un gorro, y se duerme.*

# Escena Novena

*Un café que prolongan empañados espejos. Mesas de mármol. Divanes rojos. El mostrador en el fondo, y detrás un vejete rubiales, destacado el busto sobre la diversa botillería. El Café tiene piano y violín. Las sombras y la música flotan en el vaho de humo, y en el lívido temblor de los arcos voltaicos. Los espejos multiplicadores están llenos de un interés folletinesco. En su fondo, con una geometría absurda, estravaga el Café. El compás canalla de la música, las luces en el fondo de los espejos, el vaho de humo penetrado del temblor de los arcos voltaicos cifran su diversidad en una sola expresión. Entran extraños, y son de repente transfigurados en aquel triple ritmo, Mala-Estrella y Don Latino.*

| MAX | ¿Qué tierra pisamos? |
| --- | --- |
| DON LATINO | El Café Colón. |
| MAX | Mira si está Rubén. Suele ponerse enfrente de los músicos. |
| DON LATINO | Allá está como un cerdo triste. |
| MAX | Vamos a su lado, Latino. Muerto yo, el cetro de la poesía pasa a ese negro. |
| DON LATINO | No me encargues de ser tu testamentario. |

|           | Dieguito, know nothing of all this because you were not born a poet. |
|-----------|----------------------------------------------------------------------|
| DIEGUITO  | Heaven forbid! |
| MINISTER  | Ah, Dieguito, you will never understand what it is to live the bohemian life, to feed on dreams. You were born an institutionalist.[132] You're not a renegade from the world of dreams. I am! |
| DIEGUITO  | Do you regret it, Don Francisco? |
| MINISTER  | Yes, I think I do. |
| DIEGUITO  | So His Excellency the Minister of the Interior would change places with the poet Ill-starred Max? |
| MINISTER  | So our law graduate, Don Diego del Corral, has donned his barrister's gown and lace cuffs! Well, my learned friend can suspend the cross-examination for a moment and apply his mind to the problem of how to justify the money we are going to give to Max Estrella. |
| DIEGUITO  | We'll take it from the Police funds. |
| MINISTER  | Delicious irony! |

*His Excellency sinks into an armchair in front of the fireplace where the flames cast their flickering light on to the carpet. He lights up an expensive cigar and asks for the 'Official Gazette'.[133] He puts on his glasses, runs his eyes over the paper, makes it into a hat and falls asleep.*

# Scene Nine

*A café elongated by reflections in tarnished mirrors.[134] Marble-topped tables. Red plush divans. At the back, a bar, and behind the bar the torso of a light-haired old man against a variegated array of bottles. A piano and violin are playing. Shadowy figures drift in the smoky atmosphere and the music pulsates in the pale, flickering light of the arc lamps. The multiplying mirrors add a note of melodramatic interest as the café recedes into infinite depths of extravagant geometric forms. The decadent beat of the music, the lights reflected in the mirrors, the flickering arc lamps filtering through the pall of smoke blend their diversity in a single unified expression. Enter two outsiders, who are abruptly transfigured by the triple rhythm of the context: Ill-starred Max and Don Latino.*

| MAX        | Whose ground are we standing on? |
|------------|----------------------------------|
| DON LATINO | The Café Columbus.[135] |
| MAX        | Look and see if Rubén is here. He usually sits in front of the musicians. |
| DON LATINO | There he is, like a melancholic pig. |
| MAX        | Let's join him, Latino. When I'm gone, the crown and sceptre of poetry will pass into that negro's hands.[136] |
| DON LATINO | Then don't ask me to be your executor. |

| | |
|---|---|
| MAX | ¡Es un gran poeta! |
| DON LATINO | Yo no lo entiendo. |
| MAX | ¡Merecías ser el barbero de Maura! |

*Por entre sillas y mármoles llegan al rincón donde está sentado y silencioso Rubén Darío. Ante aquella aparición, el poeta siente la amargura de la vida, y con gesto egoísta de niño enfadado, cierra los ojos, y bebe un sorbo de su copa de ajenjo. Finalmente, su máscara de ídolo se anima con una sonrisa cargada de humedad. El ciego se detiene ante la mesa y levanta su brazo, con magno ademán de estatua cesárea.*

| | |
|---|---|
| MAX | ¡Salud, hermano, si menor en años, mayor en prez! |
| RUBÉN | ¡Admirable! ¡Cuánto tiempo sin vernos, Max! ¿Qué haces? |
| MAX | ¡Nada! |
| RUBÉN | ¡Admirable! ¿Nunca vienes por aquí? |
| MAX | El café es un lujo muy caro, y me dedico a la taberna, mientras llega la muerte. |
| RUBÉN | Max, amemos la vida, y mientras podamos, olvidemos a la Dama de Luto. |
| MAX | ¿Por qué? |
| RUBÉN | ¡No hablemos de Ella! |
| MAX | ¡Tú la temes, y yo la cortejo! ¡Rubén, te llevaré el mensaje que te plazca darme para la otra ribera de la Estigia! Vengo aquí para estrecharte por última vez la mano, guiado por el ilustre camello Don Latino de Hispalis. ¡Un hombre que desprecia tu poesía, como si fuese Académico! |
| DON LATINO | ¡Querido Max, no te pongas estupendo! |
| RUBÉN | ¿El señor es Don Latino de Hispalis? |
| DON LATINO | ¡Si nos conocemos de antiguo, maestro! ¡Han pasado muchos años! Hemos hecho juntos periodismo en *La Lira Hispano-Americana*. |
| RUBÉN | Tengo poca memoria, Don Latino. |
| DON LATINO | Yo era el redactor financiero. En París nos tuteábamos, Rubén. |
| RUBÉN | Lo había olvidado. |
| MAX | ¡Si no has estado nunca en París! |
| DON LATINO | Querido Max, vuelvo a decirte que no te pongas estupendo. Siéntate e invítanos a cenar. ¡Rubén, hoy este gran poeta, nuestro amigo, se llama Estrella Resplandeciente! |
| RUBÉN | ¡Admirable! ¡Max, es preciso huir de la bohemia! |
| DON LATINO | ¡Está opulento! ¡Guarda dos pápiros de piel de contribuyente! |
| MAX | ¡Esta tarde tuve que empeñar la capa, y esta noche te convido a cenar! ¡A cenar con el rubio Champaña, Rubén! |

| MAX | He's a great poet! |
| DON LATINO | I can't understand him. |
| MAX | You should have been Maura's barber! |

*Threading their way through chairs and marble table-tops, they reach the corner where Rubén Darío[137] sits in silence. Confronted with their appearance, Rubén feels the bitterness of experience and, with the petulant expression of a self-centred child, shuts his eyes and takes a sip of his absinthe. Finally, his idol's mask softens into a dewy smile. The blind man pauses in front of the table and raises his arm in a grand imperial gesture.*

| MAX | Salutations, brother, though younger in years, the greater in glory! |
| RUBEN | Admirable![138] It's been a long time, Max! What are you doing these days? |
| MAX | Nothing! |
| RUBEN | Admirable! Don't you come here any more? |
| MAX | The café is a very expensive luxury, I wait in the tavern till death turns up to take me home. |
| RUBEN | Max, we must love life and forget the Lady in Black for as long as we can. |
| MAX | Why? |
| RUBEN | Please, let's not speak of Her! |
| MAX | You fear her and I woo her like a lover. Rubén, I'll take any message you care to give me for the other bank of the Styx.[139] I am here to shake your hand for the last time, guided by the illustrious camel Don Latino de Hispalis. A man who despises your poetry as if he were a member of the Academy! |
| DON LATINO | My dear Max, don't be quite so magnificent! |
| RUBEN | So you must be Don Latino de Hispalis. |
| DON LATINO | But we know each other from way back, maestro! It was many years ago. We worked together on the *Spanish-American Lyre*. |
| RUBEN | I have a very poor memory, Don Latino. |
| DON LATINO | I was the financial editor. In Paris we were very close friends, Rubén. |
| RUBEN | I had forgotten. |
| MAX | You've never been to Paris in your life! |
| DON LATINO | My dear Max, I repeat: spare us the magnificent wit. Just sit down and invite us to supper. Rubén, today our great poet friend Estrella is the brightest star in the firmament! |
| RUBEN | Admirable! Max, you must abandon the bohemian life! |
| DON LATINO | He's rolling in money! He's got two sheets of taxpayer's skin in his pocket![140] |
| MAX | This evening I had to pawn my cape, and tonight I invite you to dine with me. And dine with golden champagne, Rubén! |

RUBÉN          ¡Admirable! Como Martín de Tours, partes conmigo la capa, transmudada en cena. ¡Admirable!

DON LATINO     ¡Mozo, la carta! Me parece un poco exagerado pedir vinos franceses. ¡Hay que pensar en el mañana, caballeros!

MAX            ¡No pensemos!

DON LATINO     Compartiría tu opinión, si con el café, la copa y el puro nos tomásemos un veneno.

MAX            ¡Miserable burgués!

DON LATINO     Querido Max, hagamos un trato. Yo me bebo modestamente una chica de cerveza, y tú me apoquinas en pasta lo que me había de costar la bebecua.

RUBÉN          No te apartes de los buenos ejemplos, Don Latino.

DON LATINO     Servidor no es un poeta. Yo me gano la vida con más trabajo que haciendo versos.

RUBÉN          Yo también estudio las matemáticas celestes.

DON LATINO     ¡Perdón entonces! Pues sí, señor, aun cuando me veo reducido al extremo de vender entregas, soy un adepto de la Gnosis y la Magia.

RUBÉN          ¡Yo lo mismo!

DON LATINO     Recuerdo que alguna cosa alcanzabas.

RUBÉN          Yo he sentido que los Elementales son Conciencias.

DON LATINO ¡Indudable!    ¡Indudable!    ¡Indudable!    ¡Conciencias, Voluntades y Potestades!

RUBÉN          Mar y Tierra, Fuego y Viento, divinos monstruos, ¡Posiblemente Divinos porque son Eternidades!

MAX            Eterna la Nada.

DON LATINO     Y el fruto de la Nada: Los cuatro Elementales, simbolizados en los cuatro Evangelistas. La Creación, que es pluralidad, solamente comienza en el Cuatrivio. Pero de la Trina Unidad, se desprende el Número. ¡Por eso el Número es Sagrado!

MAX            ¡Calla, Pitágoras! Todo eso lo has aprendido en tus intimidades con la vieja Blavatsky.

DON LATINO ¡Max, esas bromas no son tolerables! ¡Eres un espíritu profundamente irreligioso y volteriano! Madama Blavatsky ha sido una mujer extraordinaria, y no debes profanar con burlas el culto de su memoria. Pudieras verte castigado por alguna camarrupa de su karma. ¡Y no sería el primer caso!

RUBÉN          ¡Se obran prodigios! Afortunadamente no los vemos ni los entendemos. Sin esta ignorancia, la vida sería un enorme sobrecogimiento.

MAX            ¿Tú eres creyente, Rubén?

RUBÉN          ¡Yo creo!

MAX            ¿En Dios?

RUBÉN          ¡Y en el Cristo!

MAX            ¿Y en las llamas del Infierno?

| | |
|---|---|
| RUBEN | Admirable! Like St Martin bishop of Tours you divide your cape with me, miraculously transmuted into supper.[141] Admirable! |
| DON LATINO | Waiter, the menu! It seems a little extravagant to order French wines. We must think of the morrow, gentlemen. |
| MAX | Let us not think of the morrow! |
| DON LATINO | I would share your view, if, along with the coffee, liqueurs and cigars, we also took a dose of arsenic. |
| MAX | Miserable bourgeois! |
| DON LATINO | Very well, my dear fellow, we'll do a deal. I'll just have a small beer and you give me what my share of the other booze would have cost in cash! |
| RUBEN | Let us not depart from the norms of good taste, Don Latino! |
| DON LATINO | I am your humble servant, Rubén, but no poet. I earn my living by harder graft than writing verse. |
| RUBEN | I am also a student of celestial mathematics.[142] |
| DON LATINO | In that case, I beg your pardon. Yes, sir, I may be reduced to selling these serials and penny dreadfuls, but I am a devout follower of the Gnostics[143] and the Occult. |
| RUBEN | And I the same. |
| DON LATINO | I seem to recall that you had an inkling. |
| RUBEN | I have sensed that the Elements are Consciences. |
| DON LATINO | Indubitably! Indubitably! Indubitably! Consciences, Wills and Forces! |
| RUBEN | Land and Sea, Fire and Wind, monstrous divinities. Possibly divine because they are eternal! |
| MAX | Nothingness is the only eternity there is. |
| DON LATINO | And the fruit of that Nothingness, namely the four Elements symbolized in the four Gospels. Creation, which is plurality, can only begin in Quaternity.[144] But from tri-unity stems the concept of Number. Hence the Number is sacred! |
| MAX | Oh, shut up, Pythagoras![145] You picked all that up in bed with old Madame Blavatsky.[146] |
| DON LATINO | Max, this irreverence is intolerable! You have a thoroughly irreligious and Voltarian spirit. Madame Blavatsky was an extraordinary woman and you should not profane her memory with cheap jibes. You might find yourself punished by some influence from her Karma.[147] It wouldn't be the first time it had happened! |
| RUBEN | Strange mysteries do occur. Fortunately we neither see nor understand them. Without this ignorance we would live in a constant state of terror. |
| MAX | Are you a believer, Rubén? |
| RUBEN | I believe! |
| MAX | In God? |
| RUBEN | And in Christ! |
| MAX | And in the fires of Hell? |

| | |
|---|---|
| RUBÉN | ¡Y más todavía en las músicas del Cielo! |
| MAX | ¡Eres un farsante, Rubén! |
| RUBÉN | ¡Seré un ingenuo! |
| MAX | ¿No estás posando? |
| RUBÉN | ¡No! |
| MAX | Para mí, no hay nada tras la última mueca. Si hay algo, vendré a decírtelo. |
| RUBÉN | ¡Calla, Max, no quebrantemos los humanos sellos! |
| MAX | Rubén, acuérdate de esta cena. Y ahora, mezclemos el vino con las rosas de tus versos. Te escuchamos. |

*Rubén se recoge estremecido, el gesto de ídolo, evocador de terrores y misterios. Max Estrella, un poco enfático, le alarga la mano. Llena los vasos Don Latino. Rubén sale de su meditación con la tristeza vasta y enorme esculpida en los ídolos aztecas.*

| | |
|---|---|
| RUBÉN | Veré si recuerdo una peregrinación a Compostela... Son mis últimos versos. |
| MAX | ¿Se han publicado? Si se han publicado, me los habrán leído, pero en tu boca serán nuevos. |
| RUBÉN | Posiblemente no me acordaré. |

*Un joven que escribe en la mesa vecina, y al parecer traduce, pues tiene ante los ojos un libro abierto y cuartillas en rimero, se inclina tímidamente hacia Rubén Darío.*

| | |
|---|---|
| EL JOVEN | Maestro, donde usted no recuerde, yo podría apuntarle. |
| RUBÉN | ¡Admirable! |
| MAX | ¿Dónde se han publicado? |
| EL JOVEN | Yo los he leído manuscritos. Iban a ser publicados en una revista que murió antes de nacer. |
| MAX | ¿Sería una revista de Paco Villaespesa? |
| EL JOVEN | Yo he sido su secretario. |
| DON LATINO | Un gran puesto. |
| MAX | Tú no tienes nada que envidiar, Latino. |
| EL JOVEN | ¿Se acuerda usted, maestro? |

*Rubén asiente con un gesto sacerdotal, y tras de humedecer los labios en la copa, recita lento y cadencioso, como en sopor, y destaca su esfuerzo por distinguir de eses y cedas.*

| | |
|---|---|
| RUBÉN | ¡¡¡La ruta tocaba a su fin, |
| | en el rincón de un quicio oscuro, |
| | nos repartimos un pan duro |
| | con el Marqués de Bradomín!!! |

RUBEN            And even more in the music of the spheres![148]
MAX              You're a fraud, Rubén.
RUBEN            Naive, possibly.
MAX              Not a pose?
RUBEN            No!
MAX              For me, there is nothing beyond that final grimace. If there is,
                 I'll come back and let you know.
RUBEN            Shh, Max! Let us not break the seals of our mortality!
MAX              Rubén, I want you to remember this supper. And now let us
                 mingle the wine with the roses of your poetry. We are
                 listening.

*Rubén shudders and withdraws within himself. His idol-like features evoke a
world of primeval terrors and mysteries. Max Estrella, with a somewhat
theatrical gesture, extends his arm towards him. Don Latino fills the glasses.
Rubén emerges from his meditation with all the immense sadness carved on the
face of an Aztec god.*

RUBEN            I'll see if I can remember *A pilgrimage to Compostela...* It's
                 my last poem.
MAX              Has it been published? They will have read it to me, if it has.
                 But on your lips it will be new.
RUBEN            I may not remember it.

*A young man who has been writing at the next table, apparently translating
since he has an open book and a pile of papers in front of him, leans shyly across
towards Rubén Darío .*

YOUNG MAN   Maestro, where you don't remember, I could prompt you.
RUBEN          Admirable!
MAX            Where was it published?
YOUNG MAN   I read it in manuscript. It was going to be published in a
               review that died before it was born.
MAX            Not one of Paco Villaespesa's, by any chance?[149]
YOUNG MAN   I was his secretary.
DON LATINO   And a grand post too.
MAX            You've got nothing to be jealous about, Latino.
YOUNG MAN   Do you remember, maestro?

*Rubén nods with sacerdotal solemnity and, moistening his lips in his glass,
recites with slow cadences, as if in a trance, making a conscious effort to
distinguish the s from the Castilian z.*[150]

RUBEN                        The road was coming to its end.
                            In some dark doorway of the dead,
                            We shared a final crust of bread
                            With Bradomín, our friend.[151]

EL JOVEN     Es el final, maestro.
RUBÉN        Es la ocasión para beber por nuestro estelar amigo.
MAX          ¡Ha desaparecido del mundo!
RUBÉN        Se prepara a la muerte en su aldea, y su carta de despedida fue
             la ocasión de estos versos. ¡Bebamos a la salud de un exquisito
             pecador!
MAX          ¡Bebamos!

*Levanta su copa, y gustando el aroma del ajenjo, suspira y evoca el cielo lejano
de París. Piano y violín atacan un aire de opereta, y la parroquia del café lleva
el compás con las cucharillas en los vasos. Después de beber, los tres
desterrados confunden sus voces hablando en francés. Recuerdan y proyectan
las luces de la fiesta divina y mortal. ¡París! ¡Cabaretes! ¡Ilusión! Y en el
ritmo de las frases, desfila, con su pata coja, Papá Verlaine.*

# Escena Décima

*Paseo con jardines. El cielo raso y remoto. La luna lunera. Patrullas de
caballería. Silencioso y luminoso, rueda un auto. En la sombra clandestina de
los ramajes, merodean mozuelas pingonas y viejas pintadas como caretas.
Repartidos por las sillas del paseo, yacen algunos bultos durmientes. Max
Estrella y Don Latino caminan bajo las sombras del paseo. El perfume
primaveral de las lilas embalsama la humedad de la noche.*

UNA VIEJA PINTADA  ¡Morenos! ¡Chis!... ¡Morenos! ¿Queréis venir un
             ratito?
DON LATINO   Cuando te pongas los dientes.
LA VIEJA PINTADA  ¡No me dejáis siquiera un pitillo!
DON LATINO   Te daré *La Corres*, para que te ilustres; publica una carta de
             Maura.
LA VIEJA PINTADA  Que le den morcilla.
DON LATINO   Se la prohíbe el rito judaico.
LA VIEJA PINTADA  ¡Mira el camelista! Esperaros, que llamo a una amiguita.
             ¡Lunares! ¡Lunares!

*Surge La Lunares, una mozuela pingona, medias blancas, delantal, toquilla y
alpargatas. Con risa desvergonzada se detiene en la sombra del jardinillo.*

LA LUNARES   ¡Ay, qué pollos más elegantes! Vosotros me sacáis esta noche
             de la calle.
LA VIEJA PINTADA  Nos ponen piso.
LA LUNARES   Dejadme una perra, y me completáis una peseta para la cama.

YOUNG MAN   That's the end, maestro.
RUBEN           It is time to drink to the divine Marquis of Bradomín,[152] our
                     stellar friend.
MAX              He has withdrawn from the world!
RUBEN           He is preparing himself for death alone in his village, and his
                     farewell letter was the inspiration for these lines. Let us drink
                     to the health of an exquisite sinner!
MAX              Let's drink!

*Max raises his glass and, savouring the bouquet of the absinthe, sighs and
recalls the distant skies of Paris. The piano and violin strike up an operatic air
and the customers of the café beat time with their spoons on the glasses. After
the toast, the voices of the three exiles, speaking in French, mingle in a general
blurr of conversation. They recall and rekindle the torches of divine and mortal
bacchanalia. Paris! Cabarets! All the hope of youth! And in the rise and fall
of the phrases, on his game leg, limps the shade of Papa Verláine.[153]*

# Scene Ten

*Public promenade and gardens.[154] A 'romantic' moon in a high, cloudless sky.
Mounted patrols. A motor car with its headlights on slides silently by. Ragged
young tarts and old hags painted like masks maraud furtively in the shadows of
the bushes. Sleeping human forms lie dotted about on the park benches. Max
Estrella and Don Latino walk along the shadowy avenue. A springtime
fragrance of lilac embalms the dewy night.*

PAINTED TART  Eh, my 'andsomes! Psst! Want to come for a little ride, my
                        darlin's?
DON LATINO  When you put your teeth in.
PAINTED TART  Give us a fag at least!
DON LATINO  I'll give you the *Correspondent* for your further education.
                     There's a letter by Maura in it.[155]
PAINTED TART  He can stuff a sausage up his arse!
DON LATINO  It's against his Jewish religion.
PAINTED TART  Bit of a tease, aren't you? 'Ere, 'ang on, I'll call a friend.
                        Lunares! Lunares!

*Lunares emerges, a young tart of shabby appearance, dressed in white stockings,
apron, knitted headscarf and rope-soled sandals. She pauses for a moment in
the shadows and gives a brazen laugh.*

LUNARES       Ay, ay, a couple of smart cock robins here! You'll get me off
                     the streets tonight, won't you, my darlin's?
PAINTED TART  They'll set us up in a flat.
LUNARES       Just give me ten cents and I'll have enough for the bed.

LA VIEJA PINTADA  ¡Roñas, siquiera un pitillo!
MAX          Toma un habano.
LA VIEJA PINTADA  ¡Guasíbilis!
LA LUNARES  Apáñalo, panoli.
LA VIEJA PINTADA  ¡Si que lo apaño!  ¡Y es de sortija!
LA LUNARES  Ya me permitirás alguna chupada.
LA VIEJA PINTADA  Éste me lo guardo.
LA LUNARES  Para el Rey de Portugal.
LA VIEJA PINTADA  ¡Infeliz!  ¡Para el de la Higiene!
LA LUNARES  ¿Y vosotros, astrónomos, no hacéis una calaverada?

*Las dos prójimas han evolucionado sutiles y clandestinas, bajo las sombras del paseo. La Vieja Pintada está a la vera de Don Latino de Hispalis. La Lunares a la vera de Mala Estrella.*

LA LUNARES  ¡Mira qué limpios llevo los bajos!
MAX          Soy ciego.
LA LUNARES  ¡Algo verás!
MAX          ¡Nada!
LA LUNARES  Tócame. Estoy muy dura.
MAX          ¡Un mármol!

*La mozuela, con una risa procaz, toma la mano del poeta, y la hace tantear sobre sus hombros, y la oprime sobre los senos. La vieja sórdida, bajo la máscara de albayalde, descubre las encías sin dientes, y tienta capciosa a Don Latino.*

LA VIEJA PINTADA  Hermoso, vente conmigo, que ya tu compañero se
          entiende con la Lunares. No te receles. ¡Ven! Si se acerca
          algún guindilla, lo apartamos con el puro habanero.

*Se lo lleva sonriendo, blanca y fantasmal. Cuchicheos. Se pierden entre los árboles del jardín. Parodia grotesca del jardín de Armida. Mala Estrella y la otra prójima quedan aislados sobre la orilla del paseo.*

LA LUNARES  Pálpame el pecho... No tengas reparo... ¡Tú eres un poeta!
MAX          ¿En qué lo has conocido?
LA LUNARES  En la peluca de Nazareno. ¿Me engaño?
MAX          No te engañas.
LA LUNARES  Si cuadrase que yo te pusiese al tanto de mi vida, sacabas una
          historia de las primeras. Responde: ¿Cómo me encuentras?
MAX          ¡Una ninfa!
LA LUNARES  ¡Tienes el hablar muy dilustrado!  Tu acompañante ya se
          concertó con la Cotillona. Ven. Entrégame la mano. Vamos a

PAINTED TART  Stingy bastards!  Just a miserable cigarette!
MAX                 Have a cigar.
PAINTED TART  You're having me on!
LUNARES         Grab it, muggins!
PAINTED TART  Not 'alf I won't!  It's got a band on it!
LUNARES         Let me have a drag later on.
PAINTED TART  I'm 'anging on to this one.
LUNARES         For the King of Portugal.
PAINTED TART  Don't be daft!  For the 'ealth inspector!
LUNARES         Well, how about it, my star gazers?  What about a bit of
                'orizontal refreshment?

*Subtly and unobtrusively, in the shadows of the avenues, the two prostitutes have manoeuvred themselves into position.  The Painted Tart is beside Don Latino and Lunares beside the Ill-starred Max.*

LUNARES         I've got nice clean underwear, look!
MAX                 I'm blind.
LUNARES         You must be able to see something.
MAX                 Nothing.
LUNARES         Feel me then.  I'm real firm.
MAX                 Like marble!

*With an obscene laugh, the girl takes the poet by the hand, makes him feel her shoulders, then presses it hard against her breasts.  The old hag, under her white-leaded mask, displays her toothless gums and entices Don Latino.*

PAINTED TART  You come with me, 'andsome, seeing as your mate's getting
                off with Lunares.  Don't be shy.  Come on!  If some rozzer
                comes along, we'll buy him off with this havana cigar.

*With a smile of ghostly pallor, she leads him off into the night.  Whispers as they disappear amongst the trees.  A grotesque parody of the garden of Armida.*[156] *Ill-starred Max and the other prostitute are left alone on the edge of the pathway.*

LUNARES         Feel my breast...  Don't be bashful...  You're a poet, aren't
                you?
MAX                 How did you know?
LUNARES         That long-haired wig[157] of yours.  Am I wrong?
MAX                 No, you're not wrong.
LUNARES         If I had a mind to tell you all about my life, you could write a
                really good story.  Tell me something:  what do you think of
                me?
MAX                 A veritable nymph!
LUNARES         You've got a real educated way of talking!  'Ere, your friend's
                got fixed up with Old Gossip Guts there.  Come on.  Give me

|              | situarnos en un lugar más oscuro. Verás cómo te cachondeo. |
|--------------|------------|
| MAX          | Llévame a un banco para esperar a ese cerdo hispalense. |
| LA LUNARES   | No chanelo. |
| MAX          | Hispalis es Sevilla. |
| LA LUNARES   | Lo será en cañí. Yo soy chamberilera. |
| MAX          | ¿Cuántos años tienes? |
| LA LUNARES   | Pues no sé los que tengo. |
| MAX          | ¿Y es siempre aquí tu parada nocturna? |
| LA LUNARES   | Las más de las veces. |
| MAX          | ¡Te ganas honradamente la vida! |
| LA LUNARES   | Tú no sabes con cuántos trabajos. Yo miro mucho lo que hago. La Cotillona me habló para llevarme a una casa. ¡Una casa de mucho postín! No quise ir... Acostarme no me acuesto... Yo guardo el pan de higos para el gachó que me sepa camelar. ¿Por qué no lo pretendes? |
| MAX          | Me falta tiempo. |
| LA LUNARES   | Inténtalo para ver lo que sacas. Te advierto que me estás gustando. |
| MAX          | Te advierto que soy un poeta sin dinero. |
| LA LUNARES   | ¿Serías tú, por un casual, el que sacó las coplas de Joselito? |
| MAX          | ¡Ése soy! |
| LA LUNARES   | ¿De verdad? |
| MAX          | De verdad. |
| LA LUNARES   | Dilas. |
| MAX          | No las recuerdo. |
| LA LUNARES   | Porque no las sacaste de tu sombrerera. Sin mentira, ¿cuáles son las tuyas? |
| MAX          | Las del Espartero. |
| LA LUNARES   | ¿Y las recuerdas? |
| MAX          | Y las canto como un flamenco. |
| LA LUNARES   | ¡Que no eres capaz! |
| MAX          | ¡Tuviera yo una guitarra! |
| LA LUNARES   | ¿La entiendes? |
| MAX          | Para algo soy ciego. |
| LA LUNARES   | ¡Me estás gustando! |
| MAX          | No tengo dinero. |
| LA LUNARES   | Con pagar la cama concluyes. Si quedas contento y quieres convidarme a un café con churros, tampoco me niego. |

*Máximo Estrella, con tacto de ciego, le pasa la mano por el óvalo del rostro, la garganta y los hombros. La pindonga ríe con dejo sensual de cosquillas. Quítase del moño un peinecillo gitano, y con él peinando los tufos, redobla la risa y se desmadeja.*

|       | your hand. Let's find somewhere darker. I'll soon make you randy, see if I don't. |
|-------|-----------------------------------------------------------------------------------|
| MAX   | Take me to a seat where I can wait for that Hispalenic swine. |
| LUNARES | Don't follow you. |
| MAX   | Hispalis is Seville. |
| LUNARES | It's all Greek to me. I was born on the slum side of town.[158] |
| MAX   | What age are you? |
| LUNARES | I don't know how old I am. |
| MAX   | Is this your usual patch? |
| LUNARES | Mostly. |
| MAX   | At least, you earn an honest living! |
| LUNARES | You've no idea how hard that is! I'm very careful what I do. Old Gossip Guts talked to me about going to a house. High-class house too! But I wouldn't go... Just lying on your back, not for me... I keep my jampot for the bloke who can talk me into it. Why don't you have a go? |
| MAX   | I haven't got enough time. |
| LUNARES | Just try and see how far you get. I'm beginning to fancy you, I can tell you. |
| MAX   | And I'm telling you I'm a poet with no money. |
| LUNARES | Hey, you wouldn't be the one who made up them rhymes about Joselito the matador,[159] would you? |
| MAX   | The very one! |
| LUNARES | Honest? |
| MAX   | Honest. |
| LUNARES | Say them. |
| MAX   | I don't remember them. |
| LUNARES | 'Cos you didn't make 'em up out of your own loaf. No kidding, which ones did you make? |
| MAX   | The ones about El Espartero.[160] |
| LUNARES | Can you remember them? |
| MAX   | And I can sing them like a gypsy! |
| LUNARES | I bet you can't! |
| MAX   | If I had a guitar...! |
| LUNARES | Can you play? |
| MAX   | I'm not blind for nothing, you know. |
| LUNARES | I really fancy you. |
| MAX   | I've got no money. |
| LUNARES | Just pay for the bed and we'll call it quits. If you're satisfied and want to treat me to coffee and doughnuts, I wouldn't say no. |

*Máximo Estrella, with a blind man's touch, passes him hands round the oval of her face, her throat and shoulders. The tart giggles with a vestige of ticklishness and sensuality. She removes a gypsy comb from her bun and, using it to comb out her locks, redoubles her laughter and shakes down her hair.*

LA LUNARES  ¿Quieres saber como soy? ¡Soy muy negra y muy fea!
MAX        ¡No lo pareces! Debes tener quince años.
LA LUNARES  Esos mismos tendré. Ya pasa de tres que me visita el nuncio.
           No lo pienses más y vamos. Aquí cerca hay una casa muy
           decente.
MAX        ¿Y cumplirás tu palabra?
LA LUNARES  ¿Cuála? ¿Dejar que te comas el pan de higos? ¡No me pareces
           bastante flamenco! ¡Qué mano tienes! No me palpes más la
           cara. Pálpame el cuerpo.
MAX        ¿Eres pelinegra?
LA LUNARES  ¡Lo soy!
MAX        Hueles a nardos.
LA LUNARES  Porque los he vendido.
MAX        ¿Cómo tienes los ojos?
LA LUNARES  ¿No lo adivinas?
MAX        ¿Verdes?
LA LUNARES  Como la Pastora Imperio. Toda yo parezco una gitana.

*De la oscuridad surge la brasa de un cigarro y la tos asmática de Don Latino.*
*Remotamente, sobre el asfalto sonoro, se acompasa el trote de una patrulla de*
*Caballería. Los focos de un auto. El farol de un sereno. El quicio de una verja.*
*Una sombra clandestina. El rostro albayalde de otra vieja peripatética.*
*Diferentes sombras.*

# Escena Undécima

*Una calle del Madrid austriaco. Las tapias de un convento. Un casón de*
*nobles. Las luces de una taberna. Un grupo consternado de vecinas, en la*
*acera. Una mujer, despechugada y ronca, tiene en los brazos a su niño muerto,*
*la sien traspasada por el agujero de una bala. Max Estrella y Don Latino hacen*
*un alto.*

MAX             También aquí se pisan cristales rotos.
DON LATINO      ¡La zurra ha sido buena!
MAX             ¡Canallas!... ¡Todos!... ¡Y los primeros nosotros, los poetas!
DON LATINO      ¡Se vive de milagro!
LA MADRE DEL NIÑO  ¡Maricas, cobardes! ¡El fuego del Infierno os abrase
                las negras entrañas! ¡Maricas, cobardes!
MAX             ¿Qué sucede, Latino? ¿Quién llora? ¿Quién grita con tal
                rabia?
DON LATINO      Una verdulera, que tiene a su chico muerto en los brazos.
MAX             ¡Me ha estremecido esa voz trágica!

| | |
|---|---|
| LUNARES | Do you want to know what I look like? I'm all dark-skinned and ugly. |
| MAX | It doesn't feel like it. You must be about fifteen years old. |
| LUNARES | I must be about that. It's more than three years since I started the curse.[161] Anyway, stop thinking about it and let's go. There's a very decent house just down the road. |
| MAX | And you'll keep your word? |
| LUNARES | Which one? About tasting my jampot, you mean? You don't seem much like a gypsy to me. You haven't got much of a hand either! Stop feeling my face. Feel my body. |
| MAX | Is your hair black? |
| LUNARES | It is. |
| MAX | You smell of flowers. |
| LUNARES | That's 'cos I've been selling them. |
| MAX | What colour are your eyes? |
| LUNARES | Can't you guess? |
| MAX | Green? |
| LUNARES | All black and green-eyed.[162] I'm gypsy all over. |

*The red glow of a cigar and the asthmatic cough of Don Latino come out of the darkness. In the distance, the hooves of the mounted police patrol clatter rhythmically on the asphalt. The headlights of a car. The lantern of a nightwatchman. The squeak of a gate hinge. A furtive shadow. The white-lead mask of another peripatetic drab. Different shadows.*

# Scene Eleven

*A street in the old Austrian quarter of Madrid.[163] Walls surrounding a convent. Façade of an aristocratic mansion. The lights of a tavern. On the pavement, a distraught gathering of local people. A woman, with uncovered breast and her voice hoarse from shouting, is holding her dead child in her arms with a bullet-hole through its temple. Max Estrella and Don Latino come to a halt.*

| | |
|---|---|
| MAX | We're treading on broken glass again. |
| DON LATINO | They've had a real set-to here! |
| MAX | Barbarian rabble! All of them! All of us! The poets ... we're the greatest rabble of the lot! |
| DON LATINO | It's a miracle we're still alive! |
| MOTHER OF CHILD | Bastards! Cowards! May the fires of Hell burn your black hearts! Bastards! Cowards! |
| MAX | What's happening, Latino? Who's crying? Who's shouting with such rage? |
| DON LATINO | Some costermonger with a dead child in her arms. |
| MAX | That voice, that grief, sends a shudder down my spine! |

LA MADRE DEL NIÑO  ¡Sicarios! ¡Asesinos de criaturas!
EL EMPEÑISTA  Está con algún trastorno, y no mide palabras.
EL GUARDIA  La Autoridad también se hace el cargo.
EL TABERNERO  Son desgracias inevitables para el restablecimiento del orden.
EL EMPEÑISTA  Las turbas anárquicas me han destrozado el escaparate.
LA PORTERA  ¿Cómo no anduvo usted más vivo en echar los cierres?
EL EMPEÑISTA  Me tomó el tumulto fuera de casa. Supongo que se acordará el pago de daños a la propiedad privada.
EL TABERNERO  El pueblo que roba en los establecimientos públicos, donde se le abastece, es un pueblo sin ideales patrios.
LA MADRE DEL NIÑO  ¡Verdugos del hijo de mis entrañas!
UN ALBAÑIL  El pueblo tiene hambre.
EL EMPEÑISTA  Y mucha soberbia.
LA MADRE DEL NIÑO  ¡Maricas, cobardes!
UNA VIEJA  ¡Ten prudencia, Romualda!
LA MADRE DEL NIÑO  ¡Que me maten como a este rosal de Mayo!
LA TRAPERA  ¡Un inocente sin culpa! ¡Hay que considerarlo!
EL TABERNERO  Siempre saldréis diciendo que no hubo los toques de Ordenanza.
EL RETIRADO  Yo los he oído.
LA MADRE DEL NIÑO  ¡Mentira!
EL RETIRADO  Mi palabra es sagrada.
EL EMPEÑISTA  El dolor te enloquece, Romualda.
LA MADRE DEL NIÑO  ¡Asesinos! ¡Veros es ver al verdugo!
EL RETIRADO  El Principio de Autoridad es inexorable.
EL ALBAÑIL  Con los pobres. Se ha matado, por defender al comercio, que nos chupa la sangre.
EL TABERNERO  Y que paga sus contribuciones, no hay que olvidarlo.
EL EMPEÑISTA  El comercio honrado no chupa la sangre de nadie.
LA PORTERA  ¡Nos quejamos de vicio!
EL ALBAÑIL  La vida del proletario no representa nada para el Gobierno.
MAX  Latino, sácame de este círculo infernal.

*Llega un tableteo de fusilada. El grupo se mueve en confusa y medrosa alerta. Descuella el grito ronco de la mujer, que al ruido de las descargas aprieta a su niño muerto en los brazos.*

LA MADRE DEL NIÑO  ¡Negros fusiles, matadme también con vuestros plomos!
MAX  Esa voz me traspasa.
LA MADRE DEL NIÑO  ¡Que tan fría, boca de nardo!
MAX  ¡Jamás oí voz con esa cólera trágica!
DON LATINO  Hay mucho de teatro.
MAX  ¡Imbécil!

MOTHER OF CHILD  Killers! Child murderers!

PAWNBROKER  She is rather upset and not weighing her words.

POLICEMAN  The Authorities are fully aware of the situation.

BAR OWNER  These misfortunes are inevitable in the restoration of law and order.

PAWNBROKER  The anarchist mobs have wrecked my shop window.

CONCIERGE  Why didn't you get your shutters down quicker!

PAWNBROKER  I was out when the rioting started. I assume there will be compensation for damage to private property.

BAR OWNER  A people that loots any establishment which serves the public is a people without national ideals.

MOTHER OF CHILD  Butchers of my little baby!

BRICKLAYER  The people are hungry!

PAWNBROKER  And too proud for their own good!

MOTHER OF CHILD  Bastards! Cowards!

OLD WOMAN  Mind what you're saying, Romualda!

MOTHER OF CHILD  Let them kill me, like my innocent little lamb!

RAG AND BONE WOMAN  That's true enough. Poor innocent soul, what harm had he done?

BAR OWNER  I suppose you'll claim that the regulation warnings weren't given.

RETIRED OFFICER  I heard them.

MOTHER OF CHILD  Liar!

RETIRED OFFICER  My word as an officer is sacred.

PAWNBROKER  The grief is turning your mind, Romualda.

MOTHER OF CHILD  Murderers! You are the butchers! You!

RETIRED OFFICER  The Rule of Law is absolute and unswerving.

BRICKLAYER  Only for the poor. They shoot us down defending the commercial interests that suck us dry.

BAR OWNER  And pay their taxes. Don't you forget it!

PAWNBROKER  Honest-to-goodness business never sucks anybody dry.

CONCIERGE  No, we just complain for the sake of it!

BRICKLAYER  The Government doesn't care twopence how the working man lives.

MAX  For God's sake, Latino, get me out of this infernal circle!

*A volley of rifle fire. The group disperses amidst alarm and confusion. At the sound of the firing, the woman presses her dead child to her and raises her broken cry.*

MOTHER OF CHILD  Come on then, you black bastard rifles! Kill me with your bullets!

MAX  That voice goes through me like a knife.

MOTHER OF CHILD  How cold your lips are, my little flower!

MAX  I never heard a voice with such tragic anger!

DON LATINO  There's a good deal of play-acting in all this!

MAX  Imbecile!

*El farol, el chuzo, la caperuza del sereno, bajan con un trote de madreñas por la acera.*

EL EMPEÑISTA  ¿Qué ha sido, sereno?
EL SERENO      Un preso que ha intentado fugarse.
MAX            Latino, ya no puedo gritar... ¡Me muero de rabia!... Estoy
               mascando ortigas. Ese muerto sabía su fin... No le asustaba,
               pero temía el tormento... La Leyenda Negra, en estos días
               menguados, es la Historia de España. Nuestra vida es un
               círculo dantesco. Rabia y vergüenza. Me muero de hambre,
               satisfecho de no haber llevado una triste velilla en la trágica
               mojiganga. ¿Has oído los comentarios de esa gente, viejo
               canalla? Tú eres como ellos. Peor que ellos, porque no tienes
               una peseta y propagas la mala literatura, por entregas. Latino,
               vil corredor de aventuras insulsas, llévame al Viaducto. Te
               invito a regenerarte con un vuelo.
DON LATINO     ¡Max, no te pongas estupendo!

## Escena Duodécima

*Rinconada en costanilla y una iglesia barroca por fondo. Sobre las campanas negras, la luna clara. Don Latino y Max Estrella filosofan sentados en el quicio de una puerta. A lo largo de su coloquio, se torna lívido el cielo. En el alero de la iglesia pían algunos pájaros. Remotos albores de amanecida. Ya se han ido los serenos, pero aún están las puertas cerradas. Despiertan las porteras.*

MAX            ¿Debe estar amaneciendo?
DON LATINO     Así es.
MAX            ¡Y qué frío!
DON LATINO     Vamos a dar unos pasos.
MAX            Ayúdame, que no puedo levantarme. ¡Estoy aterido!
DON LATINO     ¡Mira que haber empeñado la capa!
MAX            Préstame tu carrik, Latino.
DON LATINO     ¡Max, eres fantástico!
MAX            Ayúdame a ponerme en pie.
DON LATINO     ¡Arriba, carcunda!
MAX            ¡No me tengo!
DON LATINO     ¡Qué tuno eres!
MAX            ¡Idiota!
DON LATINO     ¡La verdad es que tienes una fisonomía algo rara!

*With a clip-clop of clogs, the lantern, staff and pointed hood of the Nightwatchman come hurrying along the pavement.*

PAWNBROKER  What was that, Nightwatchman?
NIGHTWATCHMAN  A prisoner attempting to escape.
MAX　　　　　Latino, I'm chewing on nettles... I'm dying of rage... but I can't even scream any more. That man knew what his end would be. He wasn't afraid of death but he feared torture... In these degenerate times, the Black Legend of Spain is no more than the literal truth of its history. Our life is a circle of Dante's *Inferno*. The circle of Anger and Shame. At least, I shall die of hunger, knowing that I didn't carry a candle in this tragic carnival procession.[164] Did you hear what they were saying, you old louse? You're as bad as they are. Worse because you haven't got a bean and you propagate lousy literature by instalments. Latino, vile pedlar of romantic rubbish, lead on to the Viaduct.[165] I invite you to be reborn in one spectacular leap!
DON LATINO  Max, please don't be so magnificent!

# Scene Twelve

*Corner of a narrow, sloping street with a baroque church in the background. Dark bells against a bright moonlit sky. Don Latino and Max Estrella philosophize, huddled in the corner of a doorway. During their conversation, the sky slowly takes on the pale light of dawn. On the eaves of the church some birds are chirping. Distant glimmers of daybreak. The nightwatchmen have gone home, though the street doors remain locked. The concierges are beginning to stir.*

MAX　　　　　It must be getting light.
DON LATINO  So it is.
MAX　　　　　It's so cold!
DON LATINO  Let's stretch our legs a bit.
MAX　　　　　Give me a hand, I can't get up. I'm frozen stiff.
DON LATINO  You really shouldn't have pawned your cape!
MAX　　　　　Lend me your overcoat, Latino.
DON LATINO  Max, your imagination is running wild again!
MAX　　　　　Help me to get on my feet.
DON LATINO  Upsa-daisy, you old reactionary![166]
MAX　　　　　My legs won't hold me!
DON LATINO  Come off it, you old fraud!
MAX　　　　　Idiot!
DON LATINO  True though, you do look somewhat green about the gills!

MAX                ¡Don Latino de Hispalis, grotesco personaje, te inmortalizaré en una novela!
DON LATINO   Una tragedia, Max.
MAX                La tragedia nuestra no es tragedia.
DON LATINO   ¡Pues algo será!
MAX                El Esperpento.
DON LATINO   No tuerzas la boca, Max.
MAX                ¡Me estoy helando!
DON LATINO   Levántate. Vamos a caminar.
MAX                No puedo.
DON LATINO   Deja esa farsa. Vamos a caminar.
MAX                Échame el aliento. ¿Adónde te has ido, Latino?
DON LATINO   Estoy a tu lado.
MAX                Como te has convertido en buey, no podía reconocerte. Échame el aliento, ilustre buey del pesebre belenita. ¡Muge, Latino! Tú eres el cabestro, y si muges vendrá el Buey Apis. Le torearemos.
DON LATINO   Me estás asustando. Debías dejar esa broma.
MAX                Los ultraístas son unos farsantes. El esperpentismo lo ha inventado Goya. Los héroes clásicos han ido a pasearse en el callejón del Gato.
DON LATINO   ¡Estás completamente curda!
MAX                Los héroes clásicos reflejados en los espejos cóncavos dan el Esperpento. El sentido trágico de la vida española sólo puede darse con una estética sistemáticamente deformada.
DON LATINO   ¡Miau! ¡Te estás contagiando!
MAX                España es una deformación grotesca de la civilización europea.
DON LATINO   ¡Pudiera! Yo me inhibo.
MAX                Las imágenes más bellas en un espejo cóncavo son absurdas.
DON LATINO   Conforme. Pero a mí me divierte mirarme en los espejos de la calle del Gato.
MAX                Y a mí. La deformación deja de serlo cuando está sujeta a una matemática perfecta. Mi estética actual es transformar con matemática de espejo cóncavo las normas clásicas.
DON LATINO   ¿Y dónde está el espejo?
MAX                En el fondo del vaso.
DON LATINO   ¡Eres genial! ¡Me quito el cráneo!
MAX                Latino, deformemos la expresión en el mismo espejo que nos deforma las caras y toda la vida miserable de España.
DON LATINO   Nos mudaremos al callejón del Gato.

MAX             Don Latino de Hispalis, grotesque specimen of the species, I
                shall immortalize you in a novel!
DON LATINO      In a tragedy, surely Max!
MAX             Our tragedy is not a tragedy.
DON LATINO      What is it then? It must be something!
MAX             A travesty.[167]
DON LATINO      Stop twisting your mouth, Max!
MAX             I'm freezing!
DON LATINO      Up you get. Let's walk.
MAX             I can't.
DON LATINO      Stop fooling around. Let's walk.
MAX             Warm me with your breath. Where have you gone, Latino?
DON LATINO      I'm here beside you.
MAX             You've changed into an ox, so I couldn't recognize you.
                Breathe on me, illustrious ox from the stall of Bethlehem.
                Low, Latino! You are the bell-ox, and if you low perhaps Bull
                Apis will come. We'll challenge him in the arena.[168]
DON LATINO      Now you're beginning to alarm me. The joke's gone far
                enough.
MAX             These avant-garde merchants[169] are full of pretentious twaddle.
                Travesty in art, the artistic grotesque, was invented by Goya.[170]
                All our cherished classical heroes have wandered into a hall of
                distorting mirrors.[171]
DON LATINO      You're completely stoned!
MAX             Classical heroes travestied in concave mirrors! That's the only
                way to express the tragic sense of Spanish life. It needs an
                aesthetic criterion which distorts systematically.
DON LATINO      Get away with you! The twaddle is beginning to rub off on
                you!
MAX             Spain is a travesty of European civilization.[172]
DON LATINO      Maybe it is. What do I care!
MAX             Reflected in a concave mirror, even the most beautiful images
                become absurd.
DON LATINO      Granted. But I happen to enjoy looking at myself in fairground
                mirrors.
MAX             So do I. Because distortion determined by strict mathematical
                norms is no longer distortion. That's my aesthetic creed from
                now on: to transform all the classical norms with the strictly
                mathematical impartiality of a concave mirror.
DON LATINO      And where do you find your mirror?
MAX             At the bottom of a glass.[173]
DON LATINO      You're a genius! I take my head off to you!
MAX             Latino, we must distort our expression of reality in the same
                mirrors that distort our reflections and the whole miserable
                charade of Spanish life.
DON LATINO      We'll go and live in an amusement park.

| | |
|---|---|
| MAX | Vamos a ver qué palacio está desalquilado. Arrímame a la pared. ¡Sacúdeme! |
| DON LATINO | No tuerzas la boca. |
| MAX | Es nervioso. ¡Ni me entero! |
| DON LATINO | ¡Te traes una guasa! |
| MAX | Préstame tu carrik. |
| DON LATINO | ¡Mira cómo me he quedado de un aire! |
| MAX | No me siento las manos y me duelen las uñas. ¡Estoy muy malo! |
| DON LATINO | Quieres conmoverme, para luego tomarme la coleta. |
| MAX | Idiota, llévame a la puerta de mi casa y déjame morir en paz. |
| DON LATINO | La verdad sea dicha, no madrugan en nuestro barrio. |
| MAX | Llama. |

*Don Latino de Hispalis, volviéndose de espaldas, comienza a cocear en la puerta. El eco de los golpes tolondrea por el ámbito lívido de la costanilla, y como en respuesta a una provocación, el reloj de la iglesia da cinco campanadas bajo el gallo de la veleta.*

| | |
|---|---|
| MAX | ¡Latino! |
| DON LATINO | ¿Qué antojas? ¡Deja la mueca! |
| MAX | ¡Si Collet estuviese despierta!... Ponme en pie para darle una voz. |
| DON LATINO | No llega tu voz a ese quinto cielo. |
| MAX | ¡Collet! ¡Me estoy aburriendo! |
| DON LATINO | No olvides al compañero. |
| MAX | Latino, me parece que recobro la vista. ¿Pero cómo hemos venido a este entierro? ¡Esa apoteosis es de París! ¡Estamos en el entierro de Víctor Hugo! ¿Oye, Latino, pero cómo vamos nosotros presidiendo? |
| DON LATINO | No te alucines, Max. |
| MAX | Es incomprensible cómo veo. |
| DON LATINO | Ya sabes que has tenido esa misma ilusión otras veces. |
| MAX | ¿A quién enterramos, Latino? |
| DON LATINO | Es un secreto que debemos ignorar. |
| MAX | ¡Cómo brilla el sol en las carrozas! |
| DON LATINO | Max, si todo cuanto dices no fuese una broma, tendría una significación teosófica... En un entierro presidido por mí, yo debo ser el muerto... Pero por esas coronas, me inclino a pensar que el muerto eres tú. |
| MAX | Voy a complacerte. Para quitarte el miedo del augurio, me acuesto a la espera. ¡Yo soy el muerto! ¿Qué dirá mañana esa canalla de los periódicos? se preguntaba el paria catalán. |

| MAX | Let's go and see if there's a vacant palace to let. Prop me up against the wall. Shake me! |
| DON LATINO | Don't twist your mouth. |
| MAX | It's a nervous tic. I don't even know I'm doing it. |
| DON LATINO | You're having a fine game, aren't you? |
| MAX | Lend me your overcoat. |
| DON LATINO | Sorry, I've caught a chill and gone deaf. |
| MAX | My hands have gone numb and my fingernails hurt. I'm a sick man! |
| DON LATINO | Pull the other leg! You're just trying to make me feel sorry for you. |
| MAX | Idiot, take me home and let me die in peace. |
| DON LATINO | The fact is, there are very few early risers in our neighbourhood. |
| MAX | Knock on the door. |

*Don Latino de Hispalis, with his back to the door, begins to kick against it. The blows reverberate through the gleamy silence of the street and, as if in reply to a provocation, the church clock strikes five under its weather vane.*

| MAX | Latino! |
| DON LATINO | Now what? Stop pulling that face! |
| MAX | Supposing Collet were awake!... Get me on my feet so that I can give her a shout. |
| DON LATINO | Your voice will never reach the fifth floor. |
| MAX | Collet! I'm getting bored stiff down here! |
| DON LATINO | Your old pal's here, remember! |
| MAX | Latino, I think my sight is coming back. But what are we doing at this funeral? This is an apotheosis worthy of Paris! This is like the funeral of Victor Hugo.[174] But, just a minute, Latino. Why are we presiding? |
| DON LATINO | Don't start getting hallucinations, Max. |
| MAX | It's uncanny how well I can see! |
| DON LATINO | You know you've had these delusions before. |
| MAX | Who is being buried, Latino? |
| DON LATINO | That is a secret we should not seek to know. |
| MAX | Just look at those carriages gleaming in the sun! |
| DON LATINO | Max, if all you are saying weren't just a big hoax, it could have a theosophical significance... In a funeral presided over by me, I should be the corpse. But judging by those wreaths over there, I'm inclined to think that the body is yours. |
| MAX | I'll do you a favour. To set your mind at rest, I'll lie down and wait. I am the corpse! And what will those bastards of the press say tomorrow? That's what the Catalan prisoner was asking himself.[175] |

*Máximo Estrella se tiende en el umbral de su puerta. Cruza la costanilla un perro golfo que corre en zigzag. En el centro, encoge la pata y se orina. El ojo legañoso, como un poeta, levantado al azul de la última estrella.*

| | |
|---|---|
| MAX | Latino, entona el gori-gori. |
| DON LATINO | Si continúas con esa broma macabra, te abandono. |
| MAX | Yo soy el que se va para siempre. |
| DON LATINO | Incorpórate, Max. Vamos a caminar. |
| MAX | Estoy muerto. |
| DON LATINO | ¡Que me estás asustando! Max, vamos a caminar. Incórporate, ¡no tuerzas la boca, condenado! ¡Max! ¡Max! ¡Condenado, responde! |
| MAX | Los muertos no hablan. |
| DON LATINO | Definitivamente, te dejo. |
| MAX | ¡Buenas noches! |

*Don Latino de Hispalis se sopla los dedos arrecidos y camina unos pasos encorvándose bajo su carrik pingón, orlado de cascarrias. Con una tos gruñona retorna al lado de Max Estrella. Procura incorporarle hablándole a la oreja.*

DON LATINO    Max, estás completamente borracho y sería un crimen dejarte la cartera encima, para que te la roben. Max, me llevo tu cartera y te la devolveré mañana.

*Finalmente se eleva tras de la puerta la voz achulada de una vecina. Resuenan pasos dentro del zaguán. Don Latino se cuela por un callejón.*

| | |
|---|---|
| LA VOZ DE LA VECINA | ¡Señá Flora! ¡Señá Flora! Se le han apegado a usted las mantas de la cama. |
| LA VOZ DE LA PORTERA | ¿Quién es? Esperarse que encuentre la caja de mixtos. |
| LA VECINA | ¡Señá Flora! |
| LA PORTERA | Ahora salgo. ¿Quién es? |
| LA VECINA | ¡Está usted marmota! ¿Quién será? ¡La Cuca, que se camina al lavadero! |
| LA PORTERA | ¡Ay, qué centella de mixtos! ¿Son horas? |
| LA VECINA | ¡Son horas y pasan de serlo! |

*Se oye el paso cansino de una mujer en chanclas. Sigue el murmullo de las voces. Rechina la cerradura y aparecen en el hueco de la puerta dos mujeres. La una, canosa, viva y agalgada, con un saco de ropa cargado sobre la cadera. La otra, jamona, refajo colorado, pañuelo pingón sobre los hombros, greñas y chancletas. El cuerpo del bohemio resbala y queda acostado sobre el umbral al abrirse la puerta.*

| | |
|---|---|
| LA VECINA | ¡Santísimo Cristo, un hombre muerto! |
| LA PORTERA | Es Don Max el poeta, que la ha pescado. |

*Máximo Estrella lies down on the doorstep. A vagrant dog zigzags across the street. He stops half-way, cocks his hind leg and urinates, his bleary eyes, like a poet's, raised towards the last star before dawn.*

MAX            Latino, intone a solemn dirge.
DON LATINO  If you persist in this macabre farce, I'm going.
MAX            I am the one who is going, forever.
DON LATINO  Sit up, Max. Let's walk a bit.
MAX            I am dead.
DON LATINO  You're frightening me now! Come on, Max, let's walk a bit.
                Sit up, and don't twist your mouth, damn you! Max! Max!
                Answer me, damn you!
MAX            Dead men don't talk.
DON LATINO  Once and for all, I'm leaving you.
MAX            Good night!

*Don Latino de Hispalis blows on his frozen fingers and takes a few paces hunched under his ragged, mud-spattered overcoat. With a dry cough, he returns to Max Estrella's side. He tries to prop him up, while talking into his ear.*

DON LATINO  Max, you are completely drunk and it would be a crime to
                leave your wallet on you. Somebody might rob you. Max, I'm
                taking your wallet. I'll return it tomorrow.

*At length the sound of a raucous female voice is heard from behind the door. Footsteps echo in the hallway. Don Latino slides away down a side street.*

NEIGHBOUR'S VOICE  Flora! Flora! Are you stuck to the bedsheets this
                morning?
VOICE OF CONCIERGE  Who's that? Hang on while I find a box of matches.
NEIGHBOUR  Flora!
CONCIERGE   I'm coming! Who is it?
NEIGHBOUR   You're half asleep! Who would it be now? It's Cuca, off to
                the wash-house!
CONCIERGE   Where are those blasted matches! Is it time?
NEIGHBOUR   It was time hours ago!

*The weary footsteps of a woman in carpet slippers. The murmur of voices continues. The key grates in the lock and two women appear in the doorway. One of them, grey-haired, agile and lean as a whippet, with a bundle of washing on her hip. The other, brawny and dishevelled, dressed in a red skirt, frayed headscarf around her shoulders and slippers. The body of the bohemian slips and falls across the threshold as the door opens.*

NEIGHBOUR   Holy Mother of God! A dead man!
CONCIERGE   It's only Don Max the poet. Dead drunk more like.

LA VECINA     ¡Está del color de la cera!

LA PORTERA     Cuca, por tu alma, quédate a la mira un instante, mientras subo el aviso a Madama Collet.

*La Portera sube la escalera chancleando. Se la oye renegar. La Cuca, viéndose sola, con aire medroso, toca las manos del bohemio y luego se inclina a mirarle los ojos entreabiertos bajo la frente lívida.*

LA VECINA     ¡Santísimo Señor! ¡Esto no lo dimana la bebida! ¡La muerte talmente representa! ¡Señá Flora! ¡Señá Flora! ¡Que no puedo demorarme! ¡Ya se me voló un cuarto de día! ¡Que se queda esto a la vindicta pública, señá Flora! ¡Propia la muerte!

# Escena Decimatercia

*Velorio en un sotabanco. Madama Collet y Claudinita, desgreñadas y macilentas, lloran al muerto, ya tendido en la angostura de la caja, amortajado con una sábana, entre cuatro velas. Astillando una tabla, el brillo de un clavo aguza su punta sobre la sien inerme. La caja, embetunada de luto por fuera, y por dentro, de tablas de pino sin labrar ni pintar, tiene una sórdida esterilla que amarillea. Está posada sobre las baldosas, de esquina a esquina, y las dos mujeres, que lloran en los ángulos, tienen en las manos cruzadas el reflejo de las velas. Dorio de Gadex, Clarinito y Pérez, arrimados a la pared, son tres fúnebres fantoches en hilera. Repentinamente, entrometiéndose en el duelo, cloquea un rajado repique, la campanilla de la escalera.*

DORIO DE GADEX    A las cuatro viene la funeraria.

CLARINITO     No puede ser esa hora.

DORIO DE GADEX    ¿Usted no tendrá reloj, Madama Collet?

MADAMA COLLET    ¡Que no me lo lleven todavía! ¡Que no me lo lleven!

PÉREZ     No puede ser la funeraria.

DORIO DE GADEX    ¡Ninguno tiene reloj! ¡No hay duda que somos unos potentados!

*Claudinita, con andar cansado, trompicando, ha salido para abrir la puerta. Se oye rumor de voces, y la tos de Don Latino de Hispalis. La tos clásica del tabaco y del aguardiente.*

DON LATINO    ¡Ha muerto el Genio! ¡No llores, hija mía! ¡Ha muerto y no ha muerto! ... ¡El Genio es inmortal!... ¡Consuélate, Claudinita, porque eres la hija del primer poeta español! ¡Que te sirva de consuelo saber que eres la hija de

NEIGHBOUR    His face is like wax!

CONCIERGE    Cuca, be a good soul and keep an eye on things while I pop up and tell Madama Collet.

*The concierge goes up the staircase, her slippers slapping on the steps. She can be heard muttering and cursing. Cuca, left alone, fearfully touches the bohemian's hands and then leans over and peers into his eyes, half-closed under his pale forehead.*

NEIGHBOUR    Holy God! It's not the drink at all that's done this! It's the face of death itself! Flora! Flora! I can't afford the time. I've lost half the day as it is! The public authorities can take care of this, Flora! It's the face of death itself!

# Scene Thirteen

*Funeral wake in a garret. Madama Collet and Claudinita, drawn and dishevelled, mourn the deceased, who now lies wrapped in a sheet in a narrow coffin surrounded by four candles. The sharp, bright tip of a nail, splintering the wood, points at his unprotected temple.*[176] *The coffin, stained black on the outside and revealing on the inside its rough, unpainted pine boards, is lined only by a squalid, yellowing mat. It lies diagonally across the tiles, while the two women weep in the corners of the room with the candlelight reflecting on their crossed hands. Dorio de Gadex, Clarinito and Pérez are lined up against the wall like three funereal puppets. The discordant clatter of the doorbell on the landing abruptly interrupts the silent weeping.*

DORIO DE GADEX    The undertaker is due at four.

CLARINITO    It can't be that time yet.

DORIO DE GADEX    I don't suppose you have a watch, Madama Collet?

MADAMA COLLET    Don't let them take him away yet!  Don't let them take him away!

PEREZ    It can't be the undertaker.

DORIO DE GADEX    So no one has a watch! We *are* a crew of capitalists and no mistake!

*Faltering a little, Claudinita shuffles wearily out of the room to answer the door. There is a murmur of voices, followed by the cough of Don Latino de Hispalis, with its traditional blend of tabacco and cheap brandy.*

DON LATINO    The Genius is dead! Weep not, my child! He has died and yet he has not died!... Genius is immortal! Console yourself, Claudinita, in the knowledge that you are the daughter of the greatest poet in Spain! Be comforted that you are the daughter

Victor Hugo! ¡Una huérfana ilustre! ¡Déjame que te abrace!
CLAUDINITA  ¡Usted está borracho!
DON LATINO  Lo parezco. Sin duda lo parezco. ¡Es el dolor!
CLAUDINITA  ¡Si tumba el vaho de aguardiente!
DON LATINO  ¡Es el dolor! ¡Un efecto del dolor, estudiado científicamente por los alemanes!

*Don Latino tambaléase en la puerta, con el cartapacio de las revistas en bandolera y el perrillo sin rabo y sin orejas, entre las cañotas. Trae los espejuelos alzados sobre la frente y se limpia los ojos chispones con un pañuelo mugriento.*

CLAUDINITA  Viene a dos velas.
DORIO DE GADEX  Para el funeral. ¡Siempre correcto!
DON LATINO  Max, hermano mío, si menor en años...
DORIO DE GADEX  Mayor en prez. Nos adivinamos.
DON LATINO  ¡Justamente! Tú lo has dicho, bellaco.
DORIO DE GADEX  Antes lo había dicho el maestro.
DON LATINO  ¡Madama Collet, es usted una viuda ilustre, y en medio de su intenso dolor debe usted sentirse orgullosa de haber sido la compañera del primer poeta español! ¡Murió pobre, como debe morir el Genio! ¡Max, ya no tienes una palabra para tu perro fiel! ¡Max, hermano mío, si menor en años, mayor en...
DORIO DE GADEX  Prez!
DON LATINO  Ya podías haberme dejado terminar, majadero. ¡Jóvenes modernistas, ha muerto el maestro, y os llamáis todos de tú en el Parnaso Hispano-Americano! ¡Yo tenía apostado con este cadáver frío sobre cuál de los dos emprendería primero el viaje, y me ha vencido en esto como en todo! ¡Cuántas veces cruzamos la misma apuesta! ¿Te acuerdas, hermano? ¡Te has muerto de hambre, como yo voy a morir, como moriremos todos los españoles dignos! ¡Te habían cerrado todas las puertas, y te has vengado muriéndote de hambre! ¡Bien hecho! ¡Que caiga esa vergüenza sobre los cabrones de la Academia! ¡En España es un delito el talento!

*Don Latino se dobla y besa la frente del muerto. El perrillo, a los pies de la caja, entre el reflejo inquietante de las velas, agita el muñón del rabo. Madama Collet levanta la cabeza con un gesto doloroso dirigido a los tres fantoches en hilera.*

MADAMA COLLET  ¡Por Dios, llévenselo ustedes al pasillo!

of Victor Hugo! An illustrious orphan! Allow me to embrace you!

CLAUDINITA  You're drunk!

DON LATINO  It only looks that way. Indubitably, I appear to be drunk. It's the grief!

CLAUDINITA  Your breath would stop a tram!

DON LATINO  It's the grief! An effect of grief, scientifically studied by the Germans!

*Don Latino totters in the doorway with his satchel full of magazines slung across his back and his tailless, earless little dog between his spindly legs. With his spectacles raised on to his forehead, he wipes his beady eyes with a grimy handkerchief.*

CLAUDINITA  All lit up, like a candle in the wind.[177]

DORIO DE GADEX  Very appropriate for a funeral. Correct to the last.

DON LATINO  Max, my brother, though younger in years...

DORIO DE GADEX  ...the greater in glory! We read each other like a book.

DON LATINO  Exactly! You said it, my scurvy friend!

DORIO DE GADEX  The maestro said it first.

DON LATINO  Madama Collet, you are an illustrious widow, and in the midst of your intense grief, you must feel proud to have been the companion of the greatest Spanish poet! He died a poor man, as is fitting for a genius! Max, have you no word of comfort for your faithful dog! Max, my brother, though younger in years, the greater in...

DORIO DE GADEX  ...glory!

DON LATINO  You might have let me finish, buffoon! Young Modernists, your maestro and leader is dead, leaving behind only the young and inexperienced in the Spanish-American Parnassus! I had a wager with this lifeless corpse as to which of us would be first to embark on the eternal journey and he has defeated me in this, as in everything else! How many times we made that same wager! Do you remember, my brother? You died of hunger, as I shall die, as all Spaniards worthy of the name will die! They slammed all the doors in your face and you have avenged yourself by dying of hunger! Well done! Let this shame fall on those bastards of the Academy! In Spain, being found in the possession of talent is a criminal offence!

*Don Latino bends over and kisses the dead man on the forehead. The little dog, at the foot of the coffin, wags its stump in the flickering light of the candles. Madama Collet raises her head and, with a pained expression, looks towards the row of puppets.*

MADAMA COLLET  For God's sake, take him out into the passage!

DORIO DE GADEX  Habrá que darle amoniaco. ¡La trae de alivio!
CLAUDINITA  ¡Pues que la duerma! ¡Le tengo una hincha!
DON LATINO  ¡Claudinita! ¡Flor temprana!
CLAUDINITA  ¡Si papá no sale ayer tarde, está vivo!
DON LATINO  ¡Claudinita, me acusas injustamente! ¡Estás ofuscada por el dolor!
CLAUDINITA  ¡Golfo! ¡Siempre estorbando!
DON LATINO  ¡Yo sé que tú me quieres!
DORIO DE GADEX  Vamos a darnos unas vueltas en el corredor, Don Latino.
DON LATINO  ¡Vamos! ¡Esta escena es demasiado dolorosa!
DORIO DE GADEX  Pues no la prolonguemos.

*Dorio de Gadex empuja al encurdado vejete y le va llevando hacia la puerta. El perrillo salta por encima de la caja y los sigue, dejando en el salto torcida una vela. En la fila de fantoches pegados a la pared queda un hueco lleno de sugestiones.*

DON LATINO  Te convido a unas tintas. ¿Qué dices?
DORIO DE GADEX  Ya sabe usted que soy un hombre complaciente, Don Latino.

*Desaparecen en la rojiza penumbra del corredor, largo y triste, con el gato al pie del botijo y el reflejo almagreño de los baldosines. Claudinita los ve salir encendidos de ira los ojos. Después se hinca a llorar con una crisis nerviosa y muerde el pañuelo que estruja entre las manos.*

CLAUDINITA  ¡Me crispa! ¡No puedo verlo! ¡Ese hombre es el asesino de papá!
MADAMA COLLET  ¡Por Dios, hija, no digas demencias!
CLAUDINITA  El único asesino. ¡Le aborrezco!
MADAMA COLLET  Era fatal que llegase este momento, y sabes que lo esperábamos... Le mató la tristeza de verse ciego... No podía trabajar, y descansa.
CLARINITO  Verá usted cómo ahora todos reconocen su talento.
PÉREZ  Ya no proyecta sombra.
MADAMA COLLET  Sin el aplauso de ustedes, los jóvenes que luchan pasando mil miserias, hubiera estado solo estos últimos tiempos.
CLAUDINITA  ¡Más solo que estaba!
PÉREZ  El maestro era un rebelde como nosotros.
MADAMA COLLET  ¡Max, pobre amigo, tú solo te mataste! ¡Tú solamente, sin acordar de estas pobres mujeres! ¡Y toda la vida has trabajado para matarte!
CLAUDINITA  ¡Papá era muy bueno!
MADAMA COLLET  ¡Sólo fue malo para sí!

DORIO DE GADEX  We'll have to give him ammonia. He's as drunk as a
    fiddler's bitch!
CLAUDINITA  Then he can go and sleep it off. I loathe his guts!
DON LATINO  Claudinita! My tender little flower!
CLAUDINITA  If papa hadn't gone out last night, he would still be alive!
DON LATINO  Claudinita, you accuse me unjustly! You are blinded with
    grief!
CLAUDINITA  Parasite! Always there when you're least wanted!
DON LATINO  I know you love me really!
DORIO DE GADEX  Let's take a stroll in the corridor, Don Latino.
DON LATINO  Yes, let's. This scene is too painful!
DORIO DE GADEX  Then let's not prolong it.

*Dorio de Gadex ushers the old drunk towards the door. The little dog jumps
over the coffin and follows them out, leaving a twisted candlestick behind it. In
the row of puppets along the wall there remains a gap charged with mind-
teasing suggestions.*

DON LATINO  I'll buy you a glass or two. What do you say?
DORIO DE GADEX  Always willing to oblige, Don Latino. You know that.

*They are swallowed up in the reddish half-light of the long, dreary passage, with
the dull red sheen of its tiles and the cat curled up against the earthenware
drinking jug. Claudinita watches them leave, her eyes blazing with anger. Then
she breaks down and sobs hysterically, biting the handkerchief which she
squeezes in her hand.*

CLAUDINITA  He grates on my nerves! I can't stand the sight of him! That
    man is my father's murderer!
MADAMA COLLET  For goodness sake, child! Don't talk such nonsense!
CLAUDINITA  The only murderer. I hate him!
MADAMA COLLET  The moment had to come. It was inevitable and you
    know we were expecting it... It was the sorrow of being blind
    that killed him... He couldn't work, and now he is at peace.
CLARINITO  They'll all recognize his talent now, you'll see.
PEREZ  Now that he no longer casts a shadow.
MADAMA COLLET  Without the appreciation of you young people, struggling
    and suffering hardships like him, he would have been alone
    these last years.
CLAUDINITA  Even more alone than he was!
PEREZ  The maestro was a rebel like us.
MADAMA COLLET  Max, my poor darling, you killed yourself! You alone,
    without a thought for us poor women! All your life you
    worked to kill yourself!
CLAUDINITA  Papa was a very good man!
MADAMA COLLET  He was only bad to himself!

*Aparece en la puerta un hombre alto, abotonado, escueto, grandes barbas rojas de judío anarquista y ojos envidiosos, bajo el testuz de bisonte obstinado. Es un fripón periodista alemán, fichado en los registros policiacos como anarquista ruso y conocido por el falso nombre de Basilio Soulinake.*

BASILIO SOULINAKE  ¡Paz a todos!

MADAMA COLLET  ¡Perdone usted, Basilio! ¡No tenemos siquiera una silla que ofrecerle!

BASILIO SOULINAKE  ¡Oh! No se preocupe usted de mi persona. De ninguna manera. No lo consiento, Madama Collet. Y me dispense usted a mí si llego con algún retraso, como la guardia valona, que dicen ustedes siempre los españoles. En la taberna donde comemos algunos emigrados eslavos, acabo de tener la referencia de que había muerto mi amigo Máximo Estrella. Me ha dado el periódico el chico de Pica Lagartos. ¿La muerte vino de improviso?

MADAMA COLLET  ¡Un colapso! No se cuidaba.

BASILIO SOULINAKE  ¿Quién certificó la defunción? En España son muy buenos los médicos y como los mejores de otros países. Sin embargo, una autoridad completamente mundial les falta a los españoles. No es como sucede en Alemania. Yo tengo estudiado durante diez años medicina, y no soy doctor. Mi primera impresión al entrar aquí ha sido la de hallarme en presencia de un hombre dormido, nunca de un muerto. Y en esa primera impresión me empecino, como dicen los españoles. Madame Collet, tiene usted una gran responsabilidad. ¡Mi amigo Max Estrella no está muerto! Presenta todos los caracteres de un interesante caso de catalepsia.

*Madama Collet y Claudinita se abrazan con un gran grito, repentinamente aguzados los ojos, manos crispadas, revolantes sobre la frente las sortijillas del pelo. Seña Flora, la portera, llega acezando. La pregonan el resuello y sus chancletas.*

LA PORTERA  ¡Ahí está la carroza! ¿Son ustedes suficientes para bajar el cuerpo del finado difunto? Si no lo son, subirá mi esposo.

CLAUDINITA  Gracias, nosotros nos bastamos.

BASILIO SOULINAKE  Señora portera, usted debe comunicarle al conductor del coche fúnebre que se aplaza el sepelio. Y que se vaya con viento fresco. ¿No es así como dicen ustedes los españoles?

MADAMA COLLET  ¡Que espere!... Puede usted equivocarse, Basilio.

LA PORTERA  ¡Hay bombines y javiques en la calle, y si no me engaño, un coche de galones! ¡Cuidado lo que es el mundo, parece el entierro de un concejal! ¡No me pensaba yo que tanto representaba el finado! Madama Collet, ¿qué razón le doy al

*There appears at the door a tall, gaunt individual, buttoned to the neck, with the bushy red beard of a Jewish anarchist and small envious eyes peering from beneath the implacable brow of a buffalo. He is a rascally journalist of German origin, registered on police files as a Russian anarchist and known by the alias of Basilio Soulinake.*[178]

BASILIO SOULINAKE  Peace to all!

MADAMA COLLET  I am sorry, Basilio. We can't even offer you a chair!

BASILIO SOULINAKE  Oh! Do not trouble yourself about my person. Not at all. I will not consent to it, Madama Collet. You must pardon me if I arrive a little late and miss the bus,[179] as you say in your country. In the tavern where we Slavonic emigrés eat, I have just received notification that my friend Máximo Estrella has died. The boy of Lizard-Slicer has shown me the newspaper. The death, it came unexpectedly?

MADAMA COLLET  A sudden collapse! He didn't look after himself.

BASILIO SOULINAKE  Who signed the death certificate? In Spain the doctors are very good, as good as the best in other countries. Nevertheless, the Spaniards lack a universally recognized authority in this field. This is not the case in Germany. I have studied medicine for ten years, and I am not a doctor. My first impression on entering this room was that of being in the presence of a man asleep, not of a dead man. And in this first impression, I am adamant, as you say in your country. Madama Collet, you have a great responsibility. My friend Max Estrella is not dead! He presents all the symptoms of an interesting case of catalepsy.

*Madama Collet and Claudinita embrace each other with a great shriek, their eyes suddenly bright, fingers tightly clenched and ringlets flopping about their foreheads. Heavy breathing and the slapping of carpet slippers herald the arrival of Señora Flora, the Concierge. She arrives panting for breath.*

CONCIERGE  The hearse is outside! Are there enough of you to carry the body of the late deceased downstairs? If not, my husband will come up.

CLAUDINITA[180]  Thank you, we can manage.

BASILIO SOULINAKE  My dear concierge, you must inform the driver of the hearse that the interment is postponed. And that he can bizz off. Is that not how you say in your country?

MADAMA COLLET  No, tell him to wait! You could be wrong, Basilio.

CONCIERGE  There's a load of frock coats and bowler hats out there in the street, and, if these eyes don't deceive me, one of them fancy hearses with stripes on! It's just like a councillor's funeral.[181] It's a funny old world and no mistake! I'd never have dreamt that the deceased was so important! Madama Collet, what shall I say to the bloke on the hearse?    Because he

gachó de la carroza? ¡Porque ese tío no se espera! Dice que tiene otro viaje en la calle de Carlos Rubio.

MADAMA COLLET ¡Válgame Dios! Yo estoy incierta.

LA PORTERA ¡Cuatro Caminos! ¡Hay que ver, más de una legua, y no le queda tarde!

CLAUDINITA ¡Que se vaya! ¡Que no vuelva!

MADAMA COLLET Si no puede esperar... Sin duda...

LA PORTERA Le cuesta a usted el doble, total por tener el fiambre unas horas más en casa. ¡Deje usted que se lo lleven, Madama Collet!

MADAMA COLLET ¡Y si no estuviese muerto!

LA PORTERA ¿Que no está muerto? Ustedes sin salir de este aire no perciben la corrupción que tiene.

BASILIO SOULINAKE ¿Podría usted decirme, señora portera, si tiene usted hechos estudios universitarios acerca de medicina? Si usted los tiene, yo me callo y no hablo más. Pero si usted no los tiene, me permitirá de no darle beligerancia, cuando yo soy a decir que no está muerto, sino cataléptico.

LA PORTERA ¡Que no está muerto! ¡Muerto y corrupto!

BASILIO SOULINAKE Usted, sin estudios universitarios, no puede tener conmigo controversia. La democracia no excluye las categorías técnicas, ya usted lo sabe, señora portera.

LA PORTERA ¡Un rato largo! ¿Conque no está muerto? ¡Habría usted de estar como él! Madama Collet, ¿tiene usted un espejo? Se lo aplicamos a la boca, y verán ustedes cómo no lo alienta.

BASILIO SOULINAKE ¡Ésa es una comprobación anticientífica! Como dicen siempre ustedes todos los españoles: un me alegro mucho de verte bueno. ¿No es así como dicen?

LA PORTERA Usted ha venido aquí a dar un mitin y a soliviantar con alicantinas a estas pobres mujeres, que harto tienen con sus penas y sus deudas.

BASILIO SOULINAKE Puede usted seguir hablando, señora portera. Ya ve usted que yo no la interrumpo.

*Aparece en el marco de la puerta el cochero de la carroza fúnebre: narices de borracho, chisterón viejo con escarapela, casaca de un luto raído, peluca de estopa y canillejas negras.*

EL COCHERO ¡Que son las cuatro, y tengo otro parroquiano en la calle de Carlos Rubio!

BASILIO SOULINAKE Madama Collet, yo me hago responsable, porque he visto y estudiado casos de catalepsia en los hospitales de Alemania. ¡Su esposo de usted, mi amigo y compañero Max Estrella, no está muerto!

LA PORTERA ¿Quiere usted no armar escándalo, caballero? Madama Collet, ¿dónde tiene usted un espejo?

won't wait, I can tell you! Says he's got another job in Carlos
Rubio Street.[182]

MADAMA COLLET  Lord help me! I am not sure...

CONCIERGE  That's in Cuatro Caminos.[183] More than three miles from here.
And it'll soon be dark!

CLAUDINITA  Tell him to go away! And he needn't come back!

MADAMA COLLET  If he can't wait... Then of course...

CONCIERGE  It'll cost you twice the price, just for the sake of keeping the
stiff at home a few hours longer. Let them take him, Madama
Collet!

MADAMA COLLET  But supposing he isn't dead!

CONCIERGE  Not dead? You people haven't been outside this room, you
don't notice the stink he's making.

BASILIO SOULINAKE  Perhaps you could tell me, madame concierge, whether
you have studied medicine at the University. If you have, I
shall remain silent and say no more. But if you have not, you
must permit me to say, without any desire to enter into an
argument with you, that he is not dead, but merely cataleptic.

CONCIERGE  Not dead? Dead and putrified, more like!

BASILIO SOULINAKE  Without university studies, you are not qualified to
dispute my diagnosis. You must understand, madame
concierge, that the principles of democracy do not exclude
categories of technical expertise.

CONCIERGE  Not half they don't! So he's not dead, isn't he! You should be
in his shoes, then you'd know! Madama Collet, have you got a
mirror? We'll put it to his mouth, and you'll see how he
doesn't cloud it up!

BASILIO SOULINAKE  That is an unscientific proof! As meaningless as
saying: 'I am glad to see you looking so good', as you always
say in your country. Is that not how you say it?

CONCIERGE  You've just come here to give a lecture, as if these poor women
hadn't got enough to put up with, with all their debts and
troubles, without you raising their hopes with a lot of eyewash!

BASILIO SOULINAKE  You may continue talking, madame concierge. As you
see, I do not interrupt you.

*The hearse driver appears in the doorway: nose like a beacon, old top hat with
a rosette, black threadbare frock coat, tow wig, black drainpipe trousers.*

HEARSE DRIVER  It's four o'clock, and I've got another client in Carlos Rubio
Street!

BASILIO SOULINAKE  Madama Collet, I will hold myself responsible,
because I have seen and studied cases of catalepsy in German
hospitals. Your husband, my friend and companion, Max
Estrella, is not dead!

CONCIERGE  I'll thank you to keep your voice down, sir! Madama Collet,
where have you got a mirror?

BASILIO SOULINAKE ¡Es una prueba anticientífica!

EL COCHERO Póngale usted un mixto encendido en el dedo pulgar de la mano. Si se consume hasta el final, está tan fiambre como mi abuelo. ¡Y perdonen ustedes si he faltado!

*El Cochero fúnebre arrima la fusta a la pared y rasca una cerilla. Acucándose ante el ataúd, desenlaza las manos del muerto y una vuelve por la palma amarillenta. En la yema del pulgar le pone la cerilla luciente, que sigue ardiendo y agonizando. Claudinita, con un grito estridente, tuerce los ojos y comienza a batir la cabeza contra el suelo.*

CLAUDINITA ¡Mi padre! ¡Mi padre! ¡Mi padre querido!

# Escena Decimacuarta

*Un patio en el cementerio del Este. La tarde fría. El viento adusto. La luz de la tarde, sobre los muros de lápidas, tiene una aridez agresiva. Dos sepultureros apisonan la tierra de una fosa. Un momento suspenden la tarea; sacan lumbre del yesquero, y las colillas de tras la oreja. Fuman sentados al pie del hoyo.*

UN SEPULTURERO Ese sujeto era un hombre de pluma.

OTRO SEPULTURERO ¡Pobre entierro ha tenido!

UN SEPULTURERO Los papeles lo ponen por hombre de mérito.

OTRO SEPULTURERO En España el mérito no se premia. Se premia el robar y el ser sinvergüenza. En España se premia todo lo malo.

UN SEPULTURERO ¡No hay que poner las cosas tan negras!

OTRO SEPULTURERO ¡Ahí tienes al Pollo del Arete!

UN SEPULTURERO ¿Y ése qué ha sacado?

OTRO SEPULTURERO Pasarlo como un rey siendo un malasangre. Míralo, disfrutando a la viuda de un concejal.

UN SEPULTURERO Di un ladrón del Ayuntamiento.

OTRO SEPULTURERO Ponlo por dicho. ¿Te parece que una mujer de posición se chifle así por un tal sujeto?

UN SEPULTURERO Cegueras. Es propio del sexo.

OTRO SEPULTURERO ¡Ahí tienes el mérito que triunfa! ¡Y para todo la misma ley!

UN SEPULTURERO ¿Tú conoces a la sujeta? ¿Es buena mujer?

OTRO SEPULTURERO Una mujer en carnes. ¡Al andar, unas nalgas que le tiemblan! ¡Buena!

UN SEPULTURERO ¡Releche con la suerte de ese gatera!

BASILIO SOULINAKE  It is an unscientific proof!
HEARSE DRIVER  Put a lighted match under his thumbnail.[184] If it burns
    down to the finish, he's as dead as my old grandad.  No
    disrespect intended, I'm sure.

*The Hearse Driver props his whip against the wall and strikes a match.*
*Squatting beside the coffin, he unclenches the dead man's hands and turns*
*upwards one of the yellowing palms. Between tip and thumbnail he sticks the*
*lighted match, which continues to burn and then goes out. Claudinita gives a*
*piercing shriek, rolls her eyes, and starts to bang her head against the floor.*

CLAUDINITA  My father! My father! Oh, my dear father!

# Scene Fourteen

*A patio in a cemetery in the east end of Madrid. A cold evening and a raw wind.*
*The evening light on the rows of gravestones has a harsh, arid quality. Two*
*gravediggers are busy treading down the earth on a grave. They break off for a*
*moment, take cigarette ends from behind their ears and light up from their*
*tinderboxes. They sit down at the foot of the grave for a smoke.*

FIRST GRAVEDIGGER  This geezer was some sort of writer.
SECOND GRAVEDIGGER  Didn't have much of a burial![185]
FIRST GRAVEDIGGER  Papers say he was a man of great talent.
SECOND GRAVEDIGGER  You get no prizes for talent here.  Robbery and
    cheating's all that's rewarded.  Everything bad is rewarded in
    Spain.
FIRST GRAVEDIGGER  There's no need to paint things so black!
SECOND GRAVEDIGGER  Well, take that young what's 'is name with the
    earring!
FIRST GRAVEDIGGER  Why, what did he get out of it?
SECOND GRAVEDIGGER  Lives like a prince, don't he?  And he's a right
    bastard.  Kipping up with the widow of a councillor.
FIRST GRAVEDIGGER  Town Hall thief, you mean.
SECOND GRAVEDIGGER  Granted.  Can you imagine a woman of her
    position falling for a bloke like that?
FIRST GRAVEDIGGER  Dazzled by the glamour, I s'pose. Just like a woman.
SECOND GRAVEDIGGER  That's how your virtue is rewarded!  And it's the
    same in everything.
FIRST GRAVEDIGGER  Do you know the bird? Bit of all right, is she?
SECOND GRAVEDIGGER  Plenty to get hold of.  When she walks, her arse
    shakes like a jelly! Smashin'!
FIRST GRAVEDIGGER  Some bastards have all the luck!

*Por una calle de lápidas y cruces, vienen paseando y dialogando dos sombras rezagadas, dos amigos en el cortejo fúnebre de Máximo Estrella. Hablan en voz baja y caminan lentos, parecen almas imbuídas del respeto religioso de la muerte. El uno, viejo caballero con la barba toda de nieve, y capa española sobre los hombros, es el céltico Marqués de Bradomín. El otro es el índico y profundo Rubén Darío.*

RUBÉN            ¡Es pavorosamente significativo que al cabo de tantos años nos hayamos encontrado en un cementerio!

EL MARQUÉS   En el Camposanto. Bajo ese nombre adquiere una significación distinta nuestro encuentro, querido Rubén.

RUBÉN            Es verdad. Ni cementerio ni necrópolis. Son nombres de una frialdad triste y horrible, como estudiar Gramática. Marqués, ¿qué emoción tiene para usted necrópolis?

EL MARQUÉS   La de una pedantería académica.

RUBÉN            Necrópolis, para mí es como el fin de todo, dice lo irreparable y lo horrible, el perecer sin esperanza en el cuarto de un Hotel. ¿Y Camposanto? Camposanto tiene una lámpara.

EL MARQUÉS   Tiene una cúpula dorada. Bajo ella resuena religiosamente el terrible clarín extraordinario, querido Rubén.

RUBÉN            Marqués, la muerte muchas veces sería amable si no existiese el terror de lo incierto. ¡Yo hubiera sido feliz hace tres mil años en Atenas!

EL MARQUÉS   Yo no cambio mi bautismo de cristiano por la sonrisa de un cínico griego. Yo espero ser eterno por mis pecados.

RUBÉN            ¡Admirable!

EL MARQUÉS   En Grecia quizá fuese la vida más serena que la vida nuestra...

RUBÉN            ¡Solamente aquellos hombres han sabido divinizarla!

EL MARQUÉS   Nosotros divinizamos la muerte. No es más que un instante la vida, la única verdad es la muerte... Y de las muertes, yo prefiero la muerte cristiana.

RUBÉN            ¡Admirable filosofía de hidalgo español!  ¡Admirable! ¡Marqués, no hablemos más de Ella!

*Callan y caminan en silencio. Los Sepultureros, acabada de apisonar la tierra, uno tras otro beben a chorro de un mismo botijo. Sobre el muro de lápidas blancas, las dos figuras acentúan su contorno negro. Rubén Darío y El Marqués de Bradomín se detienen ante la mancha oscura de la tierra removida.*

RUBÉN            Marqués, ¿cómo ha llegado usted a ser amigo de Máximo Estrella?

EL MARQUÉS   Max era hijo de un capitán carlista que murió a mi lado en la guerra. ¿Él contaba otra cosa?

RUBÉN            Contaba que ustedes se habían batido juntos en una revolución, allá en Méjico.

*Up the avenue of headstones and crosses stroll two figures deep in conversation,
two friends left behind after the funeral cortège of Máximo Estrella. They talk in
hushed tones and walk slowly, as if possessed by the religious awe of death. One
of them, an old gentleman with a snow-white beard and a Spanish cape round
his shoulders, is the Celtic Marquis of Bradomín. The other is the profound and
Aztec-like Rubén Darío.*

| | |
|---|---|
| RUBEN | It is indeed awesomely significant that, after so many years, you and I should meet in a cemetery! |
| MARQUIS | On Holy Ground, my dear Rubén. With that name our meeting assumes an entirely different significance. |
| RUBEN | True. Neither Cemetery nor Necropolis will do. They are names without warmth, chill and inhuman like the study of Grammar. What does Necropolis evoke for you, Marquis? |
| MARQUIS | Academic pedantry. |
| RUBEN | Necropolis for me is like the end of everything. It speaks of all that is bleak and irreparable, without hope, like dying in a hotel bedroom. And Holy Ground? Holy Ground has a lamp. |
| MARQUIS | And a golden dome above, my dear Rubén, echoing to the sound of an awesome clarion. |
| RUBEN | You know, Marquis, death could even be a friend, were it not for the terror of uncertainty. I would have been happy three thousand years ago in pagan Athens![186] |
| MARQUIS | I would never change my Christian baptism for the smile of a Greek cynic. I hope to be eternal for my sins. |
| RUBEN | Admirable! |
| MARQUIS | Life in Ancient Greece was perhaps more serene than ours... |
| RUBEN | They were the only men in history who knew how to sanctify life. |
| MARQUIS | And we sanctify death. Life is a fleeting instant, the only truth is death... And of all its forms, I prefer the Christian death. |
| RUBEN | The philosophy of a true Spanish nobleman. Admirable! Marquis, let us speak no more of Her! |

*They walk on in silence. The Gravediggers have finished packing down the
grave and take turns drinking from the same earthenware vessel, their two forms
silhouetted in black against the white wall of gravestones. Rubén Darío and
the Marquis of Bradomín. pause in front of the dark patch of newly-dug earth.*

| | |
|---|---|
| RUBEN | Marquis, how did you come to be a friend of Máximo Estrella? |
| MARQUIS | Max was the son of a Carlist captain[187] who fell at my side in the war. Why, did he tell you something else? |
| RUBEN | He said that you had fought together in a revolution, out in Mexico.[188] |

EL MARQUÉS  ¡Qué fantasía!  Max nació treinta años después de mi viaje a
Méjico. ¿Sabe usted la edad que yo tengo? Me falta muy poco
para llevar un siglo a cuestas. Pronto acabaré, querido poeta.
RUBÉN          ¡Usted es eterno, Marqués!
EL MARQUÉS  ¡Eso me temo, pero paciencia!

*Las sombras negras de Los Sepultureros, al hombro las azadas lucientes, se
acercan por la calle de tumbas. Se acercan.*

EL MARQUÉS  ¿Serán filósofos, como los de Ofelia?
RUBÉN          ¿Ha conocido usted alguna Ofelia, Marqués?
EL MARQUÉS  En la edad del pavo todas las niñas son Ofelias.  Era muy pava
aquella criatura, querido Rubén.  ¡Y el príncipe, como todos los
príncipes, un babieca!
RUBÉN          ¿No ama usted al divino William?
EL MARQUÉS  En el tiempo de mis veleidades literarias, lo elegí por maestro.
¡Es admirable!  Con un filósofo tímido y una niña boba en
fuerza de inocencia, ha realizado el prodigio de crear la más
bella tragedia.  Querido Rubén, Hamlet y Ofelia, en nuestra
dramática española, serían dos tipos regocijados.  ¡Un tímido y
una niña boba!  ¡Lo que hubieran hecho los gloriosos hermanos
Quintero!
RUBÉN          Todos tenemos algo de Hamletos.
EL MARQUÉS  Usted, que aún galantea.  Yo, con mi carga de años, estoy más
próximo a ser la calavera de Yorik.
UN SEPULTURERO  Caballeros, si ustedes buscan la salida, vengan con
nosotros. Se va a cerrar.
EL MARQUÉS  Rubén, ¿qué le parece a usted quedarnos dentro?
RUBÉN          ¡Horrible!
EL MARQUÉS  Pues entonces sigamos a estos dos.
RUBÉN          Marqués, ¿quiere usted que mañana volvamos para poner una
cruz sobre la sepultura de nuestro amigo?
EL MARQUÉS  ¡Mañana!  Mañana habremos los dos olvidado ese cristiano
propósito.
RUBÉN          ¡Acaso!

*En silencio y retardándose, siguen por el camino de Los Sepultureros, que, al
revolver los ángulos de las calles de tumbas, se detienen a esperarlos.*

EL MARQUÉS  Los años no me permiten caminar más de prisa.
UN SEPULTURERO  No se excuse usted, caballero.
EL MARQUÉS  Pocos me faltan para el siglo.
OTRO SEPULTURERO  ¡Ya habrá usted visto entierros!
EL MARQUÉS  Si no sois muy antiguos en el oficio, probablemente más que
vosotros.  ¿Y se muere mucha gente esta temporada?

| MARQUIS | What an imagination! Max was born thirty years after my voyage to Mexico. Do you know how old I am? I shall soon carry a whole century on my back. It will not be long before I'm finished, my dear poet. |
| RUBEN | But you are immortal, Marquis! |
| MARQUIS | I fear so, but one must be patient! |

*The dark forms of the Gravediggers – spades[189] gleaming on their shoulders – walk towards them along the avenue of tombstones. They approach.*

| MARQUIS | Do you suppose they are philosophers, like those who dug Ophelia's grave? |
| RUBEN | Have you ever known an Ophelia, Marquis? |
| MARQUIS | In one's salad days, all young girls are Ophelias. And that child was as green as they come, Rubén. And the prince, like all princes, a noodle! |
| RUBEN | Do you not admire the Divine William, Marquis? |
| MARQUIS | In my period of literary pretentions, I took him as my model. He is magnificent! With a shy philosopher and a simple-minded girl in all the force of her innocence, he wrought the miracle of the most beautiful tragedy. My dear Rubén, in our dramatic tradition, Hamlet and Ophelia would become two figures of farce.[190] A timid youth and a silly girl! What would the glorious Quintero Brothers[191] have made of that? |
| RUBEN | There is something of the Hamlet in us all. |
| MARQUIS | In you, perhaps. You can still raise a spark of gallantry. With my burden of years, I am closer to being the skull of Yorick. |
| FIRST GRAVEDIGGER | If you're looking for the exit, gentlemen, you can come with us. We're closing now. |
| MARQUIS | Shall we remain inside? What do you say, Rubén? |
| RUBEN | Horrible! |
| MARQUIS | Then by all means let us follow these two. |
| RUBEN | Marquis, shall we return tomorrow and place a cross on our friend's tomb? |
| MARQUIS | Tomorrow! By tomorrow we shall both have forgotten that Christian thought! |
| RUBEN | Perhaps so. |

*In silence they follow the Gravediggers, who, seeing them fall behind, stop and wait for them before turning the corners on the avenue of tombstones.*

| MARQUIS | My years do not allow me to walk any faster. |
| FIRST GRAVEDIGGER | No need to apologize, sir. |
| MARQUIS | A few more and I shall reach my century. |
| SECOND GRAVEDIGGER | You must have seen a funeral or two in your time! |
| MARQUIS | Probably more than you, if you have not been long in the trade. Are there many people dying this season? |

UN SEPULTURERO No falta faena. Niños y viejos.

OTRO SEPULTURERO La caída de la hoja siempre trae lo suyo.

EL MARQUÉS ¿A vosotros os pagan por entierro?

UN SEPULTURERO Nos pagan un jornal de tres pesetas, caiga lo que caiga. Hoy, a como está la vida, ni para mal comer. Alguna otra cosa se saca. Total, miseria.

OTRO SEPULTURERO En todo va la suerte. Eso lo primero.

UN SEPULTURERO Hay familias que al perder un miembro, por cuidarle de la sepultura, pagan uno o dos o medio. Hay quien ofrece y no paga. Las más de las familias pagan los primeros meses. Y lo que es el año, de ciento, una. ¡Dura poco la pena!

EL MARQUÉS ¿No habéis conocido ninguna viuda inconsolable?

UN SEPULTURERO ¡Ninguna! Pero pudiera haberla.

EL MARQUÉS ¿Ni siquiera habéis oído hablar de Artemisa y Mausoleo?

UN SEPULTURERO Por mi parte, ni la menor cosa.

OTRO SEPULTURERO Vienen a ser tantas las parentelas que concurren a estos lugares, que no es fácil conocerlas a todas.

*Caminan muy despacio. Rubén, meditabundo, escribe alguna palabra en el sobre de una carta. Llegan a la puerta, rechina la verja negra. El Marqués, benevolente, saca de la capa su mano de marfil y reparte entre los enterradores algún dinero.*

EL MARQUÉS No sabéis mitología, pero sois dos filósofos estoicos. Que sigáis viendo muchos entierros.

UN SEPULTURERO Lo que usted ordene. ¡Muy agradecido!

OTRO SEPULTURERO Igualmente. Para servir a usted, caballero.

*Quitándose las gorras, saludan y se alejan. El Marqués de Bradomín, con una sonrisa, se arrebuja en la capa. Rubén Darío conserva siempre en la mano el sobre de la carta donde ha escrito escasos renglones. Y dejando el socaire de unas bardas, se acerca a la puerta del cementerio el coche del viejo Marqués.*

EL MARQUÉS ¿Son versos, Rubén? ¿Quiere usted leérmelos?

RUBÉN Cuando los haya depurado. Todavía son un monstruo.

EL MARQUÉS Querido Rubén, los versos debieran publicarse con todo su proceso, desde lo que usted llama monstruo hasta la manera definitiva. Tendrían entonces un valor como las pruebas de aguafuerte. ¿Pero usted no quiere leérmelos?

RUBÉN Mañana, Marqués.

EL MARQUÉS Ante mis años y a la puerta de un cementerio, no se debe pronunciar la palabra mañana. En fin, montemos en el coche, que aún hemos de visitar a un bandolero. Quiero que usted me

FIRST GRAVEDIGGER  We're not short of work. Young and old.
SECOND GRAVEDIGGER  Autumn always brings a good crop.
MARQUIS        Do they pay you so much per burial?
FIRST GRAVEDIGGER  They pay us three pesetas a day, whatever happens.
      With the cost of living nowadays, it's not even enough to starve
      on. Now and then something else turns up. We pick up a bit
      here, a bit there. Poverty, that's what it amounts to.
SECOND GRAVEDIGGER  It's a question of luck. That's the main thing.
FIRST GRAVEDIGGER  Some families, when they lose a relative, pay us a
      peseta or two to look after the grave. Some promise and don't
      pay. Most families pay the first few months. But as for the
      whole year, maybe one out of a hundred. They don't mourn for
      long.
MARQUIS        Have you never come across an inconsolable widow?
FIRST GRAVEDIGGER  Not one! Though there may be one somewhere.
MARQUIS        Have you never heard of Artemisia and Mausolus?[192]
FIRST GRAVEDIGGER  Never heard of 'em, myself.
SECOND GRAVEDIGGER  You get so many relations coming in here, it's
      difficult to know them all.

*They walk on very slowly. Rubén, deep in thought, has been scribbling
something on an envelope. They reach the exit and the black gate squeaks open.
The Marquis takes his ivory hand from beneath his cape and benevolently
divides some money between the gravediggers.*

MARQUIS        You may not know any mythology, but you are two stoic
      philosophers. May you live to see many more funerals.
FIRST GRAVEDIGGER  Whatever you say, sir. Much obliged!
SECOND GRAVEDIGGER  Me too, sir. At your service, sir.

*Removing their caps, they touch their forelocks and depart. With a quiet smile,
the Marquis of Bradomín.wraps himself in his cape. Rubén Darío still carries
in his hand the envelope on which he has written a few lines. Abandoning its
shelter by the wall, the old Marquis's carriage draws up to the gateway of the
cemetery.*

MARQUIS        Is it a poem, Rubén? Would you like to read it to me?
RUBEN          When I've polished it a little. It is still a monstrosity.[193]
MARQUIS        My dear Rubén, a poem should be published in all its stages,
      from what you call the monstrosity to its definitive form. They
      would then have a value similar to the proofs of an etching.
      Are you sure you would not like to read it to me?
RUBEN          Tomorrow, Marquis.
MARQUIS        The word 'tomorrow' should never be uttered in the presence
      of a man of my years, especially at the gate of a cemetery.
      However, let us climb into the carriage, we still have to pay a
      visit to a certain bandit. I would like your assistance in selling

ayude a venderle a un editor el manuscrito de mis Memorias.
Necesito dinero. Estoy completamente arruinado desde que
tuve la mala idea de recogerme a mi Pazo de Bradomín. ¡No
me han arruinado las mujeres, con haberlas amado tanto, y me
arruina la agricultura!

RUBÉN　　　　¡Admirable!

EL MARQUÉS Mis Memorias se publicarán después de mi muerte. Voy a
venderlas como si vendiese el esqueleto. Ayudémonos.

# Escena Última

*La taberna de Pica Lagartos. Lobreguez con un temblor de acetileno. Don
Latino de Hispalis, ante el mostrador, insiste y tartajea convidando al Pollo del
Pay-Pay. Entre traspiés y traspiés, da la pelma.*

DON LATINO　¡Beba usted, amigo! ¡Usted no sabe la pena que rebosa mi
corazón! ¡Beba usted! ¡Yo bebo sin dejar cortinas!

EL POLLO　　Porque usted no es castizo.

DON LATINO　¡Hoy hemos enterrado al primer poeta de España! ¡Cuatro
amigos en el cementerio! ¡Acabóse! ¡Ni una cabrona
representación de la Docta Casa! ¿Qué te parece, Venancio?

PICA LAGARTOS Lo que usted guste, Don Latí.

DON LATINO　¡El Genio brilla con luz propia! ¿Que no, Pollo?

EL POLLO　　Que sí, Don Latino.

DON LATINO　¡Yo he tomado sobre mis hombros publicar sus escritos! ¡La
honrosa tarea! ¡Soy su fideicomisario! Nos lega una novela
social que está a la altura de *Los Miserables*. ¡Soy su
fideicomisario! Y el producto íntegro de todas las obras, para
la familia. ¡Y no me importa arruinarme publicándolas! ¡Son
deberes de la amistad! ¡Semejante al nocturno peregrino, mi
esperanza inmortal no mira al suelo! ¡Señores, ni una
representación de la Docta Casa! ¡Eso, sí, los cuatro amigos,
cuatro personalidades! El Ministro de la Gobernación,
Bradomín, Rubén y este ciudadano. ¿Que no, Pollo?

EL POLLO　　Por mí, ya puede usted contar que estuvo la Infanta.

PICA LAGARTOS Me parece mucho decir que se halló la política representada
en el entierro de Don Max. Y si usted lo divulga, hasta podrá
tener para usted malas resultas.

DON LATINO　¡Yo no miento! ¡Estuvo en el cementerio el Ministro de la
Gobernación! ¡Nos hemos saludado!

EL CHICO DE LA TABERNA　¡Sería Fantomas!

|            | the manuscript of my Memoirs[194] to a publisher. I need money. I am completely ruined, ever since I had the unfortunate idea of retiring to my country estate. I was not ruined by women, in spite of loving them so much, and now I am ruined by agriculture![195] |
|------------|---|
| RUBEN      | Admirable! |
| MARQUIS    | My Memoirs will be published after my death. It's rather like selling one's skeleton. Come, let us assist one another. |

# Scene Fifteen

*Lizard-Slicer's tavern. The flicker of an acetylene lamp amidst the general gloom. Standing at the counter, Don Latino de Hispalis, with slurred speech and dogged insistence, invites his companion Fantail the Pimp to drink. Stumbling and staggering, he prattles on.*

|                | |
|----------------|---|
| DON LATINO     | Drink up, my friend! My heart is so full of grief, you can't imagine it! Drink up! See? I drink mine, lees and all! |
| FANTAIL        | That's because you are a Philistine. |
| DON LATINO     | Today we have buried the finest poet in Spain! And only four friends at the graveside! That's all! Not one lousy representative from the Atheneum![196] What do you think of that, Venancio? |
| LIZARD-SLICER  | Whatever you say, Don Latí. |
| DON LATINO     | The light of genius is sufficient unto itself! Isn't that right, dear boy? |
| FANTAIL        | That's right, Don Latino. |
| DON LATINO     | I have taken it upon myself to publish his writings. A most noble task! I am his trustee! He bequeaths us a social novel[197] of the stature of Hugo's *Les Misérables.* I am his trustee! And every penny of the proceeds will go to the family! The expense of publishing them may ruin me, but what do I care? That's the duty of friendship! Like the nocturnal pilgrim my immortal hope looks not at the ground![198] I'm telling you, gentlemen, not a single representative from the Atheneum, the 'Learned Society'! Mind you, the four friends were four personages of note! The Minister of the Interior, Bradomín, Rubén and this humble citizen. Isn't that right, dear boy? |
| FANTAIL        | You can say the Princess Royal[199] was there for all I care. |
| LIZARD-SLICER  | Coming on a bit strong, isn't it, to say there was a political presence at Don Max's funeral? If you spread that around, you could be making trouble for yourself. |
| DON LATINO     | I'm not lying! The Minister of the Interior was at the cemetery. We greeted one another! |
| POT BOY        | Must have been Fantomas,[200] the Phantom Faker! |

DON LATINO　Calla tú, mamarracho. ¡Don Antonio Maura estuvo a dar el pésame en la casa del *Gallo*!

EL POLLO　José Gómez, *Gallito*, era un astro, y murió en la plaza, toreando muy requetebién, porque ha sido el rey de la tauromaquia.

PICA LAGARTOS　¿Y *Terremoto*, u séase Juan Belmonte?

EL POLLO　¡Un intelectual!

DON LATINO　Niño, otra ronda. ¡Hoy es el día más triste de mi vida! ¡Perdí un amigo fraternal y un maestro! Por eso bebo, Venancio.

PICA LAGARTOS　¡Que ya sube una barbaridad la cuenta, Don Latí! Tantéese usted, a ver el dinero que tiene. ¡No sea caso!

DON LATINO　Tengo dinero para comprarte a ti, con tu tabernáculo.

*Saca de las profundidades del carrik un manojo de billetes y lo arroja sobre el mostrador, bajo la mirada torcida del chulo y el gesto atónito de Venancio. El Chico de la Taberna se agacha por alcanzar entre las zancas barrosas del curda un billete revolante. La Niña Pisa-Bien, amurriada en un rincón de la tasca, se retira el pañuelo de la frente, y espabilándose fisga hacia el mostrador.*

EL CHICO DE LA TABERNA　¿Ha heredado usted, Don Latí?

DON LATINO　Me debían unas pocas pesetas, y me las han pagado.

PICA LAGARTOS　No son unas pocas.

LA PISA-BIEN　¡Diez mil del ala!

DON LATINO　¿Te deben algo?

LA PISA-BIEN　¡Naturaca! Usted ha cobrado un décimo que yo he vendido.

DON LATINO　No es verdad.

LA PISA-BIEN　El 5775.

EL CHICO DE LA TABERNA　¡Ese mismo número llevaba Don Max!

LA PISA-BIEN　A fin de cuentas no lo quiso, y se lo llevó don Latí. Y el tío roña aún no ha sido para darme la propi.

DON LATINO　¡Se me había olvidado!

LA PISA-BIEN　Mala memoria que usted se gasta.

DON LATINO　Te la daré.

LA PISA-BIEN　Usted verá lo que hace.

DON LATINO　Confía en mi generosidad ilimitada.

*El Chico de la Taberna se desliza tras el patrón, y a hurto, con una seña disimulada, le tira del mandil. Pica Lagartos echa la llave al cajón y se junta con el chaval en la oscuridad donde están amontonadas las corambres. Hablan expresivos y secretos, pero atentos al mostrador con el ojo y la oreja. La Pisa-Bien le guiña a Don Latino.*

LA PISA-BIEN　Don Latí, ¡me dotará usted con esas diez mil del ala!

DON LATINO　Te pondré piso.

DON LATINO    You keep quiet, fish-face! Don Antonio Maura went to Gallito
              the bullfighter's house[201] to give his condolences, didn't he?
FANTAIL       José Gómez, alias Gallito, was a real star and a prince of the art
              of bullfighting who died in the ring fighting like a good 'un.
LIZARD-SLICER  And what about Juan Belmonte, the 'Earthquake'?[202]
FANTAIL       An intellectual!
DON LATINO    Boy, the same again! Today is the saddest day of my life! I
              have lost a mentor, a brother and a friend. That's why I'm
              drinking, Venancio.
LIZARD-SLICER  The bill is going through the roof, Don Latí. Have a feel in
              your pocket and see what money you've got. We don't want
              any trouble.
DON LATINO    I've got money, enough to buy you and your whole tabernacle!

*From the deep recesses of his overcoat, he pulls a handful of banknotes and
throws them on the counter, under the sidelong gaze of the pimp and the
astonished expression of Venancio. The Pot Boy bends down to snatch at a note
fluttering between the old soak's mud-spattered legs. Brooding in a corner of
the bar, Henrietta the Hoofer stirs herself, removes her handkerchief from her
face and peers towards the counter.*

POT BOY       Have you come into some money, Don Latino?
DON LATINO    I was owed a small sum and they've paid me back.
LIZARD-SLICER  That's not a small sum.
HENRIETTA     Ten thousand smackers!
DON LATINO    Are you owed anything?
HENRIETTA     Damned right I am! You collected on a lottery ticket I sold.
DON LATINO    I did not.
HENRIETTA     Number 5775.
POT BOY       That's the number Don Max had!
HENRIETTA     So in the end he didn't want it and Don Latino took it off his
              hands. And the stingy old bastard still hasn't given me the tip.
DON LATINO    I had forgotten about it.
HENRIETTA     Then you've got a very bad memory.
DON LATINO    I'll let you have it.
HENRIETTA     What you do is your affair.
DON LATINO    Have faith in my boundless generosity.

*The Pot Boy slips behind the landlord and tugs furtively at his apron. Lizard-
Slicer locks the cash register and goes to join the boy in the shadowy hinterland
where the wineskins are heaped up. They mime an expressive secret dialogue,
while keeping a sharp eye and ear on the goings-on at the counter. Henrietta
winks at Don Latino.*

HENRIETTA     Don Latí, you could give me a dowry with them ten thousand
              smackers.
DON LATINO    I'll set you up in a flat.

LA PISA-BIEN  ¡Olé los hombres!
DON LATINO  Crispín, hijo mío, una copa de anisete a esta madama.
EL CHICO DE LA TABERNA  ¡Va, Don Latí!
DON LATINO  ¿Te estás confesando?
LA PISA-BIEN Don Latí, ¡está usted la mar de simpático!  ¡Es usted un
          flamenco! ¡Amos, deje de pellizcarme!
EL POLLO          Don Latino, pupila, que le hacen guiños a esos capitales.
LA PISA-BIEN  ¡Si llevábamos el décimo por mitad! Don Latí una cincuenta, y
          esta servidora de ustedes, seis reales.
DON LATINO  ¡Es un atraco, Enriqueta!
LA PISA-BIEN¡Deje usted las espantás para el calvorota!   ¡Vuelta a
          pellizcarme! ¡Parece usted un chivo loco!
EL POLLO          No le conviene a usted esa gachí.
LA PISA-BIEN  En una semana lo enterraba.
DON LATINO  Ya se vería.
EL POLLO          A usted le conviene una mujer con los calores extinguidos.
LA PISA-BIEN  A usted le conviene mi mamá.  Pero mi mamá es una viuda
          decente, y para sacar algo, hay que llevarla a la calle de la Pasa.
DON LATINO  Yo soy un apóstol del amor libre.
LA PISA-BIEN  Usted se ajunta con mi mamá y conmigo, para ser el caballero
          formal que se anuncia en *La Corres*. Precisamente se cansó de
          dar la pelma un huésped que teníamos, y dejó una alcoba, para
          usted la propia. ¿Adónde va usted, Don Latí?
DON LATINO  A cambiar el agua de las aceitunas.  Vuelvo.  No te apures,
          rica. Espérame.
LA PISA-BIEN  Don Latí, soy una mujer celosa. Yo le acompaño.

*Pica Lagartos deja los secretos con el chaval, y en dos trancos cruza el vano de
la tasca.  Por el cuello del carrik detiene al curda en el umbral de la puerta.
Don Latino guiña el ojo, tuerce la jeta, y desmaya los brazos haciendo el pelele.*

DON LATINO  ¡No seas vándalo!
PICA LAGARTOS  Tenemos que hablar.  Aquí el difunto ha dejado una pella
          que pasa de tres mil reales – ya se verán las cuentas – y
          considero que debe usted abonarla.
DON LATINO  ¿Por qué razón?
PICA LAGARTOS  Porque es usted un vivales, y no hablemos más.

*El Pollo del Pay-Pay se acerca ondulante.  A intento deja ver que está
empalmado, tose y se rasca ladeando la gorra. Enriqueta tercia el mantón y
ocultamente abre una navajilla.*

| | |
|---|---|
| HENRIETTA | Now you're talking! |
| DON LATINO | Crispin, my son, a glass of anisette for the lady! |
| POT BOY | Coming right up, Don Latino! |
| DON LATINO | Are you making your confession? |
| HENRIETTA | Don Latino, I really like your style! There's a touch of the gypsy in you! Hey, stop pinching me, will you! |
| FANTAIL | Watch it, Don Latino! She's got her eyes on your liquidity! |
| HENRIETTA | We bought the ticket between us, straight down the middle fifty-fifty![203] |
| DON LATINO | This is daylight robbery, Henrietta! |
| HENRIETTA | So what are *you* getting so upset about?[204] There you go, pinching me again! Randy as an old goat! |
| FANTAIL | That woman would be bad for your health. |
| HENRIETTA | I would bury him in a week. |
| DON LATINO | We would see about that! |
| FANTAIL | You need a woman with her fire put out. |
| HENRIETTA | What you need is my mother. But she's a respectable widow You wouldn't get anywhere unless you took her to the altar first.[205] |
| DON LATINO | I am an apostle of free love. |
| HENRIETTA | Then come and live with the two of us, me and my mama, like the 'respectable gentleman offering his protection' who advertises in the papers.[206] Matter of fact, we just got shot of one of our lodgers. Left a room that would suit you down to the ground. Where are you off to, Don Latí? |
| DON LATINO | To see a man about a dog.[207] Don't worry, darling. I'll be right back. Wait for me here. |
| HENRIETTA | Don Latí, I'm a very jealous woman. I'm going with you. |

*Lizard-Slicer abandons his whispered conversation with the boy and crosses the floor of the bar in a couple of strides. He grabs the drunk by the collar of his overcoat in the doorway. Don Latino blinks, pulls a face and lets his arms droop like a puppet.*

| | |
|---|---|
| DON LATINO | No need to be so violent! |
| LIZARD-SLICER | We've got business to discuss. Our dear departed friend left a debt behind him of more than seven hundred – I'll show you the bills later – I think you should pay it. |
| DON LATINO | Why should I? |
| LIZARD-SLICER | Because you're a shyster and a thief, and that's all there is to it. |

*Fantail the Pimp approaches with undulating gait. He lets it be seen that he is carrying a knife in his hand. He coughs, tilts his cap at a rakish angle and scratches his head. Henrietta flicks back her shawl and secretly opens a small knife.*

EL POLLO     Aquí todos estamos con la pupila dilatada, y tenemos opción a darle un vistazo a ese kilo de billetaje.

LA PISA-BIEN Don Latí se va a la calle de ganchete con mangue.

EL POLLO     ¡Fantasía!

PICA LAGARTOS Tú, pelmazo, guarda la herramienta y no busques camorra.

EL POLLO     ¡Don Latí, usted ha dado un golpe en el Banco!

DON LATINO   Naturalmente.

LA PISA-BIEN ¡Que te frían un huevo, Nicanor! A Don Latí le ha caído la lotería en un décimo del 5775. ¡Yo se lo he vendido!

PICA LAGARTOS El muchacho y un servidor lo hemos presenciado. ¿Es verdad, muchacho?

EL CHICO DE LA TABERNA ¡Así es!

EL POLLO     ¡Miau!

*Pacona, una vieja que hace celestinazgo y vende periódicos, entra en la taberna con su hatillo de papel impreso, y deja sobre el mostrador un número de El Heraldo. Sale como entró, fisgona y callada. Solamente en la puerta, mirando a las estrellas, vuelve a gritar su pregón.*

LA PERIODISTA ¡*Heraldo de Madrid*! ¡*Corres*! ¡*Heraldo*! ¡Muerte misteriosa de dos señoras en la calle de Bastardillos! ¡*Corres*! ¡*Heraldo*!

*Don Latino rompe el grupo y se acerca al mostrador, huraño y enigmático. En el círculo luminoso de la lámpara, con el periódico abierto a dos manos, tartamudea la lectura de los títulos con que adereza el reportero el suceso de la calle de Bastardillos. Y le miran los otros con extrañeza burlona, como a un viejo chiflado.*

LECTURA DE DON LATINO El tufo de un brasero. Dos señoras asfixiadas. Lo que dice una vecina. Doña Vicenta no sabe nada. ¿Crimen o suicidio? ¡Misterio!

EL CHICO DE LA TABERNA Mire usted si el papel trae los nombres de las gachís, Don Latí.

DON LATINO   Voy a verlo.

EL POLLO     ¡No se cargue usted la cabezota, tío lila!

LA PISA-BIEN Don Latí, vámonos.

EL CHICO DE LA TABERNA ¡Aventuro que esas dos sujetas son la esposa y la hija de Don Máximo!

DON LATINO   ¡Absurdo! ¿Por qué habían de matarse?

PICA LAGARTOS ¡Pasaban muchas fatigas!

DON LATINO   Estaban acostumbradas. Solamente tendría una explicación. ¡El dolor por la pérdida de aquel astro!

PICA LAGARTOS Ahora usted hubiera podido socorrerlas.

DON LATINO   ¡Naturalmente! ¡Y con el corazón que yo tengo, Venancio!

PICA LAGARTOS ¡El mundo es una controversia!

DON LATINO   ¡Un esperpento!

EL BORRACHO  ¡Cráneo previilegiado!

FANTAIL We've all got eyes to see what's going on here, and we've all got a right to a slice of the loot.

HENRIETTA Don Latí is leaving with me, arm in arm.

FANTAIL You're dreaming!

LIZARD-SLICER Hey, you! Put that knife away and stop looking for trouble!

FANTAIL Don Latino, you've been and robbed a bank!

DON LATINO Why, naturally!

HENRIETTA Go, fry an egg,[208] you great thug. Don Latí won a lottery prize with the number 5775. I sold it to him myself!

LIZARD-SLICER Witnessed by the lad and me. Isn't that right, boy?

POT BOY That's right!

FANTAIL Yeah, yeah.

*An old woman, Pacona, part-time procuress and newspaper seller, enters the tavern with her bundle of newsprint and leaves a copy of the* Herald *on the counter. She exits, as she came in, with silent and avid curiosity. Once in the doorway, she looks up at the stars and returns to her vendor's cry.*

NEWSPAPER SELLER *Madrid Herald! Correspondent!* Mysterious death of two women in Bastardillos Street! *Herald! Correspondent!* Read all about it!

*Don Latino breaks away from the group and sidles furtively up to the counter. In the pool of light from the acetylene lamp, holding the newspaper spread wide in both hands, he haltingly reads out the headlines and sub-headings adorning the report of events in Bastardillos Street. The others look at him with a mixture of mockery and surprise, as though listening to the ramblings of a dotty old man.*

DON LATINO *(reading)* Charcoal fumes from a *brasero*. Two women found asphyxiated.[209] A neighbour tells her story. Doña Vicenta knows nothing. Suicide or foul play? Mysterious circumstances!

POT BOY Look and see if the paper gives the names, Don Latí!

DON LATINO I'm looking.

FANTAIL Don't overload the grey matter, bird-brain!

HENRIETTA Come on, Don Latí, let's go.

POT BOY Here! I bet you the two females are Don Max's wife and daughter!

DON LATINO Don't be absurd! Why should they want to kill themselves?

LIZARD-SLICER They were having a hard time!

DON LATINO They were used to that. There could only be one explanation. Grief. Grief for the loss of that guiding star!

LIZARD-SLICER And just when you could have helped them out.

DON LATINO Why, naturally! Because I've got a heart of gold, Venancio. A heart of gold.

LIZARD-SLICER It's an upside-down world, right enough!

DON LATINO A travesty!

THE DRUNK Ah, a privileged mind!

'La Puerta del Sol' *by Francisco Sancha, 1904.*

# Commentary

## Scene One

In the early scenes of the play Max reacts to his situation by striking many of the tragic and self-pitying attitudes which he will later discard. In this opening scene we see him in despairing mood after his dismissal from the newspaper. His attitude is defeatist, even somewhat pathetic, as he talks of a possible suicide pact for the whole family, laments his literary oblivion and feels a masochistic desire to wallow in self-pity, insisting on having the letter of dismissal re-read to him. Valle-Inclán makes Max subject to occasional hallucinations in his blindness, although without any suggestion of the madness that afflicted Alejandro Sawa in his last days. He indulges in nostalgic visions and reminiscences of his Parisian heyday, which merely serve to deepen his depression when he returns to reality. Although it is clear from the outset that he sees Don Latino for the two-faced rogue he is, he shows himself to be vulnerable to the latter's flattery and, to some extent, in complicity with his own exploitation.

1     **The twilight hour:** In the first version of the play, published in the review *España* (31 July - 23 October, 1920), Valle had written 'hora canicular.' ('in the heat of the day'). His decision to change this in later editions reflects a conscious aesthetic purpose of condensing or 'filling up' time (possibly under the influence of Dostoyevski), which he adopted in several of his works from about 1922. The technique is not applied to the whole of *Lights of Bohemia* in which the first twelve scenes go without interruption from evening on one day to dawn on the next and the last three occur a day or two later.

2     **around the walls:** Similar details appear in a contemporary journalist's account of the wake of Alejandro Sawa (*El País*, 7th March 1909 - quoted by Allen Phillips, *Alejandro Sawa: mito y realidad*, p.26).

3     **master of hyperbole:** The description of Max in the 1920 edition was less sympathetic: "Andalusian poet, drunkard and writer of songs".

4     **Bull Apis:** A bull-headed god of Egyptian mythology, but here evidently the nickname or pseudonym of some unidentified newspaper editor or proprietor.

5     **those articles:** Again an allusion to an actual event in the life of Alejandro Sawa. In a letter to Rubén Darío on the occasion of Sawa's death, Valle-Inclán refers to the latter's suicidal despair on being told that his contributions to the newspaper *El Liberal* had been discontinued. See Dictino Alvarez, *Cartas de Rubén Darío* (Madrid, 1963), p.72.

6     **fourpenn'orth of charcoal:** A reference to the fuel once used in *braseros* or open braziers which were placed under a table covered with a heavy cloth to keep the legs warm. According to Zamora Vicente (*Luces de bohemia*. Clásicos castellanos, 1973, p.6, n.17) inhaling the fumes of the *brasero* was a frequent cause of death and method of suicide.

7    **busts of Hermes:** Hermes is the Greek equivalent of the Roman god Mercury. Valle is here thinking of the more primitive representations of the god as a mature man with a long, bushy beard.

8    **the Moncloa:** Formerly a royal palace and gardens, now a public park, situated in the north of Madrid near the University precinct. It was built in the eighteenth-century French style.

9    **Don Latino de Hispalis:** A typical feature of Valle-Inclán's style in his later satirical phase is the blatant and deliberate contrast between pretentious myth and sordid reality, encapsulated in this instance in the gap between Don Latino's pompous name and his occupation as a vendor of lurid and sensationalist magazines. Hispalis is the Latin name for Seville.

10   **arms of Morpheus:** An example of the bookish pedantry characteristic of bohemian speech. Morpheus is Ovid's name for the son of Sleep and god of dreams.

11   **That would be good:** Madama Collet's speech is frequently unidiomatic and sometimes incorrect in the original.

12   **Zarathustra:** The bookseller's nickname alludes to the mythical Persian prophet Zoroaster popularized by Nietzsche's *Thus Spake Zarathustra*. It testifies to the vogue of Nietzsche's work amongst Spanish intellectuals during the first two decades of the twentieth century. See note 15.

13   **fancy cape-work:** The Spanish text uses a bullfighting image here.

14   **In Lizard-Slicer's bar!:** This line was conceived as a lead-in to the next scene which, in the original version, was indeed in Lizard-Slicer's bar. The line remained unaltered when the present Scene 2 was interpolated.

## Scene Two

This scene was added in the 1924 Opera Omnia edition. It is a strangely static and discursive scene which could possibly prove difficult in production. The point of Don Gay's appearance is not entirely clear and neither is the attitude of Valle-Inclán or Max Estrella towards him. The spectacle of characters agreeing with one another does not generally make for exciting drama and here character interaction seems to have little or no part to play. It could be argued that certain speeches contribute to our knowledge of Max's attitudes to Spanish life and institutions, but this alone would not constitute a justification for the scene.

One of the most significant pointers is the stage direction which describes the contrast between the abstract philosophical discussion inside the bookshop and the background of social events going on outside. Although he may well be voicing some views close to his own heart, Valle-Inclán is evidently treating the whole dialogue with a degree of irony and underlining its complete irrelevance both to the political unrest in society and to the exploitation going on under their noses. It is possible that the author's irony towards "intellectuals without a penny to their name" does not end here. There is a very abrupt change of gear in the dialogue as the discussion passes from a topic of pretentious abstraction to one of mind-numbing banality, from Spanish obscurantism and English 'enlightenment' to the comparative creature comforts of doss houses in Madrid and London. The intentional bathos of this switch in the conversation is highlighted by Don Gay's admission that, despite the spiritual and material advantages of England, he needs the Spanish sun for his rheumatism. It is noticeable that Max himself does not participate in the latter part of this dialogue and limits himself to a rather scathing comment at the end. Nevertheless, the scene does seem to imply a comment on the degree of commitment of intellectuals to their alleged convictions.

15  **Zarathustra's cave:** The character of Zarathustra is generally thought to be based on the bookseller Gregorio Pueyo, who had a shop on the corner of Jacometrazo and Mesonero Romanos, later destroyed by the creation of the the Gran Vía. Pueyo was also a publisher and financed the publication of many works by the younger generation in the early 1900s. Contemporaries such as Gómez de la Serna and Eduardo Zamacois portray him as a man who both exploited and assisted his young writers, taking his cut of the sale price, but occasionally making small loans or advances to those in financial difficulties. Zamacois speaks of him as partly identified with the bohemian world, partly detached from it, "presiding over the *tertulia,* but divorced from the conversation, absorbed in the tangled skein of his business" (*Años de miseria y de risa,* p.214). The characteristics most emphasized by contemporary observers are his enormous nose and pronounced stoop, the monumental disorder of his bookshop and his habit of huddling over a smoky brazier in the winter. Valle-Inclán reflects most of these features in his opening description of the scene as well as the bookseller's semi-detached attitude in the ensuing dialogue. His general view of the character is, however, far less sympathetic than that of Zamacois, who describes the bohemians as stealing books from Pueyo rather than the reverse and taking advantage of the more generous, sentimental side of his nature to ask for loans which would never be repaid.

16  **Most rudely. ... stranger!:** An approximate quotation from Rosaura's speech at the beginning of Calderón's *Life is a Dream* (Act 1, 17-18).

17  **old Cuban militia:** This refers to the Cuban Volunteers, who were the urban militia force of the *peninsulares* or Spanish immigrant middle class who dominated political life in Cuba. The Volunteers supported the cause of continued Spanish sovereignty in the struggles leading up to Cuban independence at the end of the nineteenth century. The uniform would thus create an anachronistic impression.

18  **Don Gay Peregrino:** This is generally thought to be an allusion to Ciro Bayo (1850-1939), adventurer, travel writer, translator, expert on old manuscripts, who was associated with the Madrid bohemia of the early part of the twentieth century. He is best known for his book *El lazarillo español* ('The Spanish Lazarillo'), referred to in this stage direction, but he was also the author of several books recording his travels in Europe and Latin America. The pseudonym 'Peregrino' (pilgrim) derives mainly from the fact that the word frequently appears in the titles of his works. The portrait which emerges from the accounts of both Pío Baroja (*Obras completas,* VII, p.846) and his brother Ricardo is a strange mixture of the conventional and the unconventional, a traditionalist who led a hand-to-mouth, bohemian existence, an inveterate mythomaniac with a strong sense of honour.

19  **Salutem plurimam!:** A Latin expression sometimes used to begin letters. The sense is paraphrased in the English translation.

20  **Palmerin...Library:** This is the title of an imaginary chivalresque novel. The British Museum (which is no doubt the library that Valle-Inclán refers to here as the Royal Library) does, in fact, possess the only surviving copy of *Palmerin of England.*

21  **the Modern Babylon:** i.e. London, so called on account of its wealth, luxury and dissipation.

22    **man in handcuffs:** The Catalan prisoner features in all three scenes interpolated in the 1924 edition: a fleeting appearance in Scene 2, as a principal character in Scene 6 and an allusion in Scene 11.

23    **demagogues of the far left:** Probably a reference to anarcho-syndicalist leaders like Francisco Ferrer (1849-1909). Max is here commenting on the essentially moral and religious (though, of course, violently anti-clerical) basis of Anarchism. (See F. Borkenau, *The Spanish Cockpit*. London, 1937, p.22.)

24    **Escorial:** San Lorenzo de El Escorial was founded by Philip II in 1563 and completed some 22 years later. It comprises a monastery, church, palace and royal mausoleum and, as Max seems to imply here, typifies the identification of Church and State in Spain.

25    **hard as granite:** The *piedra berroqueña* is the severe grey granite from which the Escorial is built.

26    **Grand Theosophical Society:** The Theosophical Society was founded by Helena Blavatsky (see note 146) in 1875. The 'sublime doctrine' (theosophy) referred to here was a blend of Hindu and Neoplatonic theories which sought to transcend all religious institutions and establish direct mystical links with divine principles. Theosophy is a term used to describe those schools of religious and philosophic thought which aim at direct insight into the ultimate oneness of the divine essence by means of contemplative meditation. Despite widespread scepticism, the doctrine enjoyed a considerable vogue amongst writers and intellectuals (Yeats, for example) in the early part of the twentieth century. Valle-Inclán's own attitude to this and other occult doctrines was ambivalent. Although he is clearly ironical in *Lights of Bohemia*, because of the intellectual charlatanism it produced, he seems to take a more serious view in his book on aesthetics, *La lámpara maravillosa* ('The Marvellous Lamp').

27    **Children of Mary:** A secular organization for young girls associated with the Catholic Church.

28    **battle-axes they call suffragettes?:** News items about the British suffragette movement were generally treated as a joke by the Spanish press.

29    **See the connection?:** Don Gay seems to be alluding to the coincidence that the address of the hostel should bear the name of the patron saint of Spain.

30    **Queen Elizabeth Hostel:** I have not been able to establish the existence of this establishment in St. James's Square between 1910 and 1920. However, Charles Booth in his *Life and Labour of the People in London* (London: Macmillan, 1898-1903), describes the Soho and St. James area as one of "poverty and wealth lying very near together, with high rents and a super-abundance of charitable assistance" (Final Volume, p.11) and comments on the large number of foreigners in this part of the city. An earlier volume refers to the presence of refuges or 'registered common lodging-houses' for down-and-outs, migrant artisans or single people of limited means in the otherwise prosperous district of St. James.

31    *The Dead Woman's Son*: Typical of the many serialized melodramas which were published in newspapers or separately in weekly parts and avidly followed by, the general public, much in the manner of today's television soap operas. Since this kind of sensationalist literature would have been Zarathustra's bread and butter, it was clearly in his economic interest not to divulge any developments in the plot.

32    **Doña Loreta, the colonel's wife:** Valle-Inclán indicates that the readership of these trashy serials extended to the well-to-do middle class. The name reappears as that of a character in *Los cuernos de don Friolera* ('The Horns of Don Friolera'), published in the present series under the title of *The Grotesque Farce of Mr Punch the Cuckold*, translated and edited by Dominic Keown and Robin Warner.

33 **Royal Decree:** Government by decree, which by-passed extremely slow and tortuous parliamentary procedures, became a feature of Spanish political life during the premiership of Antonio Maura (1907-9) and was increasingly used as parliamentary government became weaker in the years preceding the Primo de Rivera dictatorship (1923).

## Scene Three

After the intellectual or pseudo-intellectual atmosphere of the second-hand bookshop, the scene moves to that other archetypal venue of bohemian life, the tavern. We now see Max, the poet, playing to a picturesque gallery of low-life characters: drunks, pimps and prostitutes. The histrionic gestures and trenchant phrases alternate with the pathos of the self-destructive, alcoholic bohemian who pawns his cape to buy a lottery ticket. In contrast to the previous scene, the interacting dialogue of banter and repartee, with its rich blend of cultured and popular elements, evokes a lively collective atmosphere. Valle ironically underlines his sense of the contradictions and incongruities in Spanish social life with pimps and prostitutes who adopt regal nicknames and manners, drunks who profess solidarity with the proletarian revolution, and conflicting strains of farce and social violence. The background events of strikes, demonstrations, street riots and clashes between workers and right-wing vigilantes are developed from the previous scene and begin to impinge more on the stage action.

34 **turns out to be still alive!:** The boy is parodying the improbable and melodramatic plots of the serialized novels peddled by Don Latino.

35 **newspapers:** Here, as elsewhere in the play, the word *periodista* (journalist) is jocularly used in the sense of 'newspaper seller'. An indication of the profession's low public esteem.

36 **Flowers for your button-hole!:** Literally: "stem of the spikenard".

37 **sevens and fives:** *Capicúa* means a numerical palindrome or reversible number, traditionally regarded as lucky in the National Lottery.

38 **Castelar:** Emilio Castelar (1832-99), politician, writer and orator in the grand manner, was a dominant figure in Spanish politics during the first Republic and after the Restoration of the monarchy. His traditionalist attitudes and ornate style did not endear him to the writers and intellectuals of Valle-Inclán's generation.

39 **wounded stag:** A well-worn literary commonplace much abused by modernist poets and, in particular, by Francisco Villaespesa.

40 **crosses over their mouths:** The custom of making the sign of the cross over one's mouth when yawning was originally to prevent evil spirits from entering the body. As yawning was frequently the result of hunger the phrase came to mean 'go hungry'. Both the custom and the expression are now rare in contemporary Spain.

41 **Rute:** The village of Rute in the province of Cordoba is famous for its production of aniseed liqueurs.

42 **morganatic wife:** Henrietta is humorously comparing her own inferior status *vis à vis* her pimp (the 'King of Portugal') to that of a commoner who marries a reigning monarch.

43 **Manolo:** This is the familiar form of Manuel, which was the name of the last king of Portugal (Manuel II), dethroned by a revolution in 1910.

44    **losing your crown?**: The Spanish text contains a play on the word *corona*, which
      implies "crown of horns" in addition to the more obvious sense. A reference to the
      systematic cuckoldry which formed part of the King of Portugal's trade.
45    **the money ... printed on!**: An allusion to the economic recession and galloping
      inflation in Portugal after the First World War.
46    **Don Manuel Camo:** A local chemist and *cacique* (political boss) from Huesca,
      much satirized by the novelist Pío Baroja. The *cacique's* main function was to
      deliver the votes for the candidates imposed by either of the two dynastic parties
      (Liberal or Conservative) who alternated in power during the period of the Regency
      in Spain (1885-1902) and beyond. Valle is here referring to a system which had
      been rigging elections to parliament for the past forty years.
47    **College of Christian Brothers:** A religious order devoted to education founded in
      Rome at the end of the sixteenth century by the Aragonese priest and educator San
      José de Calasanz.
48    **royal prince Don Jaime:** Don Jaime de Borbón y Parma (1870-1931) was the
      Carlist pretender to the Spanish throne. His habit of travelling incognito round the
      country was a constant security problem as well as a source of interest and humour
      for the satirical sections of the Press, especially between 1907 and 1910. Hence the
      expression *de incógnito* became extremely fashionable in the popular language of
      the capital.
49    **We voted ... union meeting:** This could be a reference to the general strike called
      by the socialist trades union, Union General de Trabajadores, in August 1917. The
      socialist *casas del pueblo* (where the original specifies that the vote had taken
      place) were a cross between a working man's club and an adult education centre
      with a pronounced anti-clerical bias.
50    **Citizens' Action Group:** A right-wing vigilante group representing commercial
      and professional interests which had been formed to help the government against
      the strikers. Zamora Vicente notes references to it in the newspapers towards the
      end of 1919 (*La realidad esperpéntica*, p.101).
51    **honorary Red Cross nurse:** This passing reference reflects topical interest in the
      Red Cross and in the training of women for hospital work, inspired largely by the
      example of Alfonso XIII's queen, Victoria Eugenia de Battenberg, who devoted
      much time and energy to its organization and improvement.
52    **heroes of the second of May!:** A reference to the popular uprising against the
      French invaders which took place in the Puerta del Sol on 2 May 1808.

## Scene Four

References to the social situation continue with allusions to broken glass,
disturbances in the centre of Madrid (Cibeles) and the sound of the mounted
night patrol. The primary purpose of this scene is to show an anachronistic Max
Estrella in contact with the younger generation of bohemians and would-be
writers. While paying lip-service to him as a 'maestro' and expressing due regard
for his talent, the 'Modernists' are clearly stronger on rhetoric than they are on
substance. Max, in his turn, strikes attitudes of populist social commitment, as
well as indignation at his boycott by the press and the literary establishment. At
this stage, the audience is not inclined to take Max's claims to be a man of the
people or to have missed his true vocation as a tribune of the plebs too seriously.
His rhetorical protests against his literary oblivion and the indifference of the
Academy are seen as the flamboyant expression of the 'hyperbolical Andalusian'.

Beneath that flamboyance there is a pathetic vulnerability. We suspect that he is dependent on the grotesque audience of Modernists, whose respect he knows to be hollow and whom he affects to despise. He adopts many of the 'magnificent' and tragic postures that will later be displaced by self-deprecating humour. Assuming attitudes for the benefit of his audience, he puts on a display of mock erudition for the Captain of the Mounted Police Patrol. As Ricardo Baroja reminds us, drinking to excess and being arrested for drunk and disorderly behaviour was regarded in bohemian circles as an essential component of a successful evening's entertainment (See *Gente del '98*, pp.118-19 and Ch. XX.)

53    **sand-covered street:** As part of the government's measures for riot control, streets were often covered with sand to prevent the police horses from slipping and damaging themselves on the asphalt surface.

54    **'Roman Guard':** This was the popular name for the Madrid municipal mounted police, created in 1893 by the Count of Romanones while he was mayor of the capital. They were normally referred to as 'los romanos' or 'los romanones'. Their helmets, though black in colour, bore a certain resemblance in shape to those of the Roman legionaries.

55    **Macfarlane overcoat:** A type of loose-fitting, caped and occasionally sleeveless overcoat with slit sides, named after its inventor.

56    **three dismal dodos!:** Literally 'three sad troglodytes', an allusion to a traditional tongue-twister in the original Spanish. Henrietta appears to see herself, along with Max and Latino, as a species threatened with extinction by the social context.

57    **Romanones:** Alvaro de Figueroa y Torres or the Count of Romanones (1863-1950) was a leading Liberal politician. Several times mayor of Madrid in his early political career, he later became leader of the Liberal Party and prime minister, by appointment of Alfonso XIII, between 1912 and 1913 and between December 1915 and April 1917. Although a man of considerable fortune, he had a reputation for being stingy.

58    **in Russia:** A reference to the Bolshevic Revolution of 1917, which naturally encouraged and increased the militancy of organized labour in Spain, particularly in Barcelona. Consult Dougherty, *Un Valle-Inclán olvidado*, p.136 and p.145 where Valle expresses similar views about a forthcoming revolution in Spain.

59    **Cibeles:** A large square in the centre of Madrid and scene of many riots and demonstrations between 1917 and 1920.

60    **bourgeois liberals:** The *sindicatos amarillos* were free Catholic unions designed to break the monopoly of militant organizations like the CNT and UGT. They were formed into a national federation in 1916. Originally conceived to catholisize the working class, these unions eventually became more independent of the Church and emphasized a non-political, non-revolutionary, professional unionism. Nevertheless they failed to win the trust of the working population and were dissolved in 1929. Later the term *amarillo* acquired a broader meaning. Zamora Vicente defines it as 'those who sought solutions to social grievances by means of compromise and dialogue between the interests of capital and labour'.

61    **Epigones of the Modernist Parnassus:** The heyday of Spanish *modernismo*, the anti-naturalist literary movement of which Valle-Inclán himself had been a part, was between about 1900 and 1910. By 1920, with its leader and chief inspiration, Rubén Darío, already dead, the movement was extinct. Valle sets his play in the period of *modernismo*'s decline when it was represented only by pretentious, third-rate talents such as appear in the names listed here. Only two of these have been

conclusively identified: Dorio de Gadex and Pedro Luis de Gálvez. Dorio de Gadex was the pseudonym for Antonio Rey Moliné, a native of Cádiz. He is remembered by his contemporaries (e.g. P. Baroja, *Obras completas*, VII, 958-9) as a pretentious, untalented individual of lachrymose disposition. *Madrid Cómico* (5 November 1910) refers to his plagiarism of Anatole France and his extravagant and largely second-hand attire. Pedro Luis de Gálvez is described by Baroja (*Obras completas*, VII, 855-8) as an ex-seminarist and sonneteer of the post-Darío period, better known for his bohemian eccentricities than for his works. Baroja's account, the only one we have of Gálvez's life, records a series of petty loans, uncompleted literary projects, and jail sentences for unspecified anarcho-syndicalist activities, culminating in his death sentence and execution during the Civil War.

62      **magic ... of us all!**: A quotation from the opening line of Rubén Darío's poem *Responso a Verlaine*, written on the occasion of Verlaine's death in recognition of the inspiration he had given to the Modernist movement in Spain. According to the memoirs of Eduardo Zamacois, Dorio de Gadex frequently addressed Valle-Inclán with these words (see Zamora Vicente, *La realidad esperpéntica*, p. 128).

63      **As Ibsen says: ... at their base**: The inference is that the only possible link between a poet and the people is at the lowest level, i.e. that of the poet who degrades himself. This is probably Dorio's élitist interpretation of Ibsen's last play *When We Dead Awaken* in which climbing the mountain becomes symbolic of human aspirations to confront the ultimate truths.

64      **every petty tyrant**: The original refers to Clarín's speech to Prince Segismundo in lines 1338-9 of Calderón's *Life is a Dream*.

65      **Death to president Maura!**: Here the reference is not so much to Antonio Maura as conservative leader and prime minister as to his role as president of the Spanish Academy from 1913 to 1925. From both a political and literary/intellectual point of view, Maura's authoritarian and uncompromising personality made him the man that every liberal loved to hate during the years covered by the play.

66      **Galdós, novelist and corn merchant**: The allusion is to Benito Pérez Galdós, Spain's most distinguished nineteenth-century novelist, whose chair in the Spanish Academy became vacant on his death in 1920, the year in which the first version of *Lights of Bohemia* was published. Galdós's brand of realism was anathema to the Modernists as is clearly indicated in the nickname of 'el Garbancero' or 'Chick Pea Merchant'. Valle-Inclán himself, however, spoke well of Galdós's work on several occasions.

67      **Sergeant Basallo ... Moroccan campaign**: Francisco Basallo Becerra was a sergeant in the Spanish army who, along with a handful of other survivors, was taken prisoner after the famous disaster of Annual in July 1921, when the Spanish garrison in Morocco was almost entirely wiped out. Basallo was repatriated in 1922 and his heroic exploits during captivity, related in his *Memorias de un cautiverio* ('Memoirs of Captivity'), established him for a short time as a national hero. The point being made here is the Academy's inability to distinguish between patriotic fervour and literary merit.

68      **latest limericks. ... mighty midget?**: In Valencia, Catalonia, Aragon and Navarre, *gozos* were popular verses written in praise of the Virgin, Christ or the Saints. The *Enano de la Venta* ('Dwarf at the Inn') alludes to a folk tale in which a man with an enormous head was in the habit of threatening the patrons of a roadside inn from an upstairs window. The tale ends when one of the patrons, calling his bluff, invites him to come down and carry out his threats and it is revealed that the enormous head is attached to the body of a dwarf. Evidently some political parody is intended here, although its object remains a matter for speculation. One of the theories is that

this could be Antonio Maura and, in the interests of simplifying the many allusions in the text, I have chosen this option. Naturally, the limerick verses that follow are a very free version of the original.

69    **Puerta del Sol:** The centre of Old Madrid.

70    **bullfighter:** Rafael el Gallo was the nickname of Rafael Gómez Ortega, the well-known matador who was the brother of Joselito mentioned in Scene 10.

71    **St. John Chrysostom:** Bishop of Constantinople and Doctor of the Church who lived from c.347 to 407 AD. After a period as a hermit, he was ordained in 386 in Antioch where he became famous for his eloquent preaching and gained the epithet 'Chrysostom' (Greek for 'golden-tongued').

72    *sermo vulgaris*: Latin for 'vernacular'.

73    **Asturian troglodyte:** Nightwatchmen in the capital were frequently from remote rural areas like Asturias and had the reputation for being both primitive in manner and reactionary in outlook. The word *troglodita* at this time was frequently used to describe anyone of traditionalist or reactionary views.

74    **Saint Lucy:** Patron Saint of the blind.

75    **Mariano de Cavia:** One of the most celebrated journalists of this period, well known for his archaic literary style and his fondness for wine. Felipe Sassone recalls his custom of writing while under the influence of alcohol (*La rueda de mi fortuna*. Madrid, 1958, 305-7). He was a member of the Spanish Academy from 1915 until his death in 1920.

76    **Death to the Pharisee ... tribe!:** Maura was reputed to be descended from a family of *conversos* (converted Jews) from Mallorca.

## Scene Five

Max continues to play to the gallery of his followers at police headquarters. Here more than anywhere, at the heart of petty officialdom, it was necessary to 'épater le bourgeois' and affirm with pride the right to be a poet and dreamer. The police interrogation of Max in this scene closely resembles an episode of Valle-Inclán's own experience witnessed by Pío Baroja and recorded in his Memoirs (*Obras completas*, VII, p.757). Baroja and Valle were in a group of five men taken to the police station after creating a disturbance at the theatre:

"When he came to Valle-Inclán he asked: 'What is your name?'

'Don Ramón María del Valle-Inclán y Montenegro', replied Valle- Inclán sarcastically.

'Profession?'

'Colonel-in-Chief of the Mexican Armed Forces'.

'Domicile?'

'A palace in the Calle de Calvo Asensio.'"

Similar incidents are related in Ricardo Baroja's *Gente del '98*.

77    **Ministry of the Interior:** Police Headquarters was housed in the basement and ground floors of the Ministry of the Interior (equivalent to the British Home Office) situated in the Puerta del Sol.

78    **Redundant:** The Spanish term *cesante* was applied to civil servants who lost their jobs after a change of government. The removal of a political party from office was accompanied by the dismissal of the bureaucrats who supported them.

79  **The Victor Hugo of Spain!:** The French Romantic poet, novelist and playwright Victor Hugo (1802-85) became a conventional standard of literary excellence amongst the Spanish Modernists.

## Scene Six

This scene was added to the original 1920 version when the play was published in the *Opera Omnia* edition of 1924.

With the exception of his wife and daughter, we have seen Max surrounded up to this point by caricatures, who either cynically exploit him, treat him with hollow respect or regard him as a drunken trouble-maker. The scene with the Catalan Prisoner contrasts sharply with the previous encounters. Max's rhetoric begins to sound hollow when set against the hard social realities as seen through the eyes of the Prisoner. For the first time he comes face to face with a situation in which he sees *himself* as a caricature. His previous claim to be a man of the people is seen for the wishful thinking that it is. Deprived of his coterie of hangers-on, Max is given the first glimpse of how he appears to others, the first insight into his anachronistic irrelevance, which prepares the ground for his later self-deprecating humour.

Both visually and emotionally, this scene is cast in an altogether more sombre mood than those which precede it. The Catalan Prisoner's story is a fusion of two sets of historical events: those which led up to what has become known as the 'Tragic Week' in Barcelona in 1909 and the violent clashes between anarcho-syndicalists and the army from 1917 to 1923, events which were very much a part of Valle-Inclán's present at the time of writing. Valle places his bohemian protagonist right up against this social reality. We observe Max's efforts to equate his plight with that of an alienated urban proletariat and to bridge the gap between the artist-intellectual and the working man. Max's essential humanity emerges from beneath the histrionic posturing. His gesture of tearing off his artist's cravat and his reference to it as the "yoke of the most abject servitude" reveal his fundamental questioning of the validity of his artistic calling in times of such social injustice. Nevertheless, the gap between them remains unbridged. Max's hyperbole and the Prisoner's earnest solemnity never quite harmonize and, after a symbolically incomplete embrace with a man whose hands are handcuffed behind his back, Max is left a sad and pathetic figure, weeping with impotence and rage.

80  **Barcelona ... burst into flames:** This alludes to the social situation — particularly in Barcelona, but also in Andalusia and Madrid — which had been simmering since the 1890s. The main reasons for it were the crumbling of an outdated political system, an unpopular colonial war in Morocco and increasing tension between capital and labour. The situation was exacerbated by the economic strain imposed by the First World War and fuelled by the Russian Revolution of 1917. See Introduction p.6.

81  **I am what the law has made me:** This statement is is line with the orthodox anarchist belief that the organization of the state is the chief oppressor of the individual.

82    **The revolutionary ideal. ... property ownership:** Anarchists were generally in
      sympathy with Lenin's Bolshevic revolution, despite their ideological rejection of
      the Communist state and the dictatorship of the proletariat. Here the Catalan
      Prisoner echoes the widely-held anarchist belief that only through violent revolution
      and the destruction of the old social order could a new 'natural' order emerge, from
      which the concept of property and ownership would be completely eliminated.

83    **Spanish colonies in Latin America:** The reference is to a commercial imperialism
      exercised by the colonies of Spanish landowners and businessmen in Latin
      America, whose greed was castigated by Valle-Inclán on numerous occasions in his
      literary works and press interviews.

84    **Matthew:** The name Mateo in the Spanish is almost certainly a reference to the
      anarchist Mateo Morral, who in 1906 attempted to assassinate Alfonso XIII and his
      bride on their wedding day by throwing a bomb at their carriage in the Calle Mayor.

85    **Saul:** In both the Old and New Testaments (1 Samuel X and Acts IX) the name is
      associated with the idea of conversion, seeing the light and preaching the new
      gospel. The precise relevance of the theme of conversion to the Catalan Prisoner is
      not clear but the equation of Anarchism with a new creed or religion is obvious
      enough.

86    **Judaic spirit ... goes with it:** The main driving force behind Spanish Anarchism
      was moral and utopian rather than economic. Their fundamental aims were not
      higher wages or better working conditions, but the complete eradication of the
      capitalist structures that enslaved the proletariat (see G. Brenan, *The Spanish
      Labyrinth*, Cambridge,1967, pp. 188-93 and Franz Borkenau, *The Spanish Cockpit*,
      London,1937, pp. 18-22 and pp. 33-8). Their attitude could be described as anti-
      semitic only in so far as Jews were traditionally associated with the commercialism
      and profit motive to which anarchists were ideologically opposed.

87    *Alea iacta est!*: Caesar's famous phrase on taking the decisive step to cross the
      river Rubicon and invade Cis-alpine Gaul: 'The die is cast'.

88    **riot in the factory:** The historical situation to which this refers is most probably
      the 'Tragic Week' (1909) in Barcelona. An ill-advised call-up of reservists by
      Maura's government to defend Spanish mining interests in Morocco released a
      flood of pent-up resentment and led to a week of street-fighting and church-
      burning.

89    **'attempting to escape':** The Catalan is alluding to the infamous *ley de fugas* which
      condoned the shooting of prisoners while 'attempting to escape' (see Introduction, p.
      8).

90    **The Black Legend of Spain:** The reputation (exaggerated in the view of some
      Spaniards) which Spain acquired abroad during the sixteenth century for cruelty
      and fanaticism, particularly in connection with the treatment of the Latin American
      Indians.

## Scene Seven

The image of Max Estrella, marooned in his irrelevance and anachronism at the
end of Scene 6, remains in the audience's mind during this sharply contrasting
scene in the newspaper office. Max's irrelevance to the social situation is
underlined from a different point of view, as the 'angry protest' of the Modernists
about Max's arrest degenerates into badinage and a parade of wit, vanity and
pseudo-erudition. The irrelevance of the dialogue, however, is only an apparent
one since the banter and repartee is in deliberate contrast to the object of their
visit and throws into relief the plight of the central character. The scene also

reminds us that the play is not only about Max Estrella and his attitudes, but about the response of the social context to him, how his image is reflected in that social context. Valle-Inclán is clearly making a social comment on the controlled and pusillanimous nature of a contemporary Press which prints only news acceptable to conservative eyes, but he is also making the more general moral point that we are usually more interested in ourselves than in other people.

91    *'The People'*: In view of the reactionary opinions of its editorial staff, the name is evidently ironical.
92    *Journal*: Don Filiberto uses the word as the French for 'newspaper'.
93    **Charles the Bewitched:** Charles II (known as 'the Bewitched') was the ailing and feeble-minded son of Philip IV and the last of the Hapsburg kings. His reign from 1665 to 1700, marked by chaos at home and disastrous wars abroad, saw a spectacular decline of Spanish influence in Europe.
94    **Philip II:** Dorio goes even further back in Spanish history to the reign of Philip II (1556-98), the archetype of autocratic monarchs.
95    **the Bard of Nicaragua:** Rubén Darío (see note 137). The quotation is from one of his best known poems *Canción de otoño en primavera* ('Autumn Song in Spring').
96    **the evidence ... coat collars:** i.e. dandruff.
97    **goaded me into it:** In the original: 'sought out my tongue', which Dorio chooses to take literally and in a sexual sense.
98    **Silvela:** Francisco Silvela (1845-1905) was leader of the Conservative Party (and occasional prime minister) until Maura took over in 1903.
99    **Floral Games:** A poetry festival originally founded by the troubadours of Provence in the early part of the fourteenth century. It spread into Catalonia towards the end of that century and thereafter into other regions of Spain.
100   **Narciso Díaz:** Narciso Díaz de Escobar (1860-1935), a well-known journalist and writer who won numerous prizes for his stories and journalism. He was the author of a book on the *Juegos Florales* in Spain.
101   *Herald*: Probably the *Heraldo de Madrid*, although the verbal joust and article referred to are no doubt fictitious.
102   **Karma:** In theosophy, Karma is the name given to the cumulative consequences of a person's deeds in life operating in a cause-and-effect sequence, which will control his destiny in the next stage of existence. Valle is reflecting what was an extremely fashionable topic of conversation at the time and one which, as in this case, offered great scope to the pedant and the charlatan.
103   **Cabala:** Here used in the general sense of 'doctrine of the occult'. Latino's exposition of the mystical significance of his name is, however, an obvious parody and its alleged magical transmutation is merely Latino spelt backwards.
104   **Neo-Malthusian ... control:** The English economist Thomas Malthus (1766-1834) argued that humanity was inevitably doomed to starvation unless the rate of growth in the world's population could be substantially reduced. His theories were the origin of the birth-control movement. The English translation adds a brief sentence of explanation.
105   **iconoclast:** A vogue word during the *modernista* period, when breaking with the past and rejecting the 'classics' of Spanish literature were the necessary credentials of any aspiring young writer. See José Martínez Ruiz, 'Somos iconoclastas', *Alma Española*, 10 January 1904.
106   **Don Miguel de Unamuno:** A writer of whom the young 'iconoclasts' would doubtless approve, in Don Filiberto's view. The forthright, paradoxical and

subversive opinions of Unamuno (1864-1936) on literature, history, politics and religion did little to endear him to a conformist public.

107 **Alfonso XIII:** Alfonso XIII, who abdicated in 1931, was Spain's last constitutional monarch until the restoration of constitutional monarchy in 1977. It has been suggested that the king himself, by overriding the democratic process and personally appointing prime ministers on several occasions, undermined the authority of parliament and paved the way for the military dictatorship of Primo de Rivera in 1923.

108 **García Prieto:** Leader of the left wing of the Liberal Party who formed three extremely short-lived governments in 1917, 1918 and 1922. The occasion referred to here is most probably November 1917, when García Prieto was asked to form a coalition government in the wake of the general strike.

109 **Queen Isabel II ... exile:** Isabel II, daughter of Fernando VII, was forced to abdicate in 1868. The translation expands on the original to clarify the allusion.

110 **Garnier:** The French publishing house Garnier published around the turn of the century a series of literary works in Spanish. The names of several Spanish and Latin American writers were associated with them during this period, including Rubén Darío, the Machado brothers and Alejandro Sawa. Zamora Vicente has pointed out how Valle makes several allusions to Sawa's life in his portrayal of Don Latino (see Introduction, pp. 14-15).

111 *Spanish-American Lyre:* A fictitious review.

112 **The Marquis of Alhucemas:** i.e. García Prieto, who was given this title after concluding, as Foreign Minister, the Hispano-Moroccan treaty of 1911-12. The speech is a parody of García Prieto's oratorical style, riddled with clichés and mixed metaphors.

113 **Benlliure:** Mariano Benlliure (1862-1947) a Valencian sculptor in the classical style who had made a violent attack on Modernist art in his acceptance speech to the Academy of Fine Arts in Madrid. The Modernists, for their part, regarded his work as banal and mass-produced.

114 **Saints for sale ... very cheap!:** A translation of the cry *Santi, boniti, barati! (santi, boni, barati!* in the text), which was associated with artisans of Italian origin who hawked cheap plaster religious figurines round the streets of Madrid. In the original this phrase is used by Don Filiberto in the previous speech and Dorio's reply means "That's telling 'em in Valencian", mistaking (possibly on purpose) the Italian for Benlliure's native language, Valencian. As the complexities of this seemed to defy translation, I have opted for adaptation at this point.

115 **Cavestany:** Juan Antonio de Cavestany (1861-1924), poet, playwright and member of the Spanish Academy, much ridiculed by the younger generation of critics for the 'padding' of his literary style.

116 **One more link in the old boy network!:** Literally: 'Just another son-in-law!', a phrase which alludes to the systematic practice of nepotism in Spanish political life. Both Maura and García Prieto launched their political careers after marrying into rich and influential families.

117 **'Long live the trivial!':** The literary generation which rebelled against the pomposity and rhetoric of Restoration values was very attached to this phrase. Azorín, Pío Baroja and Valle-Inclán all use it, although it seems to have been coined originally (in French) by Lawrence Sterne in his *Sentimental Journey*.

117 **Atheneum:** Founded in 1835 as a literary club, the Madrid Atheneum became a prestigious literary, cultural and political society with a very large library and a highly distinguished membership. Valle-Inclán himself was its president for many

years. The *Ateneo* was certainly more liberal in outlook than the Spanish Academy, but could not avoid being branded as an organization of the Establishment.

118    **As the poet says ... undertaker?:** The phrase is a parody of the last line of *Canto a Teresa* by the Romantic poet José Espronceda (1808-42).

## Scene Eight

This scene constitutes the pivotal point of the play, in which we see an important shift in Max's attitude. He insists on seeing the Minister with the intention of registering his protest and demanding retribution against those who have violated his human rights, and ends up by accepting a regular payment from a government slush fund. Max's 'heroic' posture cannot survive this indignity and the knowledge of this betrayal lowers his self-esteem. Coming on top of the feeling of social irrelevance after his encounter with the Catalan prisoner, this further disillusionment with himself precipitates a shift towards the more detached, self-destructive attitude we see in later scenes. He becomes painfully aware that he is tainted by the values of the society he lives in.

It was by no means uncommon amongst artists, intellectuals and even those who could be classified as neither to receive small salaries or occasional grants from municipal, provincial or government funds. These payments were generally awarded on the basis of friendship or 'influence' and did not involve any work or conspicuous merit on the part of the recipient. According to Ricardo Baroja (*Gente del '98*, p.52), acceptance of any official subsidy was frowned upon by genuine bohemians as a denial of their independence. Max Estrella's acceptance of the Minister's handout, therefore, would undoubtedly have been regarded as a betrayal of the bohemian ethic.

The portrayal of the Minister of the Interior as a renegade from the world of literature and the arts is generally thought to be based on Julio Burell, who occupied that post in 1917 from April to June under the premiership of Eduardo Dato. Burell was a man who had come to politics via literature and journalism and always retained a respect for his former profession. In his different official capacities, he is reputed to have given financial help to writers in difficulty on several occasions. Valle-Inclán himself is alleged to have been one of these. Pío Baroja in his *Memoirs* (*Obras completas*, VII, p.405) claims that Valle was drawing a salary from a government sinecure. He recalls Valle's discomfiture, while sitting in front of a café, when one of those present pointed out Julio Burell, who was passing by at the time, with the words: "Look, there goes our boss." Baroja claims that Valle studiously ignored the remark and changed the subject of conversation. This, of course, is purely hearsay evidence and one must allow for Baroja's personal antipathy to Valle-Inclán. However, the idea that Max Estrella's uneasy conscience about accepting a salary from the 'Reptiles' slush fund' reflects circumstances of Valle-Inclán's own life remains an intriguing possibility.

This scene with the Minister and the earlier one with the Catalan anarchist seem to be conceived as a contrast to one another. Max's unsuccessful attempt to bridge the gulf between himself and the people is juxtaposed with his unwilling compromise with Authority. The embraces which conclude both scenes are surely far from coincidental. The tragic Max who embraces the man he calls his spiritual brother in the prison cell is later 'travestied' in his grotesque embrace with the Minister. The insertion of Scene 6 with the Catalan prisoner is a striking illustration of how Valle tries to balance tragedy and pathos with the grotesque.

119 **Office ... private secretary:** The office of the Minister of the Interior was also in the Puerta del Sol, next door to Police Headquarters.

120 **crackle of a bonfire:** Literally: 'a bonfire of wood-shavings'. The original alludes to a celebrated phrase used by Maura to play down the importance of the political conflagration which followed the execution of the anarchist leader Francisco Ferrer in 1909.

121 **Blind ... like Belisarius:** Belisarius (494-565) was a famous Byzantine general, conqueror of the Persians, Vandals and Goths, in the service of the Emperor Justinian. Towards the end of his life, he was accused of complicity in a plot to assassinate the Emperor, for which, according to legend, his eyes were put out. The line is a quotation from a poem by Victor Hugo.

122 **A gift ... Venus:** i.e. venereal disease.

123 **Minerva:** Roman goddess of Justice and Wisdom.

124 **My wife ... diabolical:** Jeanne Poirier, the long-suffering wife of Alejandro Sawa, was known to many of her friends as 'Santa Juana'. The epithet is confirmed by several references in Sawa's private correspondence (see A. Zamora Vicente, 'Tras las huellas de Alejandro Sawa', *Filología*, XIII, 1968-9, pp. 383- 95).

125 **Helena's window:** The real name of Alejandro Sawa's sister was Esperanza, although he did have a daughter called Elena.

126 **brings her to me:** A very free version of the original.

127 **your brother Alex:** The name by which Sawa was known to his close friends and with which he frequently signed his letters.

128 **as long ... this job:** An allusion to the unstable political atmosphere and ephemeral nature of government appointments during the period covered by the play.

129 **if in this labyrinth ... she bites:** A jocular allusion to the Cretan Labyrinth and the Minotaur.

130 **Reptiles' slush fund:** The 'fondo de los Reptiles' was the popular name given to the secret funds available to the Ministry of the Interior and other Ministries for unofficial purposes such as paying informers, bribing witnesses and buying favours or goodwill. They were also used, as in Max's case, for unofficial payments to friends.

131 **my dog:** The detail of the dog, both the one that accompanies Don Latino in the play and the metaphorical association of Don Latino with a pet dog, is another link with the real-life Alejandro Sawa. Sawa's habit of taking a dog with him everywhere he went (originally as an extension of his personality, though in later years possibly as a guide) is well documented in several contemporary accounts.

132 **institutionalist:** This is an approximation rather than a translation. *Institucionista* refers specifically to someone educated in the *Institución Libre de Enseñanza* (Free Institute of Education), a liberal and progressive school founded in 1876 by Francisco Giner de los Ríos, which was independent of both Church and State. The *Institución* had a very important influence on Spanish public and literary life up to the end of the Civil War in 1939.

133 **the *Official Gazette*:** *La Gaceta* was the official government newspaper which reported on all legislation and Civil Service activity.

## Scene Nine

This scene with Max and Rubén Darío in the café stresses the contrast between a plush contemporary establishment in Madrid, with modern décor, lighting and music, and the bohemian poets inhabiting a mental world of Paris and the poetry of Verlaine at the turn of the century. The stage directions refer to the characters as 'outsiders' and 'exiles' in what for them is an alien environment. Certainly for Max, accustomed to the tavern, the plush café with its gilt-framed mirrors is unfamiliar territory. The initial stage direction alludes to central motifs in the play which will be picked up again in Scene 12, namely the presentation of a fragmented, 'unharmonious' contemporary scene within a new aesthetic order, the imagery of reflections in mirrors and the theme of distortion by the surrounding context. The stylization of objects, people and perspectives into geometric shapes and the synthesis of light, music and movement reflect Valle-Inclán's interest in contemporary artistic practice.

The emotional impact on Max Estrella of the previous scene is visible in the abrasive and nihilistic tone he adopts with Rubén Darío. Far from feeling elated by having money in his pocket, Max indulges in a sardonic brand of humour, much of which is directed against himself. Convinced of his social irrelevance and moral degeneration, Max's thoughts turn towards his rapidly approaching death. During Max Estrella's 'last supper' with his 'disciple' Rubén, he harps constantly on the theme of death with a pronounced nihilistic emphasis. His almost jovial acceptance of his imminent extinction contrasts sharply with Rubén's terror at the very mention of the word. Rubén, too, is portrayed in the final phase of his life, with his declining poetic and intellectual powers, his mind numbed by alcohol, his memory obliterated. Isolated and remote, he lives in his own inner world compounded of orthodox Christianity, superstition and occultism, in which he tries to exorcize his obsessive fear of death. The death theme also emerges in the poetic fragment recited by Darío at the end and in the allusion to their mutual friend, the Marquis of Bradomín, whose decision to return to his native Galicia to die had inspired the poem. The whole scene, in fact, evokes, with a mixture of irony and nostalgia, the dying cadences or last glimmers of a lifestyle destined to disappear.

At the same time, the presence of Don Latino does not allow us to forget the element of pretentious charlatanism in much of what passed for literary and intellectual conversation. The discussion of theosophical doctrine is not intended to be taken too seriously. In this context, it reflects, particularly on the part of Don Latino, superficial and half-baked notions on a currently fashionable topic. The extent to which Valle himself took this kind of mysticism seriously is a larger and more complex question. The very frequency with which it surfaces in his work suggests that this was more than a casual object of his humour and satire. His theoretical work, *La lámpara maravillosa*, is entirely devoted to the relationship between mysticism and aesthetics and reveals more than a passing interest in occult doctrines, particularly in their common quest for a static unifying principle in the universe.

134  **tarnished mirrors:** This setting coincides with what Pío Baroja described as typical of many cafés in the centre of Madrid in the early part of the twentieth century: "...large mirrors with gilt frames, marble-topped tables and long bench seats upholstered in red velvet" (Pío Baroja, *Obras completas*, VII, p.1118).

135  **Café Columbus:** The Café Colón was situated in the Calle Hortaleza.

136  **negro's hands:** Max is alluding (rather loosely and inaccurately) to Rubén Darío's Indian origins, clearly reflected in his appearance.

137  **Rubén Darío:** Born in 1867, Darío was a Nicaraguan poet who became the undisputed leader of the *modernista* movement in Hispanic poetry. He came to Spain as a correspondent of *La Nación* (Buenos Aires) in 1898 and led a wandering existence in Europe, travelling between Madrid, Mallorca and Paris, until 1914. During this period he published his major works and exerted a profound influence on Spanish literature. He was a close friend of Alejandro Sawa and Valle-Inclán. He died in 1916, four years before the publication of *Lights of Bohemia*.

138  **Admirable!:** According to Valle's biographer Melchor Fernández Almagro and the poet Juan Ramón Jiménez, this exclamation was a constant feature of Rubén's conversation. It became the vogue word amongst writers of Valle-Inclán's generation for anything or anyone they approved of.

139  **Styx:** In Greek mythology, one of the subterranean rivers of Hades or the Underworld. It is commonly referred to as the river the soul had to cross on its passage to the Netherworld, the symbolic dividing line between life and death.

140  **two sheets of taxpayers' skin:** *Pápiro* was a slang term for a hundred-peseta note. The reference to 'taxpayers' skin' makes it clear that the money Max received came out of public funds.

141  **St Martin bishop of Tours ... supper:** According to legend, the young St Martin, while serving as a military tribune in Amiens, divided his cape with a beggar who came to him for alms. After converting to Christianity, he became bishop of Tours in 371. It is interesting that Max deliberately misleads Rubén here into thinking that the money comes from pawning his cape rather than the more shameful source of the 'Reptiles' slush fund'.

142  **celestial mathematics:** Although the general tone of the ensuing dialogue is certainly ironic, it reflects the central thrust of theosophy and other occult sciences to unite different branches of knowledge into a comprehensive and harmonious system: Mathematics, Science (in particular, astronomy), Nature and Religion.

143  **Gnostics:** Although Gnosticism has its origins in Greek philosophy and Jewish mysticism, its flowering in the second century was mainly of Christian inspiration. The Gnostics believed that the unconscious self of man is consubstantial with the Godhead and that, through direct intuition into the mystery of the self, man can become aware of his origins, essence and transcendental destiny.

144  **Quaternity:** A set of four persons or things. Latino is here parading a pretentious and garbled array of theosophical ideas and terminology, which is deflated by Max's interruption.

145  **Pythagoras:** Ancient Greek philosopher and mathematician of the sixth century B.C., much quoted in works of theosophy and best known for his theory of the harmony of the spheres and the doctrine of the transmigration of souls.

146  **Madame Blavatsky:** Helena Petrovna Blavatsky (1831-91) founded the Theosophical Society in New York in 1875. In her youth she had travelled widely in Turkey, Greece, Egypt, Canada, United States, Central and South America and spent some time in Tibet studying the Tibetan religion. After founding the Theosophical Society, she went to India with Colonel H.S. Olcott and established

its permanent headquarters near Madras. Her works on theosophy enjoyed great popularity in European intellectual circles from the turn of the century to the 1930s, although there was widespread scepticism about her doctrines and alleged powers.

147 **Karma:** Theosophical theory did not exclude the notion of good and evil. Although *Karma* usually means the cumulative consequences of a person's deeds in successive reincarnations, it is here used with a more specific emphasis on retribution.

148 **music of the spheres:** Pythagoras deduced that, since sound and pitch depend on movement and the rate of vibration, the planets, in their different motions, would also produce sound. He concluded that, since all things in nature were harmoniously made, the different sounds must necessarily harmonize.

149 **Paco Villaespesa:** Francisco Villaespesa (1877-1936) was a poet and dramatist of the Modernist school who alternated between periods of affluence (in which he could apparently afford to employ a secretary) and bohemian poverty. He was the founder-editor of several short-lived literary reviews in the early 1900s, e.g. *Electra* and *La revista ibérica.*

150 **to distinguish ... Castilian z:** As a Latin American, Rubén made no distinction in pronunciation between the letters s and z. In Castile and the north of Spain the z is normally pronounced with a lisp.

151 **The road ... our friend:** The translation is a free version from a late poem by Darío entitled *Peregrinaciones* ('Pilgrimages') which appears only in the *Obras Completas* (Madrid: Aguilar, 1961). The poem in question is on page 1233 and the extract quoted here is the final stanza.

152 **Marquis of Bradomín:** The ageing Don Juan, hero of Valle-Inclán's early quartet of novels, the *Sonatas,* who makes fleeting appearances in his later work and who, over the years, came to be identified with the author himself. (See note on the Marquis's appearance in Scene Fourteen) The later allusion to the Marquis's withdrawal from society closely parallels Valle's own retreat to Galicia in the years prior to the publication of *Lights of Bohemia.*

153 **Papa Verlaine:** Paul Verlaine (1844-96), whose work was the chief source of inspiration to poets of the Spanish *modernista* movement and, in particular, to Darío. It is generally accepted that Alejandro Sawa, who was a close friend of Verlaine's in Paris, was mainly responsible for introducing his poetry into Spain.

# Scene Ten

The dialogue with the prostitute Lunares provides a further example of Max's sardonic and self-destructive humour. There is certainly no playing to the gallery in this scene. On the contrary, Max detaches himself from his tragi-heroic role and ironically contemplates his situation from an outsider's viewpoint. Not unnaturally, Lunares mistakes Max for the kind of blind 'poet' who was frequently to be seen singing ballads on street corners, while accompanying himself on the guitar. These *coplas*, as they were called, were usually concerned with topics such as political scandals, notorious crimes or the exploits of well-known bullfighters. They were a kind of crude popular commentary on local or national events, generally centred around the capital. Valle-Inclán's disdain for this type of popular literature is well documented, particularly in the Prologue and Epilogue to *Los cuernos de don Friolera.* More than their crudeness of form, he disliked the values and assumptions behind them, which, he claimed, were in most cases uncritically imperialist, traditionalist and reactionary. There is every reason to suppose that Max Estrella would share this view. Yet, despite this, we see Max pretending to be the kind of poet Lunares thinks he is. He amuses himself with the degraded image that contemporary society has given him. The man who earlier had protested against his literary oblivion and affirmed his status as 'the greatest poet in Spain' now pretends to be the author of a doggerel ballad to a bullfighter.

It is sometimes claimed that this scene shows society's 'travesty' of Max's idea of love and beauty by reducing them to commercialized sex. There is not much evidence for such a view in the text, as we have little indication of what Max's idea of love and beauty is in the first place. It would be pure speculation to claim that Max is in some way compromising or degrading himself as a poet by sleeping with Lunares (if, indeed, he does). Unlike the case of the Minister, Don Latino or the Modernists, there appears to be no condemnation either explicit or implied of the two prostitutes or of their profession, which they practise in a totally honest, sympathetic, if highly matter-of-fact way. Max himself says of Lunares that she, at least, earns an honest living. Far from being a scene of strongly contrasting values or satirical condemnation, it is one of restrained emotion in which the tender, half-teasing, sexually tentative approach of Max is balanced against the sexually blatant yet naively intrigued attitude of Lunares. A strangely poetic scene without a trace of sentimentality.

154 **Public promenade and gardens:** Probably the Botanical Gardens on the south side of the Prado Museum.

155 **letter by Maura in it:** ˙An allusion to what was, in effect, an extremely commonplace ocurrence, since Maura published a statement or letter in the newspapers on an almost daily basis, particularly when he was out of office.

156 **the garden of Armida:** A reference to an episode from Tasso's *Jerusalem Delivered* in which Armida, a beautiful sorceress, seduces her victims in the voluptuous atmosphere of her palace and gardens. The scene is thus conceived as a degraded modern travesty of a classic literary episode.

157 **long-haired wig:** Literally, 'Nazarite wig'. The Nazarites were a body of Israelites (see *Numbers,* 6) who vowed themselves exclusively to God for specified periods during which they refrained from strong drink and allowed their hair and beards to grow.

158 **slum side of town:** Literally 'from Chamberí', a working-class district on the north side of Madrid.

159 **Joselito, the matador:** José Gómez, known as Joselito el Gallo, was a famous bullfighter who died in the ring at Talavera in May 1920.

160 **El Espartero:** Nickname of the nineteenth-century bullfighter, Manuel García Cuesta (1866-94), who died after being gored in the ring in Madrid. The ballad of El Espartero is a naive, crudely-written popular elegy for the bullfighter's death which is quoted in full by Pío Baroja in his Memoirs (*Obras completas,* VII, p.668).

161 **started the curse:** Literally 'since I've been visited by the papal nuncio', i.e. 'having periods'.

162 **All black and green-eyed:** The original Spanish reads 'Like Pastora Imperio', the celebrated gypsy dancer, whose green eyes, according to many contemporary accounts, fascinated and transfixed her audiences.

## Scene Eleven

Like Scenes 2 and 6, this scene was interpolated in the definitive 1924 edition of the play. It depicts what, in the post-war slump, had become a common occurrence on the streets of Madrid and Barcelona: a clash between anarcho-syndicalist workers and an army out of political control acting on behalf of the Employers' Federation. It is a scene which is significantly different from the others both in style and the attitude expressed. Instead of cut-and-thrust, interacting dialogue, we have a series of glosses and commentaries seemingly addressed directly to the audience. Many of the speeches have a lapidary air of political clichés and slogans ("A people that loots any establishment which serves the public is a people without national ideals." "The rule of law is absolute and unswerving.") Valle makes no attempt to depict a realistic group of people on a street corner. He stylizes the content to express an attitude. The Mother with her dead child is isolated in the middle of a group of representative social types: the commercial exploiters, the voices of law and authority, and the proletariat, all of whom comment on the situation while the Mother hurls her cries of pain and anger into the void. The incident recorded here was possibly inspired by a personal experience which Valle recalls in an interview for *La Noche* (Barcelona) on 20 March 1925: " I remember one of the things that made the greatest impression on me in my life was a scene I witnessed one evening as I was going to Pueyo's bookshop. A woman was coming down the street followed by some neighbours. She was a concierge who had just been told that her son had been shot dead, while out playing with some lads from the neighbourhood. That woman did not articulate words, she just cried out. And her cries were the only expression of her feelings" (Dougherty, *Un Valle-Inclán olvidado*, p.156, n.190). The Mother's tragic isolation in the middle of this group signals an unusually explicit and passionate stance on the part of Valle-Inclán. There can be no doubt, as Zamora Vicente points out (*La realidad esperpéntica*, pp.168-70), that the reality of social and political life around him was beginning to impinge on his art. The intellectual and emotional adjustments being forced on his protagonist, Max Estrella, were also, to a large extent, his own.

The social awareness and sense of his own irrelevance and inadequacy which had been building up in Max since Scene 6 now comes to a head. The self-destructive irony turns to a feeling of guilt and self-accusation. There is a suggestion, not only that Max is irrelevant to the social situation, but that his dedication to art is reprehensible in a context of social injustice. Valle reminds us of the link with Scene 6 by having his Catalan prisoner shot offstage 'while attempting to escape' at the end of the scene. This recharges Max's feelings of rage, but it also inspires a new sense of shame. In Scene 6 Max had wept with 'impotence and rage'. In Scene 11 he describes himself as being imprisoned in a dantesque circle of 'Anger and Shame'. His last speech, in which he absolves himself from all blame of "carrying a candle in the tragic carnival procession" fails to convince. His attack on Don Latino as a "vile pedlar of romantic rubbish"

COMMENTARY					175

could also be interpreted as an attack on himself, in so far as Latino, as we see later on, can be seen as a grotesque reflection of Max.

163 **Austrian quarter:** This refers to the old southern part of Madrid which stretches from Atocha to the Plaza Mayor and was originally built during the period of the Hapsburg monarchy (sixteenth and seventeenth centuries).
164 **tragic carnival procession:** Max's phrase encapsulates the duality of farce and tragedy which, for Valle-Inclán, characterized contemporary Spanish life and constituted the ambivalence of this *esperpento*.
165 **Viaduct:** The viaduct over the Calle de Segovia in the old southern district of Madrid was originally completed in 1874, though extensively modified in the 1930s. It was, as suggested here, a favourite spot for suicides.

## Scene Twelve
The nihilistic view of death, the self-destructive irony and the acceptance of his own irrelevance are all incorporated into Max's formulation of the artist's response to his circumstances in this scene. It is perhaps unwise to be too academically solemn about the theory, since it forms part of a scene in a play rather than a formal treatise and since, in any case, Max is drunk when he. formulates it. Nevertheless, the theory does illuminate the general philosophy behind the play. It can be briefly summarized as follows: The circumstances of contemporary society act like a distorting mirror on former ('classical') values and heroes, that is, makes them appear irrelevant and absurd. The grotesque present is a travesty of the past and the reality of life is a travesty of the myths we have created. This is the aspect of the *esperpento* which concerns the actual nature of the social reality Valle-Inclán saw around him. The other aspect concerns the artist's response to that degraded reality. This should be, Max claims, to distort systematically, that is, to abandon the classical concepts of beauty, harmony and proportion and reflect discord with discord, fragmentation with fragmentation. However, to be a valid aesthetic criterion, this contemporary distortion must be subject to rigorous laws and norms. The grotesque which constitutes the reflection of our contemporary world must be reduced to a principle of order. Although Max himself does not elaborate on the precise nature of this mathematical principle of distortion, contemporary examples such as Cubism in painting may help us to understand what he means.

It is important to realize that this is a denial of tragedy only in the classical sense, that is, a denial of heroic tragedy. In all other respects, Max's theory maps out an alternative route to tragedy, via the comic and the grotesque (see Introduction pp. 20-22). Valle-Inclán surrounds Max's death with deliberately anti-tragic circumstances -- Latino denying the truth of the situation and refusing to lend his overcoat, a dog urinating nearby, Latino relieving Max of his wallet, the callous indifference of the Concierge and the Neighbour. Max responds to his circumstances by 'acting out' his death scene as if he were playing an elaborate joke. The macabre charade that Max goes through -- laying himself out in preparation, ordering the funeral dirge to be sung and uttering the anti-tragic last words of 'good night' -- is Max's self-travesty, a deliberate distortion of his own ultimate tragedy.

166    **reactionary:** The Spanish *carcunda* was a derogatory term for a supporter of the absolute monarchy and, more specifically, of Carlist traditionalism (see note 187). In his earlier writings Valle-Inclán had been a fervent advocate of the Carlist cause.

167    **a travesty:** The Spanish word *esperpento* normally refers to a grotesque person or thing ('horror', 'fright', 'scarecrow'). Valle here uses it for the first time to define a literary vision. I have opted for 'travesty' as a translation because it seems to work better in the context of this scene. It is perhaps more suitable as a description of the social reality than as an artistic method of presenting it.

168    **You've changed ... arena:** The transitions in this speech are perhaps more symptomatic of a wandering mind than pregnant with symbolic meaning. The need to be warmed by Latino's breath suggests the analogy of the stable at Bethlehem, hence Latino's metamorphosis into an ox. Owing to Latino's function as a guide, the ox becomes a bell-ox, which, in turn, is invited to summon Bull Apis ('ox' in the original, not 'bull'), the editor who had removed the last crumbs of Max's livelihood, to be tormented in the bullring.

169    **avant-garde merchants:** The *ultraístas* were an avant-garde literary movement, related to Dadaism and Cubism, grouped around a poetry magazine called *Ultra*. The movement was founded in 1918 and attracted many Spanish and Latin American writers, including Jorge Luis Borges and César Vallejo.

170    **Goya:** Valle-Inclán is probably thinking of Goya's drawings, in particular the *Caprichos* and *Disparates*, in which we find examples of distorted reflections in mirrors (e.g. *Petimetre /Mono*, a fop smugly contemplating his own reflection as a monkey). Goya, like Valle-Inclán, depicts the conduct of a degraded society in which all pretensions to the 'higher values' of the former Enlightenment have become ludicrous or inoperative under the impact of later historical developments.

171    **distorting mirrors:** The original reads: "... have gone for a stroll down the Callejón del Gato". This refers to a little street called Alvarez Gato off the Plaza de Santa Ana, near the Puerta del Sol, where, according to contemporary accounts, there was an ironmonger's shop with a pair of distorting mirrors outside for the amusement of the passers-by.

172    **Spain ... civilization:** In the 1920 version this sentence ran: "Spain is a travesty of Helleno-Christian civilization". The change marks a significant shift in the definitive edition from a classical to a contemporary frame of reference. It seems to suggest that, by the time Valle came to revise the play, he saw Spanish society not only as a distortion of traditional archetypes, but as a travesty of other European models.

173    **at the bottom of a glass:** i.e. in alcohol. The reply is consistent with Max's self-deflating humour, since it appears to make light of his own theory.

174    **funeral of Victor Hugo:** Alejandro Sawa's idolization of Hugo is well documented. It is ironic that his literary counterpart should, in the depths of poverty, have hallucinations about the French poet's lavish and spectacular funeral, which took place in 1883.

175    **I'll lie down ... asking himself:** These lines, interpolated in the 1924 edition, provide further evidence of Valle's intention to link Max with the Catalan Prisoner, at least, in so far as society and the Press treat them with equal indifference.

## Scene Thirteen

Valle-Inclán takes the extremely audacious step of killing off his hero three
scenes before the end of the play. Although this may be a risky structural
innovation, it undoubtedly underlines the play's central purpose, that is a
devaluation of the hero figure and a clear signal that the emphasis does not fall
exclusively on Max and his values, but also on the social context which distorts
them.

Max's presence, however, still continues to dominate in this scene, since
the coffin containing his remains occupies the centre of the stage. This silent
presence and the simple, dignified grief of his wife and daughter are locked in a
tragi-comic tug-of-war with a whole series of farcical characters, details and
events. The detail of the protruding coffin nail is most probably taken straight
from Valle's own memory of Alejandro Sawa's funeral. The three Modernist
poets standing against the wall like 'three funereal puppets' are clearly a
caricaturesque element, as is the arrival of a drunken Don Latino and his
grotesquely rhetorical lamentations. As Latino is escorted from the room, his dog
jumps over the coffin and bends one of the candles. The absurd pedantry of the
Russian anarchist, Basilio Soulinake, introduces a note of pure farce. His claim
that Max is not dead, but merely in a state of catalepsy is hotly disputed by the
Concierge and an insane argument ensues, which is finally resolved by the
hearse driver who places a lighted match under Max's thumbnail. One might
imagine that, with such an accumulation of grotesque circumstances, all tragic
emotion would be stifled. Surprisingly, this does not happen. Set against the
solemn presence of the pine coffin and the authentic grief of Madama Collet and
Claudinita, desperately clinging to hope, the farce generates a jarringly cruel,
tragi-comic tension. Tragic feeling stubbornly survives, despite its apparent
denial by the farcical circumstances.

176   **a nail... unprotected temple:** This detail further confirms the link between Max
       Estrella and Alejandro Sawa. It is also mentioned by Eduardo Zamacois (*Años de
       miseria y de risa*, p.195) and Pío Baroja in his novelized account of Sawa's death in
       Part 6, Chapter 8 of *El árbol de la ciencia* (1911). The Zamacois account also adds
       the detail of a small trickle of blood from a wound on Sawa's temple caused by the nail.

177   **All lit up ... wind:** The original Spanish, meaning 'drunk' or 'three sheets to the
       wind', contains a pun on two different meanings of *vela* ('sail' and 'candle'). Because
       the second of these meanings is picked up in Dorio's reply, I have opted for a
       translation with 'candle'.

178   **Basilio Soulinake:** Behind this name lies the real historical identity of Ernesto
       Bark, a Russian emigré, bohemian and theoretical anarchist. Alejandro Sawa, in his
       posthumous book *Iluminaciones en la sombra*, speaks of his flaming red hair, wild
       ideas and links with revolutionary organizations. He arrived in Spain in the 1880s,
       collaborated in several literary reviews, was one of the founding members of the
       editorial board of the socialist magazine *Germinal* and wrote novels and
       sociological works under the pseudonym of A. de Santaclara. Alberto Insúa
       (*Memorias*, pp.344-5) recalls him as a teacher of French, German and English, as
       well as a publicist of the ideas of Bakunin and Kropotkin. He appears under the
       name of Pedro Soulinake in *La lámpara maravillosa* advancing the theory that the
       seeds of the Russian Revolution were sown by the impact of the French language

on Russian culture (pp. 46-7). After recognizing his portrait in *Lights of Bohemia*, Bark is reported to have attacked Valle-Inclán in the Calle de Alcalá (P. Baroja, *Obras completas*, VII, p.172).

179  **miss the bus:** In the Spanish: '... like the Walloon guard'. Basilio's speech is characterized by an uncertain use of idiom.

180  **CLAUDINITA:** In the 1920 edition this speech is attributed to Clarinito.

181  **councillor's funeral:** There is a curious discrepancy between the Concierge's description of what appears to be a well-attended and expensive funeral and the general impression of poverty conveyed by these final scenes. Max is buried in a plain pine box and the Gravediggers comment in the next scene that he "didn't have much of a funeral". If this *is* a deliberate contradiction and not an oversight on the author's part, he neglects to tell us who paid for the 'fancy hearse' or why the many well-dressed mourners mentioned by the Concierge did not attend the graveside ceremony.

182  **Carlos Rubio Street:** A street of this name still exists in the district of Cuatro Caminos.

183  **Cuatro Caminos:** In 1920 this would have been considered a remote suburb on the north-west side of Madrid.

184  **under his thumbnail:** This incident is also included by Pío Baroja in his novelized account of Sawa's death in *El árbol de la ciencia*.

# Scene Fourteen

The introduction of the Marquis of Bradomín at this point is difficult to explain in terms of the internal logic of the play. Its significance perhaps lies in the fact that both Max Estrella and the Marquis represent aspects of Valle-Inclán's own outlook. The Marquis appears in several of his early works, notably the *Sonatas*, as a kind of *alter ego,* representing an attitude of aristocratic independence, living on his own terms according to his own values, beyond the reach of organized society. In Max, on the other hand, we see something of the Valle-Inclán who realized the unattainability and even undesirability of such an ideal. The former literary ideal of aristocratic detachment — a desiccated skeletal figure who wonders whether it is worth his while to leave the cemetery — is brought into the play as an ironical postscript to the disillusioned philosophy of the bohemian poet battered by life. This valedictory tribute to the Marquis of Bradomín is undoubtedly a piece of self-indulgence on Valle's part, but the juxtaposition of past and present attitudes usefully underlines the theme of life overcoming literary ideals in the play.

In this scene in Madrid's Cementerio del Este, the tangible presence of Max Estrella recedes into the background as Valle contrasts two dialogues arising from the context of his burial. Rubén Darío and the Marquis of Bradomín, steeped in literature, are absorbed in their respective worlds of pagan and Christian metaphysics and in thoughts about their own mortality. Their awe-struck preoccupation with the mystery of death contrasts with the matter-of-fact familiarity of the two Gravediggers, for whom death is merely a way of scraping a living. The rarified meditations on death, metaphysics and aesthetics are placed in perspective by the unvarnished realism of the Gravediggers who are more concerned about where the next meal is coming from. Max is only of passing interest in these dialogues, yet, as in Scene Seven, Valle creates a sense of presence and of dramatically significant irrelevance.

The allusions to the gravedigger's scene in *Hamlet* are made quite explicit with references to the Prince, Ophelia and Yorick's skull. More than a parody of Shakespeare (as it is sometimes described), this scene is a tribute. Valle's admiration for Shakespeare and, in particular, for the graveyard scene in *Hamlet* is well documented. On many occasions he claimed Shakespeare as his model for dramatic technique. He quotes the graveyard scene as an example of allowing the scenery to create the scene, that is, to let the expression of theme emerge from direct action and a vividly-imagined physical setting. The general point that comes out of the scene is similar in many ways to the one in *Hamlet*: the vanity of all our rhetoric, myths and metaphysics when confronted with the ultimate reality of death and oblivion. The myth of love's conquest over time and death comes up against the truth of human egoism and the impermanence of all human values. The easy familiarity with death which custom has bred in the Gravediggers strips away the delusions of those with too much time to think.

185 **Didn't ... a burial!:** See note 181.

186 **pagan Athens:** In his poetry Rubén Darío reveals a more ambiguous state of internal conflict between pagan sensuality and religious mysticism. He describes his soul as poised 'between the Cathedral and the Pagan Ruins' ('Divina psiquis' in *Cantos de vida y esperanza*).

187 **Carlist captain:** The Carlists were originally the traditionalist supporters of Don Carlos de Borbón, brother of Ferdinand VII, who disputed the succession under the Salic Law of Ferdinand's daughter, Isabel II, to the throne.There were two Carlist wars, one from 1833 to 1840 and the other from 1873 to 1876. The reference here is probably to the second of these. Valle-Inclán, in his earlier heroic phase, had felt strong leanings towards the Carlist cause, although for what he described as aesthetic rather than political motives.

188 **a revolution, out in Mexico:** This certainly does not refer to the Mexican Revolution of 1910. Assuming that Max's date of birth could have been around 1870, the only revolutions coinciding with the Marquis's visit to Mexico some thirty previously would have been the minor ones that took place in the 1830s during the dictatorship of López de Santa Anna.

189 **spades:** Literally: 'adzes', but I have opted for a more usual implement in the English context.

190 **two figures of farce:** In pointing out the unheroic nature of the protagonists of Shakespeare's tragedy, Valle is anticipating definitions that he would later apply to his own *esperpentos* (particularly *Los cuernos de don Friolera*), i.e. unheroic characters who, like Hamlet, are trapped in situations which require them to play the hero.

191 **Quintero brothers:** Serafín (1871-1938) and Joaquín (1873-1944) Alvarez Quintero were extremely popular dramatists who wrote in collaboration about 150 light sentimental comedies on Andalusian life. Valle made no secret of his scorn for their brand of theatre. He once referred to them as 'Siamese gramophones' and on several occasions advocated their public execution.

192 **Artemisia and Mausolus:** An inappropriately erudite allusion to Mausolus, king of Caria, on whose death in 353 B.C., Artemisia, his wife, erected a magnificent marble tomb at Halicarnassus. This legend has become the archetypal example of

grieving widowhood and the origin of the word 'mausoleum' for any splendid sepulchral monument.

193   **monstrosity:** The translation is only an approximation. *Monstruo* in the original is a specialized term for lines of verse, often quite meaningless in themselves, with which a composer indicates to a librettist where the stresses fall in the sung passages. This practice was very common in the writing of *zarzuelas* and comic operas.

194   **Memoirs:** Valle-Inclán's early quartet of novels, entitled 'Autumn Sonata', 'Summer Sonata', 'Spring Sonata' and 'Winter Sonata' respectively, published between 1902 and 1905, was given the general subtitle of 'Memoirs of the Marquis of Bradomín'.

195   **ruined by agriculture:** possibly a reference to Valle-Inclán's own unsuccessful experiments with agriculture in 1913 when, after abandoning literature and life in the capital, he went to live in his native Galicia and rented a farm called *La Merced* near Puebla de Caramiñal. The idea of becoming a feudal lord had always appealed to Valle, but the dream was undermined by his inability to cope with the mundane practicalities of farming and the project ended in legal disputes and financial disaster.

# Scene Fifteen

The final stage of *Lights of Bohemia is* that, with Max dead, Don Latino takes over. In this last scene Max is only remembered for the money he owes. Latino has won a prize on the lottery with the ticket he removed from Max's wallet and has neglected to help Max's wife and daughter with the proceeds. Latino is also the material inheritor of Max's spiritual laurels, since, as his trustee, he also undertakes to pocket the proceeds from the publication of Max's literary works. He becomes the object of self-interested attention from all the occupants of the bar, as well as from Lizard-Slicer himself who sees him as the only hope of recovering Max's debts. He is credited with coinage of the word that Max had previously used to express his new literary philosophy (*esperpento* or 'travesty'), for which he wins the Drunk's accolade of 'privileged mind'. What we witness in this final scene is the triumph of materialism, mediocrity and, above all, inauthenticity.

196   **Atheneum:** The Spanish text uses the common journalistic formula *Docta Casa* or 'Learned Society'.

197   **social novel:** The unpublished book which Sawa left after his death was not in fact a novel, but a collection of autobiographical essays and portraits entitled 'Illuminations in the Shadows', which Valle referred to as 'the best thing he had written'. In the 1880s, before his departure for Paris, he had published several social novels in the naturalistic style.

198   **Like the nocturnal ... ground!:** A quotation from a poem by the Modernist poet Francisco Villaespesa, in whose work the figure of the pilgrim was a stock image.

199   **Princess Royal:** A reference to the *Infanta*, Isabel de Borbón (1851-1931), daughter of Queen Isabel II, who, like her mother, was renowned for her unscheduled appearances at parties and popular festivities.

200   **Fantomas:** A character created by Marcel Allain and Pierre Souvestre in 1911, Fantomas was one of several ambiguous heroes, like Fu Manchu and Arsène Lupin, currently in vogue between 1910 and 1920. He was an elegant and mysterious

practitioner of 'perfect' crimes, who constantly eluded the grasp of his police pursuers. The success of the original book inspired a long succession of stories in serial form and several films.

201 **Gallito the bullfighter's house:** The death of José Gómez (Joselito el Gallo) in the bullring at Talavera had occurred only months before the publication of the first edition of *Lights of Bohemia* in 1920. Antonio Maura's attendance at his wake and funeral was reported by the press on 19 May of that year.

202 **Juan Belmonte, the 'Earthquake':** Belmonte (1892-1962) was a bullfighter for whom Valle-Inclán had a great personal admiration. The long-standing rivalry between Joselito and Belmonte reflected a passionate debate between the advocates of two opposing styles: the spectacular and colourful style of Joselito and the pure classical elegance of Belmonte. While Belmonte generally appealed to the purists of the art, he was frequently branded as an 'intellectual' by his opponents.

203 **fifty-fifty:** Literally: 'Don Latino one peseta fifty and your humble servant six *reales'*, i.e. the same amount.

204 **So what ... upset about?:** Literally: 'Leave the panic attacks for *El calvorota'*. *El calvorota* ('Baldie') was the nickname of another well-known bullfighter, Joselito's brother Rafael Gómez (Rafael el Gallo), who was bald. Despite his eminence as a matador, Rafael was subject to moments of uncontrollable panic (*espantás* or *espantadas*), which occasionally forced him to abandon the arena. Here Latino is seized with panic at Henrietta's false assertions that she has gone halves with him over the lottery ticket and that, consequently, he owed her half the winnings. The subtext is that Don Latino's alarm is hypocritical, since 'daylight robbery' is by no means alien to his nature.

205 **took ... altar first:** Literally: 'You'd have to take her to the Calle de la Pasa'. The Calle de la Pasa ('Raisin Street') was formerly the site of the Bishop's Palace, which housed the Vicar General's Office where all the necessary documentation for a church marriage was issued.

206 **'respectable gentleman ...' in the papers:** A reference to the usual wording of offers or requests for accommodation or protection in the Press, which, according to Zamora Vicente's edition of the play, were more often the result of economic necessity than lewd intentions.

207 **To see a man about a dog:** Literally 'to change the olive water', i.e. urinate.

208 **Go fry an egg!:** The expression has an obscene connotation in Spanish.

209 **asphyxiated:** See note 6.

*Scene 7*

*Scene 11*

*Photographs by Ros Ribas*

*Scene 13*

*Scene 15*

Printed and bound by CPI Group (UK) Ltd, Croydon, CR0 4YY

13/04/2025

14656583-0001